Watching
Communism Fai

Watching Communism Fail

A Memoir of Life in the Soviet Union

GARY BERKOVICH

McFarland & Company, Inc., Publishers
Jefferson, North Carolina, and London

Translated from the Russian by David Gurevich
with contributions by Anatol Zukerman

LIBRARY OF CONGRESS CATALOGUING-IN-PUBLICATION DATA

Berkovich, Gary, 1935–
    Watching communism fail : a memoir of life in the Soviet Union /
Gary Berkovich.
        p.   cm.
    Includes index.

    ISBN 978-0-7864-4139-6
    softcover : 50# alkaline paper ∞

    1. Berkovich, Gary, 1935–   2. Soviet Union — History —1925–
1953 — Biography.   3. Soviet Union — History —1953–1985 —
Biography.   4. Soviet Union — Social conditions —1945–1991.
5. Communism — Social aspects — Soviet Union — History.
6. Totalitarianism — Social aspects — Soviet Union — History.
7. Jews, Soviet — Biography.   8. Architects — Soviet Union —
Biography.   I. Title.
DK275.B46A3   2009
947.085092 — dc22   2008044277
[B]

British Library cataloguing data are available

On the cover: Revolution Day celebration, at YUZH design office.
The author is second from left with a flute. Kharkov, Ukraine, 1957;
background ©2008 Shutterstock.

Manufactured in the United States of America

McFarland & Company, Inc., Publishers
  Box 611, Jefferson, North Carolina 28640
  www.mcfarlandpub.com

To my children
and grandchildren

Table of Contents

Prologue

Years ago, our 20-year-old daughter Lana wondered how did we ever dare to leave the USSR? It was the kind of country where, once you declared your intention to emigrate, you became an enemy of the state and could end up in jail or in a labor camp. How did we ever dare apply for the exit visa?

Well, like most citizens, we were scared. "Daring" was not easy. You have your apartment, your family, your well-modulated, settled life with friends and habits....

But we were sick and tired of the Soviet regime. We had to get away from the Soviet-Russian anti–Semitism. We wanted a future for our children. We sought professional advancement. We dreamed of seeing the big wide world out there.

But the main reason was the total, hopeless lack of prospects.

It is the same reason why people are leaving Russia to this day. They are not in an ideological conflict with the government (which is why lovers of political labels call them "kielbasa émigrés"). But at least now they are leaving without fear. Following the opening of the borders, millions of Russians left the country and thus buried the myth of the Jewish emigration. Allegedly the Jews had no emotional ties to the country. What do you expect from "alien blood"? Yet right now anybody who can leave Russia does so. It is a scenario out of any third-world country.

As I started telling my story, other questions arose: Why is life so poor in a country with the most abundant natural resources in the world? Why in Russia is one dictatorship inevitably replaced by another?

You can't answer any of these questions in twenty words or less. You need a multi-volume treatise on life in Russia and the Soviet state.

As I reflected on it, I decided to set down my own fragment of history: what I knew from personal experience, and what I thought about it. I put it all together in the form of the memoir offered here.

Some readers of early drafts told me that even now few people would be

1

interested in the information and reflections provided here, and with time their numbers would dwindle further. Besides, celebrities' memoirs are one thing, but a memoir by a common person is something different.

I have read many a memoir by members of the Soviet ruling elite, from party mandarins to artists and their children. Although not all of them seek to whitewash the past, they all have a vested interest in "correcting" reality, in justifying their life decisions that brought them material and social rewards from the regime. But a combination of narratives by "little people," the small details of their far-from-easy lives, filled with events only they are familiar with — this makes for a more genuine, more three-dimensional story of a country that history chose for a great experiment.

Our son Slava was the biggest fan of my Soviet-era stories. If it had not been for his sincere curiosity, his attention to every detail of the past I dug out, his exceptional interest in documentary prose, this story might well have remained unfinished and unpublished.

The book grew out of short stories from our family life told at the table to family and friends. Slava genuinely enjoyed them and, along with some others, never failed to remind me that the stories needed to be put down on paper. I was happy to see him enjoy them and urge me to go on. Little by little, I found myself obsessed with the idea. And now I feel great satisfaction to be completing something that he once supported with such enthusiasm. I thank him from the bottom of my heart. My greatest regret is that I cannot do it in person; unfortunately, he did not live to see this publication.

I am thankful to a number of other people who read and commented on the manuscript or its parts and suggested changes and corrections. Among them are (alphabetically) Alla Averbukh, Carol Avins, Eugenia Brown, Vladimir Donchik, Peter Gemerer, Gregory Gemerer, Alexey Klimov, Anna Lisa Crone, Galina Lisitzkaya, Ilya Rudyak, Alexander Ryabùshin, Victoria Sagalova, Frida Lutskaya-Litvak, Nina Summo, Vladimir and Galina Zilberstein, and Anatol Zukerman (who translated two of the stories). My particular gratitude goes to Margarita Fedotova, who edited the Russian version of this book, and David Gurevich for his excellent translation and very thoughtful advice. Finally, my wife Marina and our daughter Lana. Their help in writing this book, including ruthless dissection and scrupulous correction of the manuscript, cannot be overestimated.

A special preemptive thanks to relatives and friends who have not read the manuscript yet — those who may read the book in the future and run into scenes they might not like, but will, I hope, not take umbrage over things said about themselves and their families. I hope they will see that I simply tried to lay down the facts as I remembered them. I used those I deemed important to render a complete picture.

In conclusion, I cannot omit a special segment of the public which actually doesn't deserve any good words. Yet had it not been for the hard efforts of these people, I would not have realized I had a chance to live another life and would not have written this book. My hat is off to all the anti–Semites I have known.

This is neither the story of my life nor an autobiography. Rather, it is the testimony of someone who participated as a guinea pig in the experiment on a country that vanished in 1991. It is a story of this country's exotic side; a story of my family, my colleagues, my friends and foes — other guinea pigs, who are otherwise unlikely to be the subjects of anyone's writings.

1

Existence

Soviets 101

In 1951, a funny thing happened in Moscow on the way to the Kremlin. En route from his country estate, Joseph Stalin peered out the car window to look at the construction of the new Foreign Ministry high-rise. He yawned and asked: "Is there going to be a steeple at the top, too?" (Some of the six similar buildings planned then in Moscow were crowned by towers with spires.)

One of the security men mumbled: "It seems so."

"Interesting," the dictator commented vaguely. Most likely, he forgot about it right away.

However, the question had been asked, and asked audibly. That very day the project manager called an emergency meeting. The chief architect was Vladimir Gel'freikh, 68, a man well-known and respected then for his part in the design of the Soviet Building of the Century — The Palace of Soviets in Moscow. But now his opinion did not count. The acclaimed celebrity, the gray-haired academician, was ordered immediately to make all the necessary adjustments. A special design team was assembled right away. Due to the shortage of architects and engineers in the capital, more were urgently summoned from all over the country. (I heard the story two years later from some of those I happened to work with). And a tiny tower with a steeple was slapped atop the high-rise in Smolensk Square.

Gel'freikh dared not object. Of course he feared for his life; but in fact the stakes did not have to be so high.

Twenty years later, with Stalin's terror long gone, another Soviet leader, Prime Minister Alexey Kosýgin, was riding up Gorky Street in Moscow when he saw a temporary fence around a small three-story building. "When will they get rid of this fence?" he wondered aloud.

That same night the building was demolished, the debris cleaned, and the fence removed.

Only in the morning did the demolishers discover that the fenced build-

5

ing had been an eighteenth-century mansion, and one of the few historical monuments left in Moscow's downtown. The ill-fated temporary fence had been erected by the municipality to protect and conserve the building before moving it farther down the block. As usual, there had been a delay; and now there was nothing to move.

Those bizarre episodes were not abnormal. The life of Russians has always hinged on forces beyond their control. The follies of inclement nature, the whim of cruel superiors and their total unpredictability — all these created an apathetic and fatalistic Russian mentality. The three hundred years of the Tatar yoke helped turn those qualities into an almost religious fear of authority.

Thus the remarkable Russian attitude to life, crystallized in the word *avòs'* that is so hard to convey in a foreign language. (Although by now the word is devoid of religious meaning, the closest equivalent is "God willing," and Arabic *Insh'allah* comes the closest.) The most popular phrases I heard since childhood were "maybe," "let us hope," "don't worry," and "somehow." This is the moral of the most popular Russian fairy tales: Take it easy and everything will miraculously get better. Only Russian writers could come up with Oblòmov, the quintessential idle dreamer (and Gogol's Manilov in *Dead Souls* is even worse). Oblomov's counterpart is Stoltz, an entrepreneur of German extraction, which amply illustrates how the traditional Russian suspicion of anything new and unusual is combined with xenophobia.

Centuries ago, there was a small Russian principality in Eastern Europe. Gradually it conquered neighboring lands and their populations, thus forming an empire ruled by czars and emperors. The enlightened minds of the nineteenth century called it "the prison of nations." Then in October 1917 came a coup d'etat, and a different class of people came to power; yet the definition remained just as fitting.

At different times the population of the Soviet Union ranged between 150 and 250 million, representing over 150 nations and tribes. Following World War II it surrounded itself with satellite countries, whose populations also found themselves in this "prison."

The huge new empire thus created took up the eastern part of Europe and the north of Asia and called itself the "socialist camp." It spread from the Baltic Sea in the west to the Pacific in the east and from the Arctic Ocean in the north to the Black Sea, Tian Shan, and the Korean peninsula in the south.

The Soviet Union was born as an attempt to put into practice the ideas of Karl Marx, ideas based on the most attractive moral precepts: freedom, equality, and brotherhood. Unlike Judeo-Christianity, which delays the advent of paradise till the afterlife, Communism promises it here on earth. All you need to do is to join hands in class struggle, eliminate "capitalist exploiters," and build the society of universal commonweal.

The Communist society was to be constructed by Marx's followers, or

Communists. The transitional stage was to be managed by the "dictatorship of the proletariat." This Marxist invention turned out to be most convenient for future dictators, who used the formula to construct their own tyranny in the name of the proletariat.

Although by the mid–nineteenth century Communist ideas had currency throughout the entire western world, only in Russia did their followers manage to seize power and establish a dictatorship. Among many objective reasons one stands out: democratic rule was alien to the native Russian population. A person brought up in the western democratic tradition would find it hard to comprehend, but Russian society has always been receptive to dictatorship. For centuries the fate of the Russian people traditionally has been in the hands of their rulers, whose interests usually did not include their subjects' welfare. As a result, the Russian people became used to being ruled, and gradually this became a part of their national culture.

The Soviet Union, or USSR (the Union of Soviet Socialist Republics), was a "voluntary" union of fifteen republics. The union was called "Soviet" because the official form of the government was the *sòviet*, or "council." Soviets were elected by secret vote (although each ballot contained one candidate only) on all government levels, starting with Village Soviet and going up to Town Soviet to District Soviet to Regional Soviet to Republican Soviet, and, finally, to the Supreme Soviet.

Yet in fact the country was run by a well-organized mafia called the Communist Party, whose structure was as strictly hierarchical (a pyramid with the dictator on top) as that of its Sicilian analog. It was founded at the turn of the twentieth century by the Communist leader V.I. Ulyanov (Lenin) in the course of the Communist fight for power. He called it a "new kind of party." Backed by the party, Lenin and his cohort did not merely grab power in the country. They managed to hold on to it and reinforce it, they won a Civil War against their opponents, and finally they shanghaied a whole nation into the "voluntary" Socialist/Communist construction.

On the basis of Marx's doctrine, the Bolsheviks, as they then called themselves, intended to build a state where everyone would be working "according to one's abilities" and receiving "according to one's needs." Many of them sincerely believed they were building this kind of society.

But not everybody in society was willing to "build the bright future." Force had to be used. Every act of resistance, whether real or imagined, was suppressed by a special punitive force, whose name changed over the years. It started out as ChK, or "Extraordinary Commission" (pronounced *Chekà*, its agents were called "chekists"). Then it became VChK, or "National Extraordinary Commission"; NKVD (People's Commissary of Internal Affairs); and MVD (Ministry of Internal Affairs). The final version, best known at home and abroad, was the KGB (Committee for State Security).

Everything belonged to the State, which allegedly belonged to the people. Such universal socialization naturally led to comprehensive corruption, and widespread theft became the norm. A popular ditty went, "Grab whatever's not nailed down / This is your factory, this is your town." But perhaps it is unfair to hold Soviet power as the only culprit. A Russian proverb, "No living without stealing," predates 1917.

By the late '30s the entire country was covered with a network of so-called voluntary organizations with participation compulsory from an early age. The youngest schoolchildren were called Little Octobrists, after the Bolshevik coup of October 1917. At 10 they became Young Pioneers, an organization modeled after Boy Scouts with a generous dollop of ideology. At 14 they joined the *Komsomòl* (Youth Communist Union). Every adult belonged to a trade union, which, unlike their western counterparts, protected the employer — the administration or the State. Communist Party membership (the "new kind" conjured by Lenin) embraced tens of millions. Joining it became no simple thing, but the benefits were substantial.

Not everyone joined the party for careerist reasons. Some people, cheated by ubiquitous propaganda, believed in Communist ideals. But a disappointed idealist could not leave. The mafia law kicked in.

Just like the "new kind of party," Young Pioneers and *Komsomòl* were structured as pyramids, consisting of small links. Each link had a leader who monitored the members' conduct and reported it upstairs. For example, a *Komsomòl* organization consisted of "primary cells" of three members or more. The cell leader, a *komsòrg*, was formally elected, but in fact these people were pre-selected by the local Communist cell. "Primary cells" were joined in a larger unit (up to ten and more cells) led by the "secretary," to whom the *komsòrgs* reported.

That was the establishing principle for all the "voluntary" organizations. One simply could not avoid membership in at least one of them. An average citizen belonged to several, and in each case he paid dues. From age of fourteen I paid dues to the *Komsomòl*, trade unions, the Builder Athletic Society, the Red Cross, *DOSAÀF* (Voluntary Society for Aiding the Army, Air Force, and Navy), and *MOPR* (International Society for Aiding Workers — I have no idea how I got dragged into that one). One way or another, we were "embraced," as the term went, by at least one cell of these wide-cast networks. And then there was a multimillion-person force moonlighting as the KGB's paid informers. As a result, the state kept tabs on each citizen.

At the age of sixteen a Soviet citizen received an internal passport — a picture ID. Unlike in civilized countries, where a passport is required only for foreign travel, a Soviet citizen used one internally and had to surrender it to get one for foreign travel.

There were several types of foreign passports, depending on the travel

Typical Soviet voting precinct. A compulsory ritual: A Guard of Honor next to the ballot box. Moscow, 1967.

destination. Foreign states were classified according to their policy on giving asylum to Soviet escapees. Citizens deemed insufficiently loyal were issued foreign passports good only for satellite countries, from which they could easily be returned and punished. Then there were those better trusted, and they could travel abroad more freely and hold various passports at the same time.

It was illegal to be outside without a passport. If the militia (as the Soviets called the police) detained you, for example, for drunkenness or jaywalking, absence of a passport was enough to hold you in custody for up to three days. The militia (to say nothing of the KGB) could break into an apartment ostensibly to check passports without a warrant or the residents' permission.

The only people without passports were peasants. They were simply never issued passports. They were "allowed" to live without them. As a result, just like their serf ancestors, they could not leave their villages; if they traveled to town, they had to carry letters from their village councils stating their destination, their purpose, and the time allowed for them to be away. The villagers fought it every way they could, by volunteering for jobs at "special" construction projects, re-enlisting for the draft, marrying urban residents — anything to move to town and get a passport.

Urban living conditions varied, depending on the Communist mafia and state officials. They could build Potemkin villages by giving preferential treatment to locales frequented by foreigners. This covered all aspects of life, from electricity to entertainment to food available in stores. In other words, no one lived well, but some were poorer than others.

The general rule was that life in larger cities was better than in small towns. For example, living conditions in Kharkov were superior to those in Poltava; in Kiev, better than in Kharkov. Moscow boasted the best living conditions in the country. Millions of people visited Moscow daily in search of things to buy. Yet they could not remain there as permanent residents. You could only settle where you were permitted to.

This was controlled by the so-called *propìska*: police stamped your passport and entered your permanent address. It was no simple task changing *propìska*. Sometimes it was impossible even within the same locality.

If you visited a city, whether for personal or work-related reasons, you had to check in at the nearest precinct. If you didn't do it on time, you could be fined or even get a prison term up to six months for "violation of the passport regime."

When you stayed at a hotel, you were to surrender your passport immediately to the clerk for the special stamp at the militia. This took time and increased your chances of being detained on the street without a passport. Technically, you were not supposed to leave the hotel without a passport.

In my last years in the USSR, I traveled a lot on business. Out of sheer contrariness I often refused to hand over my passport for registration, on the flimsy pretext that I had no right to trust strangers with it, even temporarily. I merely echoed the rules of use of the passport, printed in black and white on the last page — as opposed to the non-existent law invoked by the KGB man at the hotel. My refusal put these people on the spot, and they conceded out of surprise. Few people thought of confronting them.

Changing jobs was not easy and was frowned upon. People who changed jobs more often than others were called "fliers," or "fly-by-nights." In order to monitor and limit such moves — as if the passport were not enough — the government came up with a workbook that every adult had to have. Unlike the passport, the workbook was stamped by the employer. You could not get a job without it. The personnel officer (always retired KGB) decided whether a person should be hired. The person's qualifications were a secondary consideration. Other things were more important, like nationality (as far as Jews were concerned) or loyalty reports that reached personnel through their own channels.

Besides passports and workbooks, Soviet citizens were issued various forms of ID — usually with a picture — by schools and workplaces. Those were to be shown to security guards at the entrance, as well as to police and KGB upon being detained. I have been collecting these IDs since childhood, as if I had known from the start that one day they would make for a fine representation of the Soviet system.

Yet passports and *propìska*, workbooks and other IDs and this whole non-freedom of Soviet life were child's play compared to the damage done by the Soviets to the cultural life of the country.

The ignorant, ill-educated leaders who were brought to power by the terror that had followed the 1917 coup d'etat were obsessed with changing the country according to their worldview and cultural level. They taught writing to writers, painting to artists, music to composers, architecture to architects, and so forth. Those who would not learn their lessons were at the very least denied the right to ply their trade; if they persisted, there was also the firing squad.

Thus perished the intelligentsia, the social stratum that carries culture. Instead came the people educated Soviet-style, resembling only very remotely the Russian intellectual elite they replaced.

Westerners familiar with the Russia of Tolstoy, Dostoyevsky, and Chekhov are thinking of people who no longer exist — not since the early twentieth century. A different breed of people has grown to replace them. And I am one of that breed.

Born in the Soviet period, we were told since infancy that we lived in the freest, the happiest, the richest, the most democratic, and the most humane state in the world. The popular Soviet song I have loved since I was a child went, "I don't know any other land / Where a man breathes so freely." Those who disagreed were repressed severely — with jail, concentration camps, and physical elimination. By the time I became conscious of our reality, these people were no longer around.

As a child, I was very gullible. I swallowed the official propaganda, even when whatever took place around me contradicted the official line (on the radio, at school, in books, in the media, or in the movies). I was a regular, run-of-the-mill conformist. I felt happy and lucky to be "building Commu-

Twice a year, on May Day and Revolution Day, every factory and office in the
country held a Celebration Night. The night had a standard state-approved for-
mat, consisting of two parts. Part One was compulsory: everyone listened to a
political report, lasting from an hour to an hour and a half. Part Two was a concert, performed by the office personnel. This is a standard stage view: the table
and the podium removed to make room for performers. The picture shows a
Revolution Day celebration, Part Two, at the YUZH design office. The author is
second from the left with a flute. Kharkov, Ukraine, 1957.

nism, the beautiful future of mankind." At home my family did not engage
in the kind of conversation that could plant the seeds of doubt.

Besides, outwardly things were not so bad. Our life had many aspects to
it and was not all trouble. We had joys, too — just like guinea pigs born and
grown in a cage do, when they get food and are allowed to have sex. Like us,
they had nothing to compare their lives with.

This was our — Soviet — way of life.

I did not know any other way and in my youth never wondered about
its essence. Gradually, as I gained life experience, I began feeling oppressed
by this order of things.

I started figuring out what was going on around me rather late — a few
years after the death of Stalin, whom I loved dearly and who turned out to

be a villain. This happened during the so-called thaw, when I was in my twenties. People who were five to six years younger were lucky. Many of them had a chance to form their views with different, more complete, information, and were able to see the cynicism underlying social relations more clearly.

A lump that rejected reality grew inside me. Like most of my fellow citizens, I was becoming exasperated. At first I tried to adjust; then I opposed the system — alone, in my own simple way. I was hoping to outplay it. My final awakening was prompted in 1968 by the Soviet invasion of Czechoslovakia. As it turned out, I was not the only one. In a few more years emigration was the only way out.

Few people managed to leave the USSR legally between the mid-twenties and late sixties. Later on, ceding to international pressure, the state started letting people go, little by little — but only Jews and only to Israel. This was a risky enterprise. Each visa applicant was persecuted and was never sure whether the outcome would be the departure or years of fighting (while being denied employment and civic rights), or even prison and exile.

Often the desire to emigrate led to family tragedies.

Soviet society was rigidly stratified. My wife Marina grew up in the family of a prominent industrial executive at a large defense factory, with all the ensuing privileges. Thus her life experience was quite different from mine. She perceived Soviet reality differently and disagreed with me about a few things. It was hard for her to make the leap of departure. By then we were at the zenith of our hard-won wealth: prestigious jobs, good salaries, and a recently purchased co-op apartment. It took us another three years to arrive at the decision.

Our family — the lucky one — was able to emigrate in early 1977, fifteen years before the collapse of the Communist enterprise. And then we finally found ourselves in America.

I hope that scholars of the subject will take my oversimplifications here leniently. The idea of presenting this rather schematic eyewitness account of the amazing Soviet Union came from answering questions posed by my grown-up, college-educated children while I told them my Soviet-time stories. Soon there will be nobody to testify to the Soviet Experiment.

I would like to believe that my testimony will help to bury the remaining Socialist myths espoused by many western intellectuals. Their views can dismay those of us who have been inoculated by Socialist demagogy. You have to try very hard to ignore the 70 years of Soviet experience. State officials were not capable of taking care of the population, and Robin Hood–like ideas of taking money from the rich and giving it to the poor yielded little benefit to the latter.

Mother

My mother was called many names: Mùsya, Mànya, or (respectfully) Maria Yàkovlevna. But her birth certificate and her tombstone — two book-ends of a person's life — read the same: Màsya Yànkelevna Schneider.

She was born in the Ukraine in 1906 in the town of Uman, outside Kiev. As a teenager, she survived the horrors of the Civil War in the Ukraine: the Reds fighting the Whites fighting the Greens fighting the Yellow-and-Blues — pogroms and violence and robbery. Her brother Iona, under the assumed name of Yakushinsky, was a commander on the Red side and was one of the first to be decorated with the Military Red Banner Medal (at the time the highest military honor), pinned on him personally by Trotsky. After his death his father was awarded a lifetime pension. Somewhere outside Belgorod, Russia, there was even a museum dedicated to him. My other uncle, Nahum, fought for the Reds and also was killed in action.

Mother was married at eighteen. Her first husband, Aron Kùz'mis, was five years older than she. He was born in the schtetl of Atàki in Moldavia and then moved to Kharkov with his parents. When someone told him that Uman had many pretty Jewish girls, he went there. In short order, he met my mother,

Maria (Màsya) Schneider, the author's mother, Uman, Ukraine, 1924.

fell in love, and they got married. Kùz'mis was a hat maker and an amateur photographer and actor. He made caps and hats and performed on stage. He got my mother into acting, too, performing at a Jewish amateur theater, which was popular in that day.

Soon mother gave birth to her first son, named Iona after her dead brother. He died at the age of two — a sudden death, in a few hours, cause unknown. Mother was sure it was the evil eye. She took it hard and jumped out of the balcony of the hospital where she had brought him. She was saved; recovery took a long time, with a temporary loss of eyesight. Then she broke up with Kùz'mis. According to her, the cause was his parents, with whom they shared one room. They got divorced, and my mother left for Moscow, where for a while she stayed with her older sister Shura, who used her for baby-sitting and housekeeping. Then she found a job at the Moscow Electrical Factory and moved into the factory dorm.

In the early '30s, as a good worker, she was sent to the Advanced Worker Congress in the Kremlin, where she had a chance to observe the entire Soviet leadership at close quarters. She was very impressionable and for the rest of her life described the leaders in pejorative terms — a unique violation of universal conformism in the Soviet Union. For example, she called Stalin "*Yòssele*" and described him as severely lacking in masculine charms: "I saw him as close up as I am seeing you now," she said. "He was short and homely, with traces of smallpox on his face and bad breath. Not like his paintings at all." (Official posters showed him as a tall, powerfully built superman.)

In the '40s and the '50s this kind of talk could easily get you ten years in a camp — or more. As a *Komsomòl* member steeped in ideology, I was aghast at this hostile libel of our "great leader and teacher," which was what I sincerely thought of Stalin.

The author's mother as an amateur actor, Kharkov, Ukraine, 1925.

My mother called Chinese Communist leader Mao Zedong *Mach ze un*, which in Yiddish means "Do them" — with an obscene connotation — which is what happened a few years later.

We fought often about her outspokenness. A few times I came to the verge of denouncing her officially. Thank God it didn't actually happen.

In 1934, mother went back to Kharkov and married — the same old Kùz'mis. The next year I was born. And two years later they broke up again; according to mother, it was caused — again — by his parents (the two families still shared the same room). They got divorced, and this time, it was for good.

After her last fight with Kùz'mis and his parents, my mother grabbed me and ran out of the room. En route she accidentally struck my head on the door frame. I was two, and this was my first memory of my life — that sparks flew out of my eyes.

Two years later, she got married for the third time. This time, it was Aron Berkovich, who adopted me.

My mother brought me up in a spirit of hostility towards Kùz'mis. She called him *meshùgga*, the Yiddish word for madman, and all her life suspected me of meeting with him behind her back (which was strictly forbidden).

In late December 1963, I visited my mother for the last time. She was only fifty-seven, but she looked much older. She was very sick. We were chatting as I sat at her bedside, and she said all of a sudden, "Did you know that Kùz'mis died? Recently, too." Her voice changed, and there were tears in her eyes.

I told her calmly that I had never heard about it — and who would have told me?

"Don't you feel anything for him?"

I shrugged — why? She had been telling me all her life he was a stranger.

She cried. "He died of cancer." (She was wrong. It was a heart attack.) "He wanted to see you very much. He kept saying your name before he died." It looked as if she had never fallen out of love with him.

My mother had a few heartfelt desires. For example, all her life she was sorry that she had refused to marry a man who was about to emigrate to America (she did not want to settle that far from her parents.)

The author's mother at work at the Moscow Electrical Plant, Moscow, 1930.

Another unrealized dream of hers was a movie career. Aron Kùz'mis and she had ambitions that went beyond the stage. I was named after their favorite actor, Gary Cooper.

The other thing she dreamed about was writing down the story of her life. She had seen and gone through so much! The Civil War, the pogroms, the marauding gangs, World War II, the loss of her family,

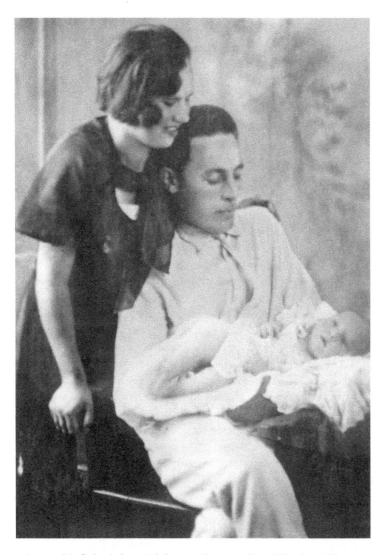

The author on his father's lap with his mother standing, Kharkov, Ukraine, 1935.

including her first son, three marriages.... She wanted to share her experiences with her future grandchildren. But she died early, at the age of fifty-eight, and didn't have a chance to do it.

It so happened that little by little I have been living out mother's dreams. First I emigrated to America. Then — strange as it may seem — I appeared in a Hollywood movie. And now, I have written a memoir.

2

War and Family

The Bridge

In 1941, playing war was the most popular game among boys in Kharkov. Since we were in diapers, we were groomed for military glory. We imagined being Civil War heroes, wearing those dashing cavalry hats and routing the "whites," and we were really frustrated that that war had ended twenty years earlier.

In the meantime, on my sixth birthday my father bought me a bike, a two-wheeler. I mastered it pretty quickly. The trouble was that the moment I would come outside, older kids would take it away from me "for a ride." I did not dare turn them down, yet I did not want to be known as a snitch. Since everybody took turns, sometimes I would get my chance, too. One day, as I was waiting for my turn, I noticed that everyone around was agitated. I was told that the war with Germany had broken out.

I was delighted: finally, a real war!

Like all my friends, I celebrated: now we'll be covered with glory, too. But why were the adults so upset, especially my mom? Also, it took me a while to figure it out: "a war *with* Germany" *against* whom? *Against* Germany, I was told. In retrospect, the question was not that dumb: only a short time earlier, the Nazis were our best friends.

Soon I got myself an exciting hobby — collecting bomb shards. We lived right in the center of the city, in what was once Old Passage, a large shopping complex converted into housing under the Soviets. Next door was Red Army House, a frequent target of German planes. During air raids we stayed at home, which was a deep basement and served as a shelter for us and our neighbors. The moment the siren sounded "all clear," all the kids ran outside in the hope of picking up a fragment of the bomb, nice and warm. We traded them, too, especially the shards that had German lettering on them.

Two and a half months later it was time for evacuation.

The author, five years old. Kharkov, Ukraine, 1940.

Not everybody wanted to go. Many Jews, used to the lies of official propaganda, were sure that the stories of Nazi anti–Semitic savagery were lies, too. My father's parents were among them. They found their end in Kharkov's Drobitsky Yar death camp.

My mother, however, did not doubt the veracity of this information. She had first-hand information from her sister Brònya, who had six months earlier visited us from Uman. She had lived in Poland for twenty years, and now her family had spent over two months under the Germans, living in indescribable fear and expecting SS men to come after them. They got out by a sheer miracle.

My stepfather did not join us. He stayed back to fight. At first he tried to volunteer in the regular army, but he was turned down. Strange as it may seem, there was no room in the army in the chaos of the early days — not enough weapons or uniforms or food supplies or commanding officers. (Just on the eve of the war, Stalin had done a good job purging the armed forces — sometimes with the Germans' help.) At forty, my stepfather was in the reserve and would not be drafted. Yet, despite my mother's begging, he signed up for a voluntary militia to defend the city — with one rifle per twelve people.

We embarked on our trek. My mother was in charge of my six-month-old baby brother Gena, her eighty-one-year-old father, me, two huge bundles of bed linens, and three large suitcases. I still don't know how she managed. I had to leave my precious bike behind, and in all my Soviet life, I never had another bicycle.

My stepfather managed to get us aboard a train with suburban train cars. The car was so jammed as to be on the verge of bursting at its seams. Even before it moved, it was permeated with the smells of sausage, sweat, and urine. Right before the departure, my stepfather brought us a big sack of rolls and two one-liter jars of butter boiled with honey. This was our means of sustenance en route, supplemented with hot water at train stops. Towards the end of the trip, the rolls got rock-hard, yet Grandpa managed to split them with a kitchen knife. Later, during the war, I would remember those rolls and that butter, as I dreamed of the good old pre-war days.

The train moved slowly, stopping several times an hour as it let trains with soldiers pass. Sometimes it would stop for hours. Other times it would be put on a reserve track, where it would sit for days. For children these stops were the main source of amusement: we would gawk at the freight cars rushing past and shout out to soldiers sitting there and dangling their legs in the open doors. We tried to fathom what kinds of weapons were hidden under the tarps on the platforms. We looked for seashells amid the pebbles between the cross-ties. I will never forget the railroad smells: a mix of the tar-soaked cross-ties, the wheel oil, and the scorched car paint.

Often, air raids caused delays. We heard the hum of the planes and the whistle and the bursting of the bombs. The Germans kept blowing up the tracks, and we had to wait for a long time until they were repaired. Then we had to wait for the army trains to pass. Long after the war, I tracked our train's progress on the map. It took us two weeks to cover the distance normally covered in six to eight hours.

Besides, our train was getting longer, with extra cars, both passenger and freight, and even platforms added. Somehow people managed to squeeze inside already jammed cars. They climbed on the roof and rode in the doorways and between the cars and hanging on to the steps.

Often during the stops I managed to give the adults the slip and run along the track before the locomotive whistled departure. Once, caught up in play, I missed the whistle and looked up only when I heard the clanging of the buffers: the train came into motion and was picking up speed. Adult passengers nimbly leaped on the steps, but I was too short to reach for them! I grabbed one, on the last car, and kept running—another moment, and I would have had to let it go! I almost lost hope of reuniting with my mother when someone grabbed my hand and pulled me inside.

It all happened too fast for me to get scared, and I calmly got on my way to my car. It took me a while as I pushed myself through the jam-packed cars and windswept passages between cars, slippery with urine. Finally, in between bodies and luggage I spied my grandfather comforting my mother, who was sobbing in despair. They could not see me. I squeezed closer and tugged at her blouse, trying to draw her attention and find out what she was crying about. Finally, she turned around, her face wet with tears.... She hugged me and then gave me a thrashing. She never let me out again, even to get hot water at long stops.

Life got boring, and I decided to write a letter to my stepfather, who was supposed to be at the front line. I already knew all the letters, but I could only print and needed to dictate. A fellow passenger lent a hand. The letter was short:

"Dear Daddy. I am alive and well. And I wish you the same. Beat the Germans hard. Kisses. Garik."

I folded the sheet into a triangle, as was the custom in those years, and wrote the address, which I remembered well: Berkovich, APO such-and-such. No return address, and no stamp — none was required for front-line mail. I asked someone to drop it in the mailbox at the nearest station.

As we learned later, my stepfather never got my mother's mail, but he did get mine, and it gave him a scare. The letter said nothing about mother or Gena or grandpa. Somehow, my stepfather concluded that I was the only one to survive the bombs (the Germans were known to chase the refugee trains) and became an errant orphan.

While the train was in motion, I tried to take a window seat. I liked watching the phone line — the way the wires seem to race each other, soaring and falling in unfathomable trajectories. As we approached the river, I could see the huge arc of the railroad line and two other refugee trains slowly proceeding towards the bridge ahead of us. One of them barely got on the bridge as the German planes appeared.

I did not get too scared. To the contrary: finally, I saw them live, and so close! They were right above us, racing ahead of the train, likely on their way to bomb the bridge and the station past it.

I could distinctly see the crosses on the body of the plane and tried to make out the pilots. Most of all I was surprised that, unlike the Soviet planes I knew, these had two tails — and for some reason it scared me. I heard the anti-aircraft fire next to the bridge. Without changing formation, the planes soared, then turned with menacing beauty, and finally went in for their target in pairs. Miraculously, neither the bridge nor the train were damaged. I am still wondering why they attacked across the bridge from the river side, rather than following the track — the latter seemed like an easier solution.

Half an hour later we got on the bridge, and the planes came back. Now they were coming straight at me. In the dead calm of the car, the machine-gun fire and the hooting sound of the anti-aircraft guns were especially loud. Like the adults, I stared outside the window, looking at the river far below. I remember trying to figure out whether I would survive the crash. I didn't know how to swim. Mom was quiet, pale-faced, gripping Gena tight. He stopped crying, gazing at us with his eyes wide open. Grandpa prayed, his lips moving without making a sound. Finally, a few horrifyingly long minutes later, the planes were gone. Everyone sighed with relief. Women cried. The train kept on moving. The planes had missed.

We were the last train to make the bridge.

The train behind us was less fortunate. By then we were some distance away, still following the arc of the railroad tracks, and we saw everything clearly, though the sounds did not reach us. Or, perhaps, that was the way I remembered it — burning cars with people were crashing into the river, along with the bridge's metal frame — like a silent movie. Adults around me looked away and wept. Many years later my mother told me that that was the day when much of her hair went gray. She was thirty-five years old.

Later in life, I relived this scene many times over in my nightmares. It was even more terrifying than the one we had gone through while on the bridge.

After that day, somehow I was never enthusiastic about playing war again.

Tashkent

It took us almost two months to get from Kharkov to Tashkent, in Central Asia, with a brief stopover in Kuybyshev (now known as Samara), where we changed to a cattle car. I think my mother and grandfather chose Tashkent for two reasons: to get as far as possible from the Germans and to avoid cold weather. Besides, Tashkent had a reputation for having plentiful food.

We settled on a bench in a vest-pocket park outside the train terminal. I enjoyed the warm dry weather in the late fall, and the green grass along the irrigation ditches. I ran along the garden paths and played with other refugee children. I don't remember what we ate, but I didn't starve. The nights were a little chilly, and the warm blankets we had brought from Kharkov came in handy. The park seemed large, and, though my mother would not let me outside its perimeter, I did not feel confined.

Once I was rolling around the iron hoop one of my new friends had given me, and I saw two familiar faces across the park. Hard to believe, but I recognized Aunt Brònya's children, my cousins — fourteen-year-old Yuzik and fifteen-year-old Nikolay — whom I had seen only in passing in Kharkov when I was not even five.

It turned out that in the chaos of escaping Uman they lost their family and were now looking for them. In Tashkent, they were about to take a train to Samarkand, where they were hoping their parents and siblings had ended up.

I proudly brought them to my mother and grandfather. Everybody was shaken up and excited by this unexpected meeting. As for me, I learned that miracles do happen.

Nikolay and Yuzik

By 1945, my eighteen- and nineteen-year-old cousins Yuzik and Nikolay Zamel were working as lathe operators at an armaments factory in the

Urals. Later, Nikolay would tell me that their monthly salary was just enough to buy a loaf of bread at the market. One day they decided to leave for Brazil. This was not something a regular Soviet person would think of.

The Zamel brothers made it to Lvov, close to Polish border. It was an amazing feat in itself, since train-station police checked not just papers and tickets, but also special traveling permits. Of course they did not have anything like that. They stopped in Lvov to seek ways to cross the border. Legal crossing was out of the question. They thought the simplest way to escape the Soviet Union would be on the bottom of the car of a westbound train.

Yuzik made it somehow. He managed to make his way through Poland, which was occupied by the Soviet Army, and then to Romania and to Italy. There he learned that the quota for Romanians entering Brazil had not been filled. Posing as a Romanian Jew named Zamelesku, he made his way to Porto Alegro, and became a millionaire there.

Nikolay was caught and sentenced to eight years of forced labor in the Donbàss coal mines. He served a full term. After release, he was denied residence registration in the areas within seventy miles of large cities and he settled at a place three hours away from Kharkov by train. He found a job as a bartender at Osnòva railroad terminal in Kharkov. The commute would have been a killer, so he had to violate the terms of release and stayed overnight at his mother Bròxnya's tiny damp basement quarters.

We saw each other frequently. The jail years taught him a lot. He turned out to be an excellent student of that university. When I visited him at Osnòva he showed me how he was making money by short-changing his customers — and without breaking the law, either. He told me that there were special standards within which the bartender could cheat his customers "legally." For example, he could pour ninety-four grams of vodka instead of a hundred and get away with it. In order to avoid suspicion, Nikolay ordered custom-made, ninety-four-gram shot glasses. He sold over three hundred shots a day, both one- and two-hundred-gram, and underpoured over six bottles of vodka, which amounted to his weekly salary. And all of this was within the law! No other bartender ever thought about it and tended to pour below the rim. By contrast, Nikolay always poured right at the rim, which brought him many grateful customers. He made similar arrangements with wine and beer and food.

But he was not happy. He often complained to me that he had different plans for his life and it hurt him to waste his years behind the bar. He dreamed of being a journalist, tried to write, and even applied to enter Kharkov University's journalism school. But that required a high-school diploma, which he didn't have, of course. I suggested that he take evening courses. But he didn't have the patience to spend another three or four years in class and asked me to take graduation exams in his name. We talked about it in all seriousness. I was apprehensive. And then I was drafted.

The author's cousin, Nikolay Zamel. Kharkov, Ukraine, 1954.

While I was in the navy, Nikolay left his bar and went into the "picture business." In the Soviet countryside, it was customary to decorate the walls with family pictures. Local photo studios were rare and portraits cost a lot of money. This was a niche ripe for exploitation.

The "picture business" was as simple as it was brilliant. "Picturemen" traveled through the countryside, picking up clients' small snapshots; then in the city they had them enlarged and retouched by professionals, and delivered the product back to clients. At first the pictures were black-and-white, but then — to the clients' great delight — they were colorized with aniline paints. The "pictureman" was not paid until the client was satisfied, which in the Soviet Union amounted to an incredible level of service.

However, private business was illegal, and "picturemen" needed a front, which was willingly supplied by the photo studios. For a cut of profits, they put the businessmen on their payrolls. With colossal orders, the costs were miniscule. The profits reached 500 to 600 percent. In a single trip to, say, the Urals, lasting four to five weeks, a pictureman could make as much money as an average Soviet engineer in two or three years.

Nikolay was one of the first people in Kharkov (if not *the* first) to discover

The author (left) and a guest from Brazil, cousin Yuzik Zamel. Moscow, 1964.

this gold vein. He traveled tirelessly, and became rich. He spent money liberally, buying expensive clothes and helping his mother.

In Kharkov, he was known as Korèiko, a reference to an underground millionaire from a popular novel. Nikolay tried to live up to the legend. He liked spending money in an obtrusive manner. Someone else with a police record might have chosen to keep a low profile, but that was not Nikolay's way. He was a show-off, period.

At the time the regional party secretary, the "viceroy" of Kharkov, tooled around in a ZIL-111, a Cadillac-like, Soviet-made luxury car, the only one of the kind in the city. Somehow Nikolay managed to befriend his chauffeur. For a hundred rubles a pop (a huge amount of money, exceeding an engineer's monthly salary), the chauffeur would drive Nikolay for a couple of blocks and drop him off on the city's main promenade — a stretch of Sumskàya Street beside the Shevchenko monument, where Nikolay's date du jour was already waiting. The car pulled over, Nikolay stepped out and dropped in a casual voice to the chauffeur: "I won't need you till tomorrow."

Nikolay would blow his earnings in a month or two and would leave again for a few weeks. And then start all over again.

In the late '50s, Nikolay, being Polish-born, got a chance to leave the

Soviet Union legally. But he did not stop at Poland and proceeded on to Brazil where his brother Yuzik lived.

By then Yuzik owned a chain of three stores in Porto Alegre. He received Nikolay happily and offered him a job at one of his stores. The idea was that Nikolay would live with Yuzik in his villa for free and set aside his earnings so that he would join the business as a partner.

Nikolay had no objection to living for free and getting paid. But he turned down the job offer outright: he reasoned he had not wasted his best years in the camp to break his back now. So he left for Rio, where, according to Yuzik, he spent days and nights on the Copacabana. Clad in a white suit and wielding a cane, he "had a girl on his left arm, a girl on his right arm, and the third one he just kicked forward — toward the hotel."

Soon he got tired of this ritzy life, too. He decided to build a fish-smoking factory. "There's a shortage of that in Brazil," he wrote me, requesting some literature. I went through every Moscow bookstore and finally found a brochure on smoking fish. Six months later, we got the news: the factory had opened. And then it had to be closed. According to Yuzik, Nikolay "poisoned half the city." It cost Yuzik a fortune to settle the case and keep Nikolay out of jail.

By then Nikolay had developed a different obsession: being a playwright. One of his plays even got produced. Yet some tireless local critic wrote that, while the play was not so bad, it was "partially" borrowed from Shakespeare. The production went down the tube. A scandal broke out, and Yuzik had to repay his investors.

This was not the last scandal. Yuzik would not talk much about it when he visited us in Moscow, but there were enough hints that Nikolay even managed to get involved in drug trafficking from Columbia.

But Nikolay's creative urges were not to be suppressed for long. He reported to me in Moscow that he "was composing one-liners" and was writing "up a storm." They sold a buck apiece, he wrote, which in Brazil was enough to lead a life of leisure. "A dollar is a thousand cruzeiro; in Brazil, with a thousand dollars, you're a millionaire." He sent me some of his product — "you can take it to a publisher and make a fortune." Some of his bon mots were quite witty, while others sounded like this: "Strolling through evening streets, I have fun looking into lit windows." It was hard for me to imagine a publisher who would jump at that.

In another letter, Nikolay wrote that Brazilians are crazy about soccer. That prompted him to write a book called *How to Make a Fortune in Soccer Betting* and, naturally, make a fortune on it. From Moscow it was not easy to tell his fantasies from truth. The Brazilians' devotion to soccer was well-known — the market was there for the taking. But that Nikolay would be the one to conquer it?

In the late '60s, Nikolay wrote me from Rio that he had met a woman of stunning beauty, "a smoldering petite hot pepper who left a billionaire husband for me. She is very jealous and packs a Beretta in case she catches me with another woman. Her name is Fira and she comes from Ufa." (Ufa is an obscure Bashkir town in the Urals, light years away from Rio in every way.) Later Yuzik would tell me that Fira and Nikolay had lived it up for two years, moving around in casinos and ritzy resorts and hanging out with film stars like Rubens De Falco, who tried to take Fira away — in vain, of course. Eventually, they ran out of her settlement money, and Nikolay — like a true *l'homme fatal*—had to leave. Inconsolable, Fira killed herself with her Beretta.

At that time, Yuzik decided to open a business with an Israeli partner and asked Nikolay to be his representative. He bought Nikolay a ticket to Tel Aviv and gave him $10,000 for the investment, promising to send him more if necessary for the business.

For a while, neither Yuzik nor his Israeli companion heard a word from Nikolay. Finally, after three months Yuzik got a wire: "The ten thousands are spent, and you promised to send more."

Yuzik got the picture and refrained from sending money or a return ticket. By default, Nikolay had to make an aliya and become an Israeli.

Another six months or a year later we in Moscow got a letter from Nikolay: he was living in Israel and he was doing fine, married to a military officer's widow, who was getting a good pension, enough to live on. But he was making out all right, too, from selling his ... paintings.

This is how we learned that Nikolay had become a painter. I was one of the first people he wrote about it. He also asked me to send him a set of oils with extra tubes of white. Only zinc whites — no lead stuff. And some extra fine brushes.

No one was surprised at this turn in Nikolay's life, as well as at the request to send the supplies that must have been in acute shortage in Israel. After a while, he started sending color pictures of his paintings. Unsurprisingly, he turned out to be leaning towards abstractionism. He signed his paintings Juan Lemaz. Since Israelis wrote from right to left, he explained, it was only logical that his last name Zamel should read as "Lemaz," and his Jewish name, Noah, as "Juan."

I sent him a couple more paint sets. Now Nikolay wrote that, as a "famous Brazilian painter," he had opened an art gallery in downtown Tel Aviv, and the opening was attended by members of the government and the "famous art critic Moshe Baam." Now we had no idea whether we should believe this or not, but we were relieved to hear that his life had acquired a certain stability.

He also wrote that he decided to buy his Kharkov nieces a car each, and suggested they should get a drivers' licenses as soon as possible. The nieces rushed to take training courses, but his older sister Irene was skeptical: "That big mouth. Just teasing the girls."

She turned out to be right. The promised cars never arrived. When they reminded him, the letters fell to a trickle.

We emigrated in the mid–'70s. Earlier, Nikolay kept urging us to come to Israel, but now he changed his tune "You belong in America, of course." As was his wont, Nikolay promised me generous financial support upon arrival in the West — enough to live on till we got to America.

A couple of months later, when the first shock of emigration wore off, I reminded him of his promise — almost as a joke and not expecting anything. But in another four months, just as we were about to leave Rome for the U.S., I got a check for $500 from him. A few years later I sent him a check to repay the loan. He took umbrage; he wrote that it was a gift, not a loan. Yet the check was cashed.

In another letter to Rome, Nikolay sent me the phone number of his "closest friend" in New York. "You don't even have to call. Find Nakhàmkin's Gallery. Tell him you are my cousin. He'll do everything for you. He'll do right by you."

I figured it was another pipe dream and never went to New York or called Nakhàmkin. Much later I would discover that Nakhàmkin was a real person, a well-known art dealer, whom Nikolay knew in Israel. Yet I never tried to discover what Nakhàmkin thought of Nikolay and whether it had been realistic to expect him to help.

By 1981, Nikolay wrote that he was tired of Israel's hot climate and had decided to move to Miami. He was invited by a millionaire friend who bought his paintings in Israel. He showed up on our doorstep in the middle of an Illinois winter. It was a bit of a shock. He bore a resemblance to the handsome devil we remembered, but in fact he was a shadow of his old self—an elderly man who had taken life's many blows. His teeth were bad, and the spark in his eye was gone.

We issued him thermal underwear, and after a week he adjusted to the cold climate. He started cracking jokes, and — without missing a beat — lecturing us on how to live. It turned out that the true purpose of his visit was to make us millionaires. He would be painting and we would be selling his paintings. How much would a painting 24x30 inches, nicely framed, go for? A hundred bucks? Materials (canvas-paints-frame) would set us back twenty to thirty dollars at the most. Labor would cost us nothing — he would paint for room and board. He could do fifteen or twenty paintings a day; a hundred a week. At seventy dollars' profit a painting, the profit came to seven thousand a week, or three hundred fifty thousand a year. Our million was a mere three years away. Then we would invest it well — he would tell us how — and in a few more years we all would be millionaires.

We bought a few canvasses stretched on frames, some paints and brushes. Nikolay locked himself in a room for a whole day and "produced" six paintings. Following his advice, my brother Gena and I, conscientious workers that we were, carried these six, along with the ones Nikolay had brought earlier, to a Ukrainian church. Why a church and why Ukrainian? Nikolay knew better, we reasoned. To our surprise, we were met by a person who was indeed selling art. He glanced at Nikolay's works and suggested that we take them to a synagogue. His reasoning was as obscure to us as Nikolay's. After speaking to a couple of gallery owners, we concluded that no one in Chicago was interested in the works of Juan Lemaz, a famous Brazilian artist from Israel.

After less than a month, Nikolay went back to Miami, and then back to Brazil. Yet he did not abandon his notion of making me a millionaire and kept sending me one idea after another. One was a sure-fire method of winning the lottery; another, a design of a car train; finally, a screenplay he had written back in Israel about an American who was made Hero of the Soviet Union. I was supposed to sell it in Hollywood and make a fortune.

In 1995, my last letter to him came back. Six months later, I learned he was dead.

His last source of income was a taxicab. He bought a car with a cab license and rented it out. The driver paid him weekly. One day he brought Nikolay money, but no one answered the door. Eventually, they had to break down the door. He had died of a heart attack at night in his own bed. He left behind a car and ten thousand dollars, which became a source of discord among his brothers and sisters, still alive.

I remembered Nikolay's visit to Moscow in '58, just before his departure from the USSR. He needed to fill out some last-minute papers, buy an inflatable boat (he heard they sold like hotcakes in Poland), and, while he was at it, bid his goodbyes to the family.

It was late autumn, it was cold, and it had been raining for weeks. We met downtown in the evening. We walked down the boulevards, strewn with wet yellow leaves, and talked about a thousand things. We had never been close, but the realization that we would never see each other again made us very sad and unwilling to say goodbye.

We talked politics. Nikolay philosophized plenty and talked about his plans and fantasized what his life would have been like if he had not been forced to try to cross the border illegally.

The subway station was abandoned. A slender girl, soaking wet, her lips blue with cold, approached us and shyly offered to sell "the last bunch" of sickly chrysanthemums. To my surprise, Nikolay patted his pockets and found a three-ruble bill. He bought the flowers, fluffed them a little, and courteously presented them to the girl, numb with surprise.

Cotton Growers

We spent two weeks in a park outside Tashkent's train terminal among other war refugee families, and in December of 1941 were put on the train, and taken to the town of Merzachul, west of Tashkent, en route to Samarkand.

Once again we were riding in a stinking, jam-packed suburban train car. Grandpa settled with our possessions at the tambour, while mother and I and my baby brother Gena were on a nearby bench inside the car.

Soon after we departed late at night we heard grandfather call for help. The scene was terrifying: Grandpa was fighting two young bandits, who, wielding knives, were trying to wrest our things away. By the time we got there, they had already got the bundle of our bedding. Then, suddenly the door opened, and their trophy fell outside. Despite his eighty-something years of age, Grandpa was no slouch and he managed to push the thug outside to follow his loot — and, to our horror, almost fell out himself. Other passengers came to our aid and sent the second robber crashing outside to chase the first one.

Grandpa's clothing and his long gray beard were covered in blood, but it turned out that all he had suffered was a few cuts. We couldn't settle down till we reached Merzachul a few hours later.

In the morning we were loaded on a cart with two huge wheels — an *arba*— driven by an exhausted-looking animal with long ears and a back covered in sores. I had seen a donkey — or, as the locals called it, *ishak*— only in pictures and in the Kharkov zoo. It flatly refused to go anywhere and indicated that it was loath to do anything in general but chase away flies and look for something to eat. It took our guide a considerable effort to make it move.

We were bound for Pakhtakor collective farm, where local authorities decided to resettle us. Mama and Gena and our possessions were on the cart, while Grandpa and I and our guide from the farm plodded along silently — the guide spoke no Russian — on the side of the dirt road. The road wove through the cotton fields that stretched to the horizon, with irrigation ditches cutting through them. Cool air was pleasantly warmed by the rising sun. I inhaled the strange smell of clay dust mixed in with camel dung. I looked around, and I rejoiced in everything that was so new.

The road was well-traveled: we ran into a number of similar carts loaded with melons and watermelons, with more donkeys, and camels, which I had seen only in the zoo, and whose riders in their exotic padded gowns seemed to be nodding off. Both donkeys and camels were loaded with huge bales of white stuff, which, I learned later, was called cotton. I had never seen cotton bushes before and kept slipping away to tear off another half-opened fruit.

The only thing that marred my joy was our donkey. It kept plodding and stopping, and was engaged in a constant fight with our guide. The donkey was absolutely opposed to going in the direction needed. He responded to whipping by braying and resisting. Then our guide, knowledgeable in the donkey's ways, would purposely drag him back. Out of stubbornness, the donkey headed forward. Ever since, whenever I hear the words "stubborn as a donkey," I think of our Pakhtakor *ishak.*

It took us four hours to cover about seven miles, and the Central Asian sun was getting to be a real scorcher.

We were put in a tiny dugout, a hole in the ground slightly larger than the kitchen in our Kharkov apartment and slightly deeper than Grandpa's height. Banks of dirt on the sides formed the top of the walls. On top of them were ricks, slightly aslant; on top of those was a thick layer of clay mixed with straw that formed the roof. A narrow sloped path was dug to the entrance — a small hole with a curtain of straw. Grandpa had to bend in half to get in.

The clay floor had two levels: about two steps wide at the entrance and then the main one that came up to my waist, where we slept on large straw pallets. Between the levels was a hearth called the *sandàl,* formed by two holes in the ground — one in the floor, and the other perpendicular to it in the vertical ledge formed by the difference in levels. The *sandàl* was quite large in diameter — I could easily hide in it. Over the sandàl was a low wooden table that did not reach to my knee and whose legs perched on the edge of the hole. It was covered with a dark cloth that descended to the floor. A flue (a hole in the roof) was approximately above the *sandàl.*

For fuel we used *kizyàks*— big round patties of animal dung, mixed with straw and dried in the sun. We found a pile of these patties not far from the hut, along with some *saxaul*—a shrub used by locals for firewood. A small stinking clay toilet without a door was nearby, with a hole in the floor and flies of frightening size.

Sandàl was used both for cooking and heating the hut, which at night got damp and cold. The Uzbek guide showed us how to use it. It was quite comfortable for warming up. When patties burned out, they turned into hot coals. We settled on the pallets next to the *sandàl* and dropped our feet in the hole under the table. The tablecloth ended on our laps, blocking the cold air from the sandàl. You could have tea at the same time on the table. For tea we tore up large homemade *lepèshki* (flat bread) the guide left for us. They seemed to me a delicacy on the order of pre-war rolls. I still remember their specific sour taste and smell.

I once saw how those *lepèshki* were made. An elderly Uzbek woman kneaded the dough, then pushed the *sandàl* table aside and slapped big round pieces of dough on the *sandàl's* still warm black walls. The *lepèshki* were considered done when they fell off the walls on the cooling coals of *kizyàks.* Then she took them out and carefully laid them out with a gray towel that gave off a strange, unpleasant smell. None of this cooled off my love for them.

We drew the water for drinking and washing from a nearby irrigation ditch. We saw the same ditch used for laundry and bathing.

Later we were visited by The Boss — "Comrade Ibragìmov," the farm chairman. He inspected our arrangements, patted Gena's head, and spoke to mom. Before he left, he instructed the man who came with him in Uzbek. The next day someone brought us a little flour and rice and a string of onions. A week later, he came back. Mother asked him to find some work for her and Grandpa that they could do at home. His answers, she reported later, were "evasive and incoherent."

After the first few days we were given to settle down, I was called in to help the farmers pick cotton.

This was women's work. I saw men only a few times — they came on donkeys to see if everything went well. The pickers followed dried ditches along the cotton shrubs with large sacks. They nimbly tore off the seed cases and dropped them into their sacks; once those filled, they would pour the contents into huge baskets that they gracefully balanced on their heads and carried to the common pile. Despite the heat, they wore sturdy long blouses over cotton pants. Their faces were hidden under nets called *paranja*. Later I learned it was an Islamic tradition and elsewhere this net was known as the hijab.

Along with other local kids, I followed the pickers with a small bag of my own, to pick up what they sometimes missed on the shrubs or dropped on the ground. I don't remember getting tired or bored. Time went fast, and I had fun with the other kids, though none of them spoke Russian. I must have picked up a few Uzbek words, which sufficed for communication. Children taught me how to pick and pop cotton seeds, which I quickly learned to like, and I even brought some home.

Somehow, the cotton, the picking, the women in *paranjas*, the life in the damp hut — somehow, all of this exotica failed to win me. It was too much, all at once, and I must have developed a defensive reaction rather quickly.

One night, two or three weeks after our arrival, Comrade Ibragimov invited us over. He lived far away, and he sent a cart to pick us up.

We walked through a terrace in the courtyard of a large house behind a tall clay wall and found ourselves in a large, rug-decorated room, well-heated and already crowded. All were men, with a few kids my age and slightly older. My mom was the only woman present. Everyone sat on the beautiful rugs. In the middle of the room was an elevation, also covered with a rug and serving as a table. We were seated in the center, facing the host, and my mom was seated at his side, sleeping baby Gena next to her.

The food was already on the table: a huge glazed dish with a mountain of steaming, delicious-smelling pilaf, with big bones and chunks of meat sticking out. There were no other dishes, no plates, and no cutlery. Everybody reached for the pilaf and grabbed pieces of it and laughed at our awkwardness.

Oily fat flowed down their arms, and they simply soaked it with their patties or licked it off. I have been to many a dinner like this since and read about them in books. But that was the first time, and I nervously looked around, trying to copy other guests' manners.

After the pilaf we drank tea out of large cups called *pialas*, held with two hands, and ate lots of grapes and honey, all brought by silent women in dark clothing and *paranjas*. They appeared and disappeared, without partaking of the feast or the conversation. My mother was talking to the host, who may have been the only one present who spoke Russian. Smiling and smacking his greasy lips, he was chatting her up as he was helping her to the tastiest pieces. I don't know if it was a routine dinner, but I felt I was at a feast. My stomach was not used to these amounts of food, and I got a stomachache and nausea. My mother noticed and made a fuss over me. We left soon afterwards.

Next day Comrade Ibragimov invited mom to his place. He sent an *arba* for her. She declined the invitation, using Gena's health as an excuse.

We left the farm a week later. The cart, the donkey, the guide, the road — everything was like the first time, but in the opposite direction.

Many years later, my mother told me that we "escaped," as she put it, because the chairman "had designs on" her.

Turkestan

In the spring of '42 we were invited by mother's sister Aunt Zhènya to join her in the Kazakh settlement of Turkestan. At the time, it consisted of two small towns. One was old, founded in times immemorial — a run-of-the-mill Central Asian village, with crooked narrow streets and small adobe houses behind huge clay walls, or *duvàls*. The new town was about seven miles to the west. It had sprung from the railroad laid down in the valley of the Syr-Darya River and centered around the train station and a rail yard. The settlement grew eastward, towards the old town, and after the war they merged, I believe.

We lived on the west side of the tracks, slightly to the north of the station, on Railroad Street, which, as the name indicates, stretched along the rail yards.

Aunt Zhènya had settled in Turkestan with an elderly Uzbek family. Their residence consisted of a few dwellings around a small rectangular courtyard, with an entrance in the northern wall of the *duvàl*. We settled in one of the dwellings, in a room next to Aunt Zhènya's. She had two children, Tòlik, 10, and Bella, 4. Zhènya's husband, Uncle Zyàma, was released from front line duty — "thank God he's been suffering from diabetes for five years" — and was instead drafted into a civilian job in Chimkent, a few hours' drive south from our place.

Our hosts had two goats and a large, good-natured dog, whom I befriended right away. My year-old brother Gena already toddled a little and spent all his time in the dust with the goats and the dog.

Tòlik immediately took me under his wing. He showed me a bazaar half an hour away, past the many rail yard tracks, where one could get quite a bit to eat by picking dried apricot pits off the ground. We filled small sacks with pits and then sat at the side of the dirt road and smashed them with rocks. Sometimes our harvest was big enough to bring some home. The inside of the pits tasted like almonds and was our main means of sustenance that summer.

Sometimes we managed to swipe a bit of fruit from a distracted vendor. Sometimes sympathetic Uzbeks would toss us bits of bread patties. In the summer, we picked up discarded apple cores. We cleaned off the dirt and finished them with pleasure. Ever since, I have eaten apples core and all.

Our main bazaar competition — besides other boys — were the so-called Polaks, who barely stayed on their feet. They were mostly old people who silently wandered around the stalls with an outstretched hand. They hardly ever got anything. Helpless and starving, groups of them, sometimes whole crowds, lay on the ground in neighboring streets. Years later I saw similar skeleton-like former camp inmates in a documentary. I didn't know it then, but they were Polish Jews who had escaped Hitler. They numbered in the thousands and they lived in the street. Every morning I saw two carts slowly making the rounds and inspecting them on the ground. Those who weren't breathing were tossed on the cart. Afterwards, the overloaded carts were taken out of town and tossed into pits, which were later covered with chlorine and dirt. A couple of times mom showed me those horrible pits on our way to the old town.

We were lucky. We slept in beds and once a week went to the public baths, where men and women washed on alternate days. Mom took Gena and me on women's day, but a girl thought I was studying her too intently, and then I started washing with Grandpa and Tòlik on men's days.

At no other time in my life have my cousin Tòlik and I been as close as that summer. Once, as usual, we were scavenging for food at the bazaar. It was a hot dusty day, with smells of rotten vegetables. The morning crowds were thinning out, except at the areas where used clothes and other inedible stuff was sold.

Suddenly, a young man broke out of the crowd, followed by a few others, and they ran towards us. As he came abreast of us, he grabbed Tòlik's hand tightly and clenched it into a fist — and then ran on, overturning stalls on the way.

Tòlik stood next to me, his eyes wide open and his mouth agape, unable to exhale or inhale. He held his hand in a fist up, in a salute of sorts. We managed to bring it down; but we could not unclench the fist. Tòlik's face grew red. He could breathe, but his hand was paralyzed.

Back home, Tòlik's mother was scared speechless. She could not unclench his fist either. On Grandpa's advice we lowered it into a bowl with warm water down to the elbow. A half-hour later Tòlik finally smiled and took his hand out of the bowl. When he unclenched the fist, there was a thirty-ruble bill in it. Everybody

The author's mother and younger brother Gena. Turkestan, Kazakhstan, 1942.

rejoiced — a regular celebration, with Tòlik in the center of it, laughing and planning what he would do with the money. He settled for a kilo of dried fruit.

Once we had a real feast. Our hosts' goat somehow managed to drink some kerosene from a container in the closet and instantly dropped dead in the middle of the yard. Little Gena shrieked with joy at a trick like that and started tugging at it. The host's wife yelled at her husband, and he ran outside, wielding a knife. I rushed to block him, but his target was not Gena. With one quick movement he slashed the goat's throat. As I was told later, he was in a hurry to do it while the goat was still alive.

The hosts dared not sell the meat of the half-dead goat. It reeked of kerosene. The goat was cut into pieces, and we got one, and we had a feast. I tasted the meat, but I couldn't eat it, though I was quite hungry. I remembered the goat too well.

Before the war, Tòlik had finished first grade and now told me a lot about his school in Kharkov. I was especially impressed by their school lunch — a roll with a little meat patty inserted. With each successive retelling, the patty grew in size and turned into a huge juicy chunk of meat. When, 35 years later, I saw my first Big Mac, it was in a sense a return to my childhood dreams.

The local school was a handsome two-story building close to the bazaar, which we passed often. In the summer it was closed, but in August we saw it open and came in. As a pro in all school things, Tòlik found the office, and we were enrolled. I followed Tòlik's advice and lied about my age. I told them I was eight. As an older child, Tòlik confirmed this. We were told to bring our birth certificates. But in the chaos of the first day of school, no one asked us about them.

There were no rolls with patties — but there was a generous spoonful of sugar that came with a cup of tea.

All of us had gone through malaria, except for baby Gena, but it was my mother who was hit the hardest. She had a bout of fever every other day, and they were so bad that Aunt Zhènya lost all hope of recovery. Quinine did not help.

Finally, in late September the disease started waning. Weak, thin, and yellow-faced, my mother stayed in bed. Now she began to talk. She called me to ask in a barely audible voice why I was away all day long. I proudly told her that I was going to school. She smiled as she patted me on the head; clearly, she did not believe me. Then she fell asleep again. When she recovered, she was surprised to see that I was indeed a student. She wept. It had been her dream to take me by hand to the first grade!

To get to school I had to cross the rail yard. There was no fence or marked crossing. Anyone who crossed the tracks took his life into his own hands.

The author with his mother and kid brother Gena. Turkestan, Kazakhstan, 1942.

The arriving train, about twenty cars long, was driven to the so called "hump yard," or a man-made hill. The cars were uncoupled, and the locomotive would lightly push the train to the edge of the hill. The lead car would slowly start on its way down. The switchman would switch the car to the track where a train was forming. Then the locomotive would push the next car to the edge of the hill. The cars moved with minimum noise. And if the coupler was absent, there was no one to warn of the approaching car.

We often stood on the track waiting for the train to the front line to pass. We were fascinated by the sight of endless cars filled with soldiers. Once we were too busy gawking to see a freight car coming from the side of the switch.

There were four of us. Tòlik and I were to the right of the approaching car, which pushed us off the earth fill; we got off with a scare and a few bumps on the head. The boy on Tòlik's left fell next to us; he twisted his foot and could not get up till some adults came by. And the fourth boy, the closest to the oncoming car, fell straight on the tracks and was killed.

This was a hell of a thing to see at the age of seven: a head rolling between the rails and a large puddle of blood next to the body on the slope.

We were hoping to conceal the incident from our parents. But soon they found out and tried to keep us away from school. But our thirst for knowledge prevailed ... to say nothing of the spoonful of sugar with the tea.

Tòlik and I did not play war. Our intentions were more serious. We would go to war. The plan was simple. We would sneak into one of the front line-bound trains as it paused at the station. When we get to the front line we would enroll in combat units. If we got turned down, we would join the partisans. We would live in the woods, pick berries and mushrooms, and blow up Nazi trains.

We actually took a few stabs at it. Once, just before the train left the station, a soldier pulled us out and took us to the station's commandant. The latter was happy to see that the "volunteers" were homespun — less hassle this way — and simply told an MP to take us home. We got home before our parents had a chance to get scared. Still, we got a good thrashing.

Frustrated with this lack of understanding, we hatched another plan: to build an airplane and fly it to the front line. We liked this plan even better. It was easier to implement.

We stole metal sheets through a hole in the barbed-wire fence from a scrap yard not far from home and glued them with clay right in our courtyard. It was a slow process; once the clay dried, the sheets got loose. And we had no other material to glue the iron together.

By the time we made a cockpit for two and a wing, it occurred to Tòlik that we might need an engine. That was a major problem. We put in a lot of time going through the scrap metal, hoping to find an engine, till we were spotted by the guard. The landlady, too, voiced her displeasure. We had made a mess of the courtyard.

Now Grandpa got involved. Tòlik suggested we invite him along. This was not a good idea. Grandpa was not enthusiastic and took our "plane," piece by piece, back to the scrap yard. By then Tòlik had cooled off, too — a girl next door was more interesting. Left alone, I had to give it up.

For his ten years of age, Tòlik showed a disproportionate interest in the opposite sex, which led to many adventures, both sad and funny. Occasionally he came back home with a bloody nose.

After the war, when he was in the seventh grade or so, he had an artistic awakening: he was a bound to be a great actor. He was in a school play.

I still remember him climbing a stool during family occasions and reciting a Pushkin poem in a still breaking voice. The family was ecstatic.

The problem was that in the year 1951, even with a major talent, a Jew had a hard time getting into theater school. He was drafted and was sent to Azerbaijan. With a name like Naphtali Lisnevsky, he could not escape the attention of the anti–Semites. After some beatings, Aunt Zhènya got on a plane. After a few rubles changed hands, Tòlik was transferred to a desk job at the headquarters.

After his service, Tòlik entered a construction trade school and became a contractor. He married a girl named Galya and shelved his acting dreams. Still, from time to time he would climb on stage and recite his Pushkin. Galya gave birth to a girl named Irene. Tòlik had to fight to get an apartment and make a living. He was hopeless. His job wasn't working out and he did not learn how to steal. They were surviving with his parents' help.

In the late '70s, his daughter and her husband decided to emigrate. By then Tòlik had divorced Galya, and, egged on by his mother, he tried to prevent them from getting an exit visa. At the authorities' suggestion, he went as far as publishing an open anti–Israel letter in a newspaper and took it to the local TV channel. Irene left anyway, but would not hear about her father again. Later on, he told me he was afraid he would lose his job. He did get to keep it. But his dignity was gone, and his daughter, too.

He remarried and had another daughter, Victoria. Soon thereafter, he started going blind. Another fifteen years later, blind, with his wife and second daughter, he found himself in Israel. His sister Bella and her husband emigrated, too.

In my memory he had not changed from the evacuation days, though we stayed in touch, more or less, and even met in Moscow in 1987 when I came back from America for the first time. He was already blind then.

His father, Uncle Zyàma, was a gentle and affable person. He never raised his voice. He was a bookkeeper, and, perhaps, a highly competent one. He always seemed to agree with everybody. He was the kind of bookkeeper who, when asked how much was two times two, would answer, "How much do you need?"

In the late fall of 1942, he finally decided to settle in Chimkent, and called us to join him. For some reason we traveled in a flatbed truck, rather than by train, and — inexplicably — at night. The bed of the truck was filled with empty boxes and barrels well above its walls. We rode atop this pile, along with our belongings, defying the laws of physics. Aunt Zhènya and Bella rode in the cab.

I could not fall asleep. I was terrified. I had overheard adults talk about a gang that robbed villages and trains and trucks. That night, I felt we would be attacked.

From time to time, as the road curved, the headlights illuminated fantastic snatches of the nighttime landscape. And each time left me more scared as I kept seeing the villains' silhouettes ahead. The night sky was cloudy, with bits of the moon showing up here and there, making the mood more ominous. Baby Gena, who rode in my mother's arms somewhere atop the cab, kept waking up and crying. Mother gave him her breast. The road was bumpy, and the truck swayed wildly from side to side. Riding atop the boxes, I felt that this time we would be tossed overboard for sure. Once my leg got stuck between the boxes. I could not get it out. Grandpa, seeing the state I was in, kept telling me stories and hugging me. Incredibly, Tòlik slept calmly next to me.

The trip took all night. To me, it lasted an eternity — like the war itself.

Uncle Yefim

Barely had we settled in Chimkent when Uncle Yefim, mother's older brother, showed up. He found himself in the army early in the war, but then was de-mobbed due to his age — fifty-eight. He found us and took mother, Gena, and me to the nearest collective farm, which hired him as a blacksmith.

The farm was a large rich village. We lived in a spacious clay hut, in a total contrast to our hole in the ground on our first Uzbek farm.

Soon I was enrolled in the village school. It was a small, modest house consisting of one room only, for about twenty students, where all four grades studied at the same time. The longer wall featured a blackboard with a Stalin picture above it. In the left corner was the teacher's small desk. We sat on two wooden benches along large tables.

The four first-graders shared the front desk with second-graders; the third- and fourth-graders sat behind us. The teacher handed us assignments in turn. While one grade was doing its assignment, she would be working with the next one. While I learned how to write letters, she would be dictating a text to fourth-graders.

Of course we didn't have any exercise notebooks or textbooks. Under the teacher's guidance, we carefully cut newspaper pages and bound them into notebooks. We used printed text for horizontal lines. We made our own ink, too. Our teacher procured a copying pencil somewhere and we chipped its lead core and dissolved it in water. Somehow she also managed to procure inkpots and pens with metal quills that we were allowed to take home to use for homework. Since everything we wrote on newsprint seeped through, we could use one page only.

There were no teaspoons of sugar during the long recess as I had expected. Instead we got a wheat bread patty and a cup of milk. I loved that school.

I spent my free time at Uncle Yefim's blacksmith shop, blowing up the bellows. Sometimes I even helped his assistant hold slabs of hot metal with pliers. Uncle Yefim showed me how to temper metal, how to heat it without overburning it, and other little tricks of the trade. I'll make a fine blacksmith out of you, he would say. I couldn't wait for that, too, though I was a little afraid of horses, and could not imagine that I'd be able to put on horseshoes as deftly as he did.

We lived on the farm for only two or three months and then went back to Chimkent. Uncle Yefim stayed back and helped us the best he could.

Uncle's real Jewish name was Haikel or Hayim. He was the oldest son in the family. Grandpa Schneider gave him a good education at the Jewish school and a decent skill, that of a mechanic, which was a lot for a poor Jewish family in the Pale. Long before World War I, Uncle Yefim started the first bicycle repair shop in Uman.

At nineteen, he married a relative, Malka, against his parents' will. He just went to another schtetl and then came back with a wife. In the tradition of the day, Grandpa cursed his favorite son — and firstborn. He disavowed him and would not talk to him for years.

The marriage turned out not exactly made in heaven. Their children kept dying. By the time the war started, out of eight or ten, only three children survived. The oldest son, Zyuma, hobbled along on crutches. Another son, Yosif (Yòssele), also had some serious disease. Only 18-year-old Yuzef, affectionately called Yuzik, grew up healthy and handsome.

The Germans occupied Uman weeks after the war broke out. Yuzik and 57-year-old Uncle Yefim were drafted, while Malka with their sons and a daughter-in-law didn't leave in time. We heard of her tragic death three years later, after Uman was liberated.

Drunken Ukrainian policemen — possibly, the boys next door who had only recently played with her own children — forced Malka

Uncle Yefim Schneider. Kharkov, Ukraine, 1950.

at gunpoint to dig a hole in her own yard. Then they pushed in her sons and her daughter-in-law and buried them alive. According to the neighbors who came in to gawk at how "the Yids will get their comeuppance," Malka lost her mind. Half-naked, with her hair undone and instantly turned gray, she was forced to dance as policemen shot at her feet. Then they shot her dead.

Yuzik changed his name to a Russian-sounding Yevgeny, joined the Party, became a paratrooper, and marched with the army as far as Prague. He was wounded many times, but survived. In the last year of the war we exchanged letters, which I saved for years, along with a few Czech wartime bank notes he sent me as souvenirs. He was my hero.

The author's cousin Yuzik (Yevgeny) Schneider. Front lines, 1945.

He came home with his chest covered in medals. He got married and had a daughter named Irene. Subsequently she became an academician and a top expert in turbine-making.

In 1955 Khrushchev called on the Soviets to develop land in Kazakhstan. Yevgeny-Yuzik, as a good Party member, heeded the call. He came back a few years later, disease-ridden, and with a brain tumor. The surgery was unsuccessful; he became disabled and gradually went blind.

When, in 1944, Uncle Yefim learned what had happened to his family in Uman, he chose not to go back and settled in Kharkov. He never remarried, though his sisters tried to introduce him to many ladies. He wouldn't have any of it. He found a job as a plumber at an elite residential building and stayed there till he was forced into retirement at the age of eighty-two. He was angry and refused to accept the pension. "I won't rip off the state!" He continued to do odd jobs: in one apartment he would fix a toilet, in another a sink.

He was religious, too. In those days observant Jews were denounced as "cosmopolite Zionists" and "vassals of Israeli aggressors." The only active synagogue in Kharkov was shut down. Studying Hebrew was transgression enough to be sent to a camp. Under these conditions, old Jews, who kept Torahs and

The very first Seder. From left are Uncle Yefim, the author and cousin Leonid Zamel. Moscow, 1975.

prayer books, organized minyans and gathered at one another's houses to pray in secret. Uncle Yefim was one of the last survivors of his minyan, and in 1974 he unexpectedly came to Moscow to hand over their religious items to the Moscow synagogue, which in those days was almost the only active one in the European Soviet Union.

When he met with us, he declared that his days were numbered, and, before he died, he wanted to show his family how to celebrate Passover properly. He was staying with Aunt Shura, and she helped him to set up a Seder. Our whole family came by. He led in Hebrew, so we didn't understand a single thing and after three hours were utterly exhausted. However, he was very happy and believed he observed his duty in the eyes of God. He was ninety then. Four years later, after many years of suffering, his son Yuzik died of the brain tumor. Soon, Yefim followed him.

In America, we became used to celebrating Passover. And each time, along with the story of Moses, I would talk about my first Seder in Moscow led by Uncle Yefim.

From left are the author's Uncle Yefim Schneider, mother Maria Schneider, and Aunt Brònya Zamel (Schneider). Kharkov, Ukraine, 1953.

Grandpa

In Chimkent, I went back to the first grade — a third school in the course of one school year — and it was rough. This one was unlike my village school. Each grade had a room of its own. The class started with being called to the blackboard. We were writing in homemade notebooks made of newspaper there also, but the teacher used special books called textbooks. Both of these books belonged to her. They had pictures and texts that students gingerly read syllable by syllable. I fell behind. A girl called Nelly, an A student, was assigned to help me. My seven-year-old male ego couldn't bear it.

My only relief was my communication with Grandpa. I remember him well: in his eighties, he was still a tall, strong, and active old man. We did not used to be close. Grandma and he had moved to Kharkov two years before the war and lived separately from us.

Now we spent a lot of time together. I grew up, and Grandpa felt he could talk to me. We became friends. We listened together to the war reports on the radio. I quickly learned to copy the voice and mannerisms of Yury Levitan, the famous announcer, and used it to entertain Grandpa. The rumors said that

Hitler hated Levitan so much that he promised to wring his neck first thing after he took Moscow. To us and many others, Levitan was like a family member.

The news reports in those days were getting grimmer and grimmer. None of this affected Grandpa's mood. Unlike everyone else, he was an optimist. As an observant Jew, he "talked" to God every day and very seriously explained to me that, according to Torah and what God was telling him, Hitler didn't have a chance. That's right. All because he had undertaken to eliminate the Jews. "He'll pay for this," Grandpa said. "It's curtains for him. Any day now." Meanwhile, the Germans were outside Moscow, about to take it any day.

"You have to remember, Grandson: whoever is plotting against the Jews — his days are numbered. It has always been this way. You grow up, you learn history, you'll see for yourself. This is what my grandfather told me when I was your age. And you should pass this to your grandchildren, too, and tell them to pass to their own grandchildren, too." Later on, I had more than one occasion to appreciate his wisdom.

I found out I was a Jew from the kids on the street in Kharkov. Grandpa explained to me that it was a serious responsibility: "You have to be the best student and the best worker. You have to make an example. This is what God orders us. Otherwise, a Jew won't have a good life."

It took me many — too many — years to recall Grandpa's advice and realize its full sense.

He was born in 1860 near Odessa in the Ukraine. In his youth, he worked as a drayman in Odessa — the kind beautifully described by Isaac Babel. Draymen transported freight in Odessa's port. Like other draymen, he had a cart and a horse. The only exception to the Babel prototype was that Grandpa would not drink or curse.

He was born Yankel Schneider. He married my grandma Gena, nee Nakhman, in Uman, outside Kiev, where they had a multitude of children. Only nine survived: my aunts Zina, Shura, Brònya, and Zhènya, and my uncles Yefim, Iona, Nahum, and Hershel (Grigory). And my mother Manya (Màsya). Iona and Nahum died in the Civil War.

My first memory of Grandpa goes back to when I was about three years old. He came to Kharkov to visit. He stayed with Aunt Zhènya and came to our place. I sat in his lap and he fed me cherries. I shot cherry pits at everybody in the room. By accident I shot one at Grandpa and split his lip. Blood flowed down his resplendent white beard, but he didn't get angry. I was smacked for it, but for some reason I laughed.

Aunt Shura from Moscow was also present at the scene, and she would pester me with this episode all my life, citing it as an example of what a brat I had always been.

Grandma died in early '41. She was about eighty. Grandpa joined us in the evacuation.

A typical picture of the time: the extended family of the author's mother. Present are (lower row, from left) cousins Yuzik (Yevgeny) Schneider, and Tosya and Zyuma, Uncle Yefim's children; (sitting from left) Malka, Uncle Yefim's wife; Uncle Yefim Schneider, Grandfather and Grandmother, Yankel Schneider and Genya Schneider (Nakhman); author's mother's sisters, Aunt Shura Kravets (Schneider) with her son Naum Kravets, and Aunt Zina Rud' (Schneider) with her adopted son Naum Rud'; (standing from left) the author's mother Maria Schneider, Uncle Grigory (Hershel) Schneider, Aunt Zhènya Lisnevskaya (Schneider), her husband Zyàma Lisnevsky, Aunt Shura's husband, Solomon Kravets, and Aunt Zina's husband Lev Rud'. Uman, Ukraine, 1925.

In Chimkent, Aunt Zhènya's family lived not far from us. For some reason we stayed at their house for a while. One morning we woke up to see we had been sleeping on a stage of sorts: the outer wall of the house was gone. It turned out there had been an earthquake, and it had collapsed. Then Grandpa decided he would build us a house — he did construction work earlier in life.

He made a deal with our Uzbek landlord — perhaps he promised they would get it for free once we went back to Kharkov after the war. He took me on as an assistant. I was responsible for getting adobe bricks. To make those, I kneaded clay with my feet, mixed it with straw, and poured it into the wooden forms Grandpa had made. Bricks would be dry in a day or two and would be ready to be used in a wall. This was my first construction job.

Yet we were not meant to live in that house. It remained unfinished.

Grandpa died. It wasn't a regular death. He willed himself dead. To be more precise, he arranged it with God.

Grandpa loved my mother very much. In the spring of '43, she stopped receiving letters from her husband Aron — my stepfather — who was at the front lines. And then, during his daily chat with God, Grandpa offered his own life in exchange for Aron's. A few days later we heard from Aron: he had been severely wounded, but his life was no longer in danger, and he was in a hospital in the rear.

Grandpa thanked God, took a bath, put on fresh clothes, lay down on his couch next to the window, and, ignoring his two daughters' hysterical protests, stopped taking meals. A few days later he was gone.

From left are Aunt Zhènya Lisnevskaya (Schneider), author's mother Maria Schneider, and Aunt Shura Kravets (Schneider). Uman, Ukraine 1923.

Stepfather

My stepfather Aron was wounded in both legs as his infantry company was attacking in a skirmish formation. According to him, a German machine gunner was hiding in the woods, and when the company came abreast of him, he enfiladed them all. When it grew dark, Aron heard the voices of the medics crawling through the snow and called them. When they saw his condition, they decided there was no sense in picking him up. Aron gripped one of them by the edge of the coat with his teeth so hard they could not shake him off. They dragged him for about fifteen hundred feet until he tripped over the edge of a shell crater. He fainted with pain and let the medic's coat go.

He came to at night at the bottom of the shell crater. At dawn he was picked up by another medic — or perhaps it was a burial team that was taking the corpses' IDs. They took him away on a sled. His blood froze in huge lumps. The bleeding stopped and they decided he did not need a bandage.

The next day he was put back on a sled and taken to the rear. They rode across a large snowy plain. The day was quiet, and the sun shone brightly. Suddenly, a German bomber flew by and coolly dropped five bombs on their cart, clearly marked with a red cross. The wounded who could walk tried to get away, but Aron could not move. He lay on his back, stared into the sky, and counted the bombs. Everyone was killed, including the horses. Aron took a few bomb fragments, including a large one that hit exactly the same spot already injured by the machine gunner and tore out a piece of flesh straight to the bone. It took years for the huge hole to heal.

In the evening, he was picked up by another cart.

Stepfather wrote us from a hospital in Saratov. He said that the doctors were afraid of gangrene and planned to amputate both his legs.

This was followed by another one, also from a hospital, but farther back in the rear — Kirgizia, a few hundred miles from us. Now there was no gangrene, one leg was saved, and he was fighting to save the other one. Mother grabbed my brother Gena and got on the train. Two weeks later she brought Aron, who was barely able to move, to Chimkent.

Although he had both legs, he was in bad shape. One leg, with a broken bone, was in a cast; the other one had bandages on, soaked in blood and pus, which my mother washed every day. I tormented Aron to tell me war stories. Gena would not let him go either and would later tell neighbors, "Bastid 'itler, 'ounded papa legs. One meat and one bone." And demonstrated on his own legs.

For a month my stepfather remained bedridden. Even before the cast was off, he started learning to walk — hopping on wooden crutches and supporting himself on the bandaged leg. Everybody helped him. Once, hobbling through pain, ignoring mother's protests, he plodded to town to look for a job. He came back late, with one crutch broken in two, and the bottom used as a cane. The top half was gone. The other one was under his arm. He was agitated and spoke in short bursts, inhaling noisily: "That parasite. I let him have it. With a crutch. Broke, sure. *First learn to walk.* Wants me to starve. Sitting on his butt. Instead of going to fight."

After a number of sorties like this, he finally was hired to work at the military office's canteen.

After he came back, he was unrecognizable — nervous, irritated, with a short fuse. Mother attributed the change to his constant pain. His wounds would not heal. She realized he was depressed by his inability to relieve our wretched poverty and by being dependent on us. But that he should be drinking so hard? Her Aron — a Jewish husband — boozing and fighting? That was not like him at all. Mother was lost. She did not know that she would have to fight his passion for the bottle — acquired at the front — through the rest of her life.

Before the war, he would down at the most a shot glass on May Day. But during fighting, right before going into combat, soldiers always got their "legit" one hundred grams. Sometimes even more — to "warm up." Then there was the alcohol taken from Germans. Usually, they would get more than few glasses a day. For example, they would receive enough for a squad of ten people — and six of them already dead. Can't pour it away, right? The hospital staff kept up patients' morale with pure medical alcohol, too. And so on.

Aron was born in 1901 into the family of a rich industrialist who owned several tanneries in the Ukraine. He was the youngest child of his elderly father's last marriage. He had three siblings: Yakov, Tuba, and Lyuba, all much older than he. Tuba emigrated to America before World War I and settled in the Bronx. Her husband was called Abraham Katz. In the 1950s, we got several letters from her with the pictures of her daughters, Claire and Florence. I tried to find her in New York in the 1980s. I even found the phone number of their business — a laundry — in the local directory in the library. The last reference went back to 1952.

Numerous children of grandfather Mark Berkovich and his first two wives scattered around the world before Aron was born, or else when he was a baby.

We almost met one of them in Mexico. In 1981, we took a bus from Mexico City to Acapulco. I bought some souvenirs at a stop in Cuernavaca. The saleswoman read my name on the credit card and exclaimed: "Are you related to Berkoviches? ... You mean old Grigory Berkovich is your relative?"

I joked in response: "How do you know our Grigory Berkovich?" In fact, I had never heard of him.

"Are you kidding? They know him even in Mexico City. He is both the oldest and the richest man in our town!"

Our son Slava immediately insisted that we go visit Grigory. But we were too lazy and did not feel like interrupting the trip.

Six years later in Moscow, Aron told me that he indeed had a half-brother named Grigory who was somewhere in America or Argentina. "I don't think he'd be alive, though. In '81 he would be well into his nineties, I believe."

With a Soviet man's average lifespan being 57 years, it was hard for him to imagine living to such old age, something that westerners find unsurprising.

Soon after the revolution, Aron was drafted. He served under Kotovsky, a famed Civil War general, in Uman and got married there. Then they got divorced, and two years later someone introduced him to my mother.

I was four years old, and we lived in a tiny room on Rybasov Street. One night we had guests: a thickset man with a full head of red hair and a thin, pale-complexioned boy, much older than I. They arrived laden with food: tasty cold cuts, cheese, cookies, honey, and butter. This was the first time I met Aron Berkovich, whom I would call "Papa" — and still do, and my future half-brother Mitya (Mark). As Mitya joked later, that was their way of wooing my mother.

The courtship did not take long. Aron introduced my mother to his sister Lyuba, who had served in the cavalry in the Civil

The author's mother, Maria Schneider, and stepfather, Aron Berkovich. Kharkov, Ukraine, 1940.

War. My mother and Lyuba took a liking to each other, and, as befits a Red Army cavalry woman, Lyuba spoke directly: "What are you pussy-footing about? What are you two, kids? License, schmicense. Move her to your place, and that's it."

While his father was alive, Aron managed to get a good Yiddish education, available to someone of his social status. After the revolution he was an orphan and had to conceal his social origin. He had to start his life anew. He knew his way about the tanning business, but Lyuba advised him against practicing it, lest he draw attention. He became a salesperson "for a while," and stayed one.

Now his occupation came in handy. We no longer starved. I had sugar for tea almost every day.

When Aron's cast was removed, it turned out that the doctors had made a mistake. They had not noticed that the ends of the broken bone had shifted and crossed each other. And that's how the bone healed — and became three inches shorter. It was unrealistic to try to fix it under the circumstances. He limped through the rest of his life.

A year after the war, he was waiting for the streetcar in Kharkov, and a group of drunks started picking on him. Short and gimpy, he seemed like a good target. The leader of the group was a tall, freckled guy who told his pals he remembered "this kike from before the war. He was a gimp all his life — got hit by a streetcar. Now he's got his medals, posing as a war hero." He grabbed Aron. "Why don't you tell us how you fought Fascists in Uzbekistan?"

Aron blew his fuse on a dime, as he was wont to after the war. He cast aside his cane, picked up the offender and tossed him hard on the ground.

The man struck his head on the streetcar rail and fell quiet. His pals ran off and brought the police.

Aron was charged with murder. But someone advised my mother she should go to Kiev and see Sidor Kovpak, a famed war hero and deputy chairman of Ukraine's government. He was rumored to be soft on veterans. The war scars were still fresh. The investigation was closed.

This was not the last occasion when mother had to bail him out. To be fair, he fought a lot of other people — not just anti–Semites.

I never queried my stepfather about his family. I can only guess from snatches of phrases that his family was well-to-do, moderately religious, and no stranger to culture. For example, Sholom Aleichem was a visitor. The children received a serious education that went beyond Yiddish.

Even before the revolution, Aron's nephew Izzy Berkovich, who was much older, became a famous Jewish author, with his own entry in the Jewish Encyclopedia. He emigrated to America and then to Palestine. I bought a book of his short stories from American life, a translation from English (or perhaps from Yiddish), published in the USSR in the '20s, at a second-hand bookstore and showed it to my stepfather. He read it, but he didn't say a word about being related to the author. After all, it was 1948. I found about that later.

Since childhood, my stepfather had loved books and read constantly. When he developed Parkinson's and it reached an advanced stage with his hands trembling uncontrollably, he could no longer hold a book and had to set it on the table in front of him. He kept reading. In my childhood I often asked him to read aloud, which he did willingly.

He read and wrote fluently in Yiddish. When, after the war, Emes Publishers released a few books in Yiddish, I bought Sholom Aleichem and David Bergelson and asked my stepfather to read them aloud. My parents spoke Yiddish to each other, too, especially if they needed to conceal something from us. We strained our ears, trying to understand. Soon both Gena and I could understand it well.

I remember very well Sholom Aleichem's collection of stories called *The Idler*, that Aron read to me from beginning to end. When I didn't understand a word or a phrase, he translated it into Russian on the fly, barely pausing in his recital. Sometimes I would simply get tired of listening to Yiddish. Then he held up the Yiddish text and read it in Russian. Sholom Aleichem sounded just as funny. Later on, I read the same stories in the author's translation and was struck at the quality of Aron's off-the-cuff translation. I thought it was better than Sholom Aleichem's.

Once, on a Jewish holiday (Yom Kippur, I believe), Uncle Yefim stopped by with a prayer book and suggested to my stepfather that they pray together. Uncle Yefim read from his book, while Aron did it from memory, and in Hebrew.

Our relations were not always smooth. I called him Papa after our first meeting — I wanted to have a father that badly. In my youth, I felt I irritated him somehow. With age, it became more obvious that I was completely unlike him, both in appearance and in nature — unlike my kid brother Gena.

Aron was intemperate, especially after a few glasses. He smacked me quite a bit, and his touch was anything but light. Gradually our relations turned to enmity. He would ask me to bring him a glass of water. "What did you bring me? Couldn't you get it from a fresh bucket?" (We did not have running water.) I would go back and bring him the same glass of water. "Now, that's better." I crawled back into my corner and cried.

By the time I was drafted, our relations improved a lot. Now, the older I became, the better he treated me. When my unit was stationed in Tallinn for two months, he even came to visit me, and we had a good time.

The last time we saw each other was in 1987, when we visited Moscow for the first time. He stayed with our friends. He was weak and hardly ever left the guestroom, sitting upright in bed and reading. Our conversations with him consisted of answers to his endless questions as he queried us about our life in America, down to the smallest quotidian details. He was especially concerned if we had enough money to live on.

I told him about the mortgage, a term unknown then in the USSR. He paused and then asked if one could add money to one's mortgage payments. If so, he would recommend we do that. Then and there, he calculated in his mind how much I would save in ten years if I were to pay an extra fifty dollars every month.

Once I remembered that he used to sing well and knew many songs. I asked him to sing something. He sang a few Ukrainian and Jewish tunes that no one any longer remembered the lyrics to. We had a good mind to tape his performance.

We were interrupted — a guest came to see the "Americans." We left the room; my stepfather produced his glasses and opened yet another freshly published book.

He died two years later.

Chimkent

We were struck by my stepfather's condition when he was brought from the hospital, but he was struck even worse by our state of poverty. Of course the small barn where we lived was scrubbed clean, the clay floor was daubed with fresh clay, and our landlady's cow and goats were no longer in the same room with us but in the shed next door. Our beds were made up with clean linen. Yet we were clearly suffering. We had sold all of the things we could sell. Nothing was left to survive on.

My main memory of those days is constant hunger.

Chimkent was a site of lead and uranium mines, where soon the raw material for the first Soviet bomb would be mined (not that we knew about it). We spent hours sifting through the pit refuse heap — a virtual mountain in the center of the city not far from the train station. We found so-called "sea clay" (as children called it) — small, patty-shaped, gray-bluish pieces that were considered edible. It tasted like chalk and assuaged hunger — though not for long.

As early as April we began raiding neighbors' vegetable plots. I was slim and short, and had no trouble finding a hole in a fence. Then I dropped on the ground between the rows and devoured everything I could find. Depending on the season, it could be onions, turnips, garlic, carrots — anything that I could dig out discreetly. Unknowingly, I was following a very healthy diet by today's standards. By May I was already raiding fruit orchards, biting through apricots so green as to set my teeth on edge.

Raiding orchards was no picnic. Their owners carried rifles loaded with salt. Once I got it full blast, when I almost made it over the high clay wall. That put a stop to my adventures for a while.

The hardest times were in the early spring and early summer, when there was no "pasturage fodder." All the leftovers from the previous year's crop at the neighbors' gardens were dug up and eaten. I did the best I could and ate anything I could procure and digest. I could not wait for the long recess in school when I would get tea with a packet of saccharin. Nobody knew then that it was carcinogenic.

The military office issued a ladle of soup a day to a member of a soldier's family — as long as you came early enough. The soup was basically warm water with traces of cornmeal and a lard compound. Standing in line was my duty, and carrying it home was a challenge. I could not help stopping for a taste every few blocks. By the time I got home, there was one portion missing. Mother sobbed, split the remnants evenly, and never punished me.

The author with his stepfather, Aron Berkovich. Tallinn, Estonia, 1955.

Soldiers' families received a small allowance,

too. We bought food with ration cards. Our main staple for which we always tried to save money was bread. We received half a loaf a day; it was damp and heavy, and half of it was bran. We also had cards for cereal, butter, and even meat. But reality was different. If in a given month there was any food in the store, we had enough cards to get something two or three times a week. Yet seldom could we afford the subsidized prices.

Before the war Chimkent was a small town, but during the war it grew considerably. For example, the Architecture Academy was evacuated there. Perhaps I had a chance to communicate with my future idols. But I didn't give much thought to architecture. It was too far from my stomach.

Another outfit evacuated to Chimkent was Odessa Musical Comedy Theater. I knew all three productions that made up its repertoire, especially *A Wedding in Malinovka*, a Civil War musical. I could recite all the lines by heart. What I don't remember is how my friends and I got to see the shows. I certainly wasn't getting an allowance.

Both the musical comedy theater and the local philharmonic — evacuated from elsewhere to Chimkent — had a special relationship with our school and sometimes gave free concerts. I remember a magician who, to the tune of an accordion, followed a few magical passes by producing real eggs out of an absolutely empty pillowcase. I asked him to do it over in slow motion. I thought I had his routine down pat!

At home I declared that our food troubles were over and asked Mother for a pillowcase. I thought I copied the magician's movements perfectly — but the eggs were not there, no matter how many times I tried. Enraged, I almost tore up the pillowcase. My mother wished she had not let me start. But I could not put up with failure. I broke into tears.

Later, I hoped to find the magician and ask him to show me the mechanics once again. I just couldn't believe that it was impossible to obtain eggs that way. Maybe it was the accordion accompaniment that had done the trick — or the magician's song about his dunce hat?

The winter of '43 was a cold one, with snow, sleet, and temperatures below zero. We were ill-equipped, but mother managed to keep us warm. She found children's galoshes, *chùni*, which were a size too small for me; she cut the rear side and wrapped them with cloth — they didn't look great, but they kept me warm. Then she picked up a needle — her sewing machine was back in Kharkov — and fashioned grandfather's jacket into an overcoat for me, with two layers of gauze and cotton between them serving as lining. For headwear, she found a little girl's fur hat with earflaps hanging down to my waist. Again, she cut through the back to fit my head and then filled the gap with the earflaps' ends, which now reached to my shoulders. We didn't have a mirror for me to see what I looked like, but I saw tears in my mother's eyes. My classmates mocked the hat, but I kept going to school and kept myself warm.

My closest friend was Nema. Although his father, like mine, was in the front lines, his mother and he were not starving. She brought men home, and they brought food. Nema hated it. He called his mother a "whore" and threatened he would tell his father when he came back. We were trying to hatch plans on how to teach her a lesson.

In what seemed like the darkest hour, mother ran into some distant relatives from Kharkov, a family named Konovàlovs. They were an elderly couple whose two sons served in combat units (later on I found out both were killed). The Konovàlovs bred rabbits and invited me to have a meal sometimes.

I recall with some surprise that, though constantly hungry, I was too shy and found numerous excuses to stay away, though they often invited me to "stop by on the way to school." I did it only a few times. They lived far away from the route to school, which meant a considerable detour.

The school could not accommodate all the students at the same time, and classes were held in three shifts. I was in the evening shift. The first time I visited the Konovàlovs, I miscalculated and missed the first class. Naively, I told the teacher I had "tried a different route." When she probed further, I sincerely told her about where exactly my route was, which for some reason ended up with the whole class, including the teacher, howling with laughter. I was reminded of this episode for a long time.

To top it off, when I was called blackboard, for some reason I brushed off all the inkpots on the floor. I got away with it. The teacher did not call my mother to come in.

Gena

My two-year-old half-brother Gena looked better in Chimkent than the rest of us. He got his meals from Aunt Zhènya. Every night I would bring him to her place at the time her husband arrived from work. In Chimkent, Uncle Zyàma, toiling at his "labor front lines," provided well for his family. He was very fond of my kid brother Gena and always brought him some tidbits, evoking jealousy from his own children Tòlik and Bella. Gena would lie in wait for Uncle Zyàma at the door. He would spot Zyàma from afar and rush at him like a puppy. For many years our family would laugh as we recalled his phrase, "Zyàma, gimme!" Unlike me, Gena would land at the table at their house and loudly demand to be fed.

Gena learned to walk and talk at the age of one, when we were still in Turkestan. I spent a lot of time with him then. Hence his first word was "Gayik." Next one was "gimme," then "eat" and "want." And only then did he say "mama." Still breast-fed at eighteen months, Gena learned the phrase "mama give tit." It was considered that babies should not be weaned in the summer heat in order to protect them from stomach infections. And so my mother suffered and waited for colder days. She was sure this saved him from the malaria that the rest of us had gone through.

Gena spent his days chasing the landlord's two goats and a dog around the courtyard. Then, tired and hungry, Gena went to our mother, prone and helpless with malaria, and bit her breast. Once he did it hard enough to make her bleed.

Those were hungry days. All of us were thin and barely walking. Gena alone was always pink-cheeked and plump and full of energy. With his blond curls, broad face and big cheeks, he looked like a young Lenin in a school textbook.

When mother went to Frunze to retrieve my wounded stepfather from the hospital, the two-year-old Gena quickly adjusted to the large hospital ward. He toddled around and entertained bedridden soldiers, who missed their own children. Gena figured it out in no time. He would come up to a patient, call him "papa," and get into the cot with him. Soldiers always saved tidbits for him — a slice of bread, a lump of sugar, a piece of toast. Once the tidbit was consumed, Gena moved on to the next cot, followed by laughter.

Gena made friends with a neighboring Uzbek boy named Maken and picked up Uzbek from him. He tried to recall it when he became an adult, but in vain.

When we came back to Kharkov, for a while Gena studied French. Mother took him to a small day care group of five children. The fiftyish, large-bodied nanny had the manners of a pre-revolution governess. She took her charges to the park, where they played under her supervision, and she taught them French. Every day, five-year-old Gena brought home a new French word and made us repeat after him: *Bonjour, merci,* and *merci beaucoup*. One night at dinner mother noted that fresh air was having a beneficial effect on Gena's already good appetite.

Gena looked at her oddly and said, "She doesn't feed us. She takes away the food you give me and eats it herself."

Apparently, the nanny was starving, and sustained herself on the children's sandwiches.

Unfortunately, I don't remember Gena's school years well. We did not get along. I was into my teenager woes, and my stepfather saved his love for Gena and little Yanna and made it a point that I was not his child. This did not encourage intimacy.

Gena was thirteen when I was drafted; sixteen, when I came back. Those were important years in his development.

In my absence, Gena was learning about life from our cousin Nikolay, who had just come back from jail. Eight years inside for an attempt to escape from the Soviet Union had turned Nikolay into a complete cynic who now firmly believed that the world owed him. A good-looking show-off and a skirt-chaser, quick-tongued, and a lover of the good life, Nikolay taught Gena that the world of 9 to 5 was not for "real men." One day his chance would come, and he'd become rich and famous without having to work for it.

Gena was thirteen years younger, and swallowed Nikolay's life philosophy hook, line, and sinker. Nikolay enjoyed having a student, too. He taught Gena, not yet fifteen, everything he knew and shared with him generously, including his girlfriends.

At fourteen, Gena followed in my footsteps and entered a construction trade school. He played horn in the school band and moonlighted by playing funeral gigs, which provided various entertaining stories that he loved to re-enact.

However, Nikolay's life lessons won over. In his third year of school, like all Soviet students, Gena was sent to work at a collective farm; there he got involved in a shady situation with his girlfriend — I do not know the details — which, in turn, led to his expulsion.

Once out of school, Gena fell in with a "bad crowd." His father had no way to influence him. My mother was appalled.

Nikolay's influence on Gena irritated me endlessly. Oddly enough, I liked Nikolay as well. I empathized with him and tried to understand him, though his philosophy was completely at odds with mine. But with Gena it was more complicated. We just were unable to have a serious heart-to-heart.

Later on, we kept coming back to the subject. We were both growing up and less prone to pick on each other. Gradually our differences were ironed over. We preserved our completely different views of life, though that did not prevent us from being loving brothers.

The author's brother Gena Berkovich. Skokie, Illinois, 1982.

Much later in America, Gena told me that one day he had come across my adoption papers — which were kept a family secret. Gena was shaken. He remembered the beatings his father had given me and our mother defending and comforting me. He remembered sitting in his father's lap, while the latter told me drunkenly, pointing at Gena: "This is my son, you bastard! My hope!"

Gena told me that when

he had read the adoption document he felt he became an adult and he felt deep sympathy and respect for me. Now he remembered how, well up to the time I was drafted, we shared the same bed in a hug.

I knew he always loved me and I felt his love even in the midst of the most heated arguments.

At fifteen, Gena and his friend Fima made a few rubles working as night watchers for an oil wildcatter team, and decided to blow it on the good life in Sochi, a famed Black Sea resort. They decided not to wait for the actual money, which they were promised by mail. Every day they kept plodding to the post office, but the money was not there. Days went by and the few rubles they had begged from their parents were vanishing. They were getting desperate ... and then Fima came up with an idea.

At nights Gena and Fima would go to an open-air dancing club. Fima would quickly locate a group of Jewish-looking boys and strike up a conversation. He would steer the conversation to the subject of Jewishness; then he would point at Gena, who was strolling about indifferently, and told them he would bet fifteen to one that Gena was Jewish. With his snub nose and blonde hair, Gena did not look like a Jewish stereotype at all. At these odds, the kids were eager to make a bet, especially since no one had an idea as to how Fima would prove it.

Fima would collect the money and bring Gena over. Without a word, Gena would unzip his pants and demonstrate the evidence. Then they were off to another club, where this started all over again.

The money still did not arrive, and just about every sporting Jew in Sochi was onto their sting. But then, a stroke of luck: Cousin Nikolay arrived. Gena was perfectly aware that Nikolay had a soft spot for him and never missed a chance to show off. His reasoning was sound; Nikolay immediately loaned them a large sum of money. Hoping their luck would hold, Fima and Gena joined a card game and lost it all. Apparently, they did not know that Sochi was a summer Mecca for cardsharps from all over the country.

Gena was ashamed to go back to Nikolay for more. Instead, he ambushed Nikolay as the latter was on a stroll with his date. Gena pretended to bump into them by accident, and, after being introduced, casually asked for a small loan. Of course Nikolay could not appear stingy to the date and supplied the money, adding that he was happy to bail out a relative and Gena should not rush to pay it back.

For a couple of weeks, this worked. But then Nikolay found Gena on the beach, gave him twenty rubles, and begged him not to do it again: his own money was running out, and he could not say "no" in a girl's company.

Gena and Fima had nothing left to do but go back to Kharkov. They had no money for tickets and had to ride the train for free, dodging the conductors.

After I left Kharkov and entered architecture school in Moscow, our communication dwindled to a trickle. We wrote each other, but rarely. From time to time I visited Kharkov, or Gena visited Moscow. My mother kept complaining that she had a hard time with him — once again he had fallen in with "bad company" — and asked me to help. I would write him a letter, but I realized I was going through the motions. I could not count on his understanding.

Finally, our mother found what she deemed was a way out. Gena was exempt from the draft for medical reasons — a bad case of cervical sciatica. So she went to the local draft board and paid someone a bribe to have him drafted. My mother firmly believed that Gena needed a taste of army discipline. Also, the police were investigating a criminal case against Gena's friends. He was a witness, but could become a defendant too. He would be safer in the army, she reasoned.

Gena spent over a year in the army. He didn't like it very much, and he wangled a medical discharge. For that, he had to agree to a spinal tap at the army training hospital. This was considered a dangerous procedure, and many patients became cripples. As a result, through the rest of his life he walked leaning slightly forward with his legs spread out wide.

In part, mother's aspiration was justified. Gena went straight. Back in Kharkov, he got a job as a lathe operator at the gas company. There he met his future wife Marina, who for a while was even his boss.

Soon he was fired for not showing up at work. He took it calmly: with its niggardly pay, the job was nothing to hold onto. With the help of some of his friends he went to train as a butcher. Butchers were paid no better than lathe operators, but they could double and triple their pay by cheating customers. Conversely, good cuts never made it to the front of the store and could be traded for other hard-to-find goods, which was a tremendous cashless benefit in a society of permanent shortages.

Since the bulk of an animal was divided into categories, a butcher would cut it in such a way that a customer would be hard put to tell where this or that piece came from and would be paying, so to speak, a filet mignon price for a standard chuck steak. Besides, all the scales were "adjusted," too.

After a brief training period, Gena and his two friends were sent to a meat store in a working-class area. Their predecessors had been fired for abuses and put under investigation. Now the store manager took his time to instruct the newcomers in how to cut the meat so that not only a customer but even an inspector could not catch them. In addition, he advised them that not only should they not cheat with the scale, but they should even "overweight" the purchase by a few ounces (by throwing in a bone or two), since "short-weighting" was easiest way to get caught.

Gena recalled that when they first showed up, the customers started complaining about their predecessors, "those crooks."

"It's all over," Gena told them. "We have been sent here by the Party to set this place straight."

Gena's finances improved substantially.

At first Gena and Marina lived with her parents; then they moved in with our mother and Yanna, while my stepfather was doing time — eighteen months — for an "economic crime" such as privately manufacturing and selling vinyl napkins. A year later Marina gave birth to a boy they named Igor.

Soon after his son's birth, Gena realized that he had to get really serious about getting an apartment. The few "free" apartments built were distributed among the Party elite or according to city's and large factories' waiting lists. As a young Jew without connections, Gena did not have a chance of getting on any of these lists. The only avenue open to him was buying a co-op. Although his butcher job paid well, he had to get deep in debt to afford a small apartment in the outskirts.

The authorities were well aware that the shortage of goods and services created an excess of cash in people's pockets, and they kept coming up with ways of extorting this money. Co-ops were one such ruse. It was dishonest, because the population had already paid for their homes by surrendering to the state the so-called "surplus value" of their labor. Now the state "legally" pumped the citizens for the same service once again.

Saving five thousand rubles for a one-bedroom apartment was unrealistic, with the average pay between a thousand and fifteen hundred rubles a year. This money was barely enough to make ends meet. Extra earnings came from the shadow economy. Everybody was moonlighting, and most of these earnings fell legally into the grey area.

It was legal to unload coal cars in your free time, but not quite legal to haul passengers' luggage at train stations (students did that a lot). The same went for construction jobs in the countryside, guarding gardens at collective farms, growing vegetables and fruit for sale, and all sorts of sundry jobs. Yet all these jobs needed to be done, and managers and directors came up with a zillion loopholes in the legislation, from part-time jobs to working on contract — and the omnipotent state had to look the other way.

What was absolutely illegal was manufacturing and selling goods that were in short supply, from food to napkins, shoes, and rugs. That could lead to a jail term or even an execution, depending on the scale, since manufacturing and selling were absolutely the state monopoly. The Soviet economy was based on shortages, and someone had to fill in the gaps. People paid officials bribes and bought discarded factory machinery and raw materials and set up their own underground production facilities. Naturally, the risks they took were justified by their incomes that exceeded any state salary. And, unsurprisingly, a lot of underground businessmen — and co-op owners — just happened to be Jewish. The Party and industry executives who solicited their bribes did not need co-ops — they got their apartments free from the state.

In 1965, when his meat store became an object of investigation again, Gena went back to trade school and graduated a year later. He got a job at a factory in the supply department. After two or three jobs like these, he became convinced that he would never feed his family on this salary, to say nothing of paying back his co-op debt. He went into the "picture" business.

This was one of the semi-legal businesses that Nikolay got him into. For a few years Gena traveled to outlying areas, getting small photos from peasants and bringing back to them enlarged, retouched photos in a frame good enough to hang on the wall. This paid handsomely. Gena was able to pay off his debts, bought a car, and started casting about for a job that would not require him to spend his life on the road.

Soon Gena got into something called Consumer Equipment Repairs, a group of shops that semi-legally manufactured the goods that could not be found in stores. Legally, Gena's shop produced dress belts; however, it used enough raw materials to also manufacture buttons and pins and buckles and whatnot — none of which showed on the books.

Everybody who worked under him or dealt with him considered him an outstanding person. He charmed them with his quick mind, sharp wit, and natural generosity. In the mid-nineties, I got a sudden reminder of Gena's past. At the wedding of a son's friend in Chicago, a visitor from Russia came up to me. With his impressive physique, flashy clothes, and menacing air, he looked a little like a stereotypical "new Russian" with mob connections. He checked to see if he had my name right and offered his hand. "I'm happy to meet the brother of Gena Berkovich," he said. "I worked for him twenty-five years ago. I'll never forget him."

Gena's last business in the USSR before he emigrated was making propaganda stands for collective farms. These stands generally featured Best Workers pictures or Socialist Promises posters. Gena used this as a cover to launch a large-scale production of plastic goods, including even cemetery monuments. By the time he emigrated (which he called "evacuation"), he had turned into a run-of-the-mill Soviet underground businessman with two or three small shops that he, as he put it, "oversaw."

He was a good manager, who knew how to get along with everybody, including financial examiners, police, the DA's office, and many other official Soviet racketeers. A thoroughly social animal, he was the life of every party. He was especially fond of telling jokes and before his death even thought of publishing a collection.

Naturally, most jokes were Jewish. "Moyshe, I heard you are fooling around with other women? Maybe our children did not come from you either?"

I started writing about my younger brother many times and had to quit. He was a mass of contradictions. It is hard to describe him correctly.

We were born to the same mother, we grew up in the same family, yet we were so different that strangers asked, "Are you really brothers?"

As far as appearance was concerned, I took after my mother, while Gena took after his father — my stepfather. Psychologically, emotionally — we had nothing in common. We were formed at different times under different conditions. From the age of two I grew up in preschool, where my mother, divorced at the time, took me six days a week. I saw her on Sunday only. And we never had enough food. Gena, from his birth, was everybody's pet and never knew hunger.

My generation was brought up to follow the example of a classic Soviet book called *How Steel Was Tempered*, whose main character says, "You should live your life in such a way so that you never feel sorry about your wasted years." I was an idealist who followed this motto: I studied hard, I trained hard to master a profession, and I volunteered for the draft.

Gena was a mere six years younger, but his generation was completely different. The rigid conformist education of the Stalin era collapsed, and the vacuum was filled by rejection of all moral values. Many of Gena's generation invested the same motto with an opposite meaning: "Grab whatever you can, wherever you can."

Gena was an avid clubgoer, especially to Russian clubs in the U.S., with their typically Russian entertainment. He died in one of them, aboard a pleasure boat, celebrating a friend's birthday.

He inherited our cousin Nikolay's belief in his luck. He kept buying lottery tickets and told us quite seriously that his "peak moment was at hand." A few days before his death he studied some diagram very seriously and concluded that on August 11 something "very important in his life" would take place. A large lottery was being drawn on that day, and Gena decided that this was It. He bought a bunch of tickets.

On August 11 he died of a heart attack. He was forty-three.

Mark

In the early fall of '43 we had a visitor in Chimkent: my stepbrother Mark. He was almost sixteen — manly, tanned, broad-shouldered, flexing his muscles, and parading his Navy cadet uniform. I followed him everywhere. I adored him.

Two years earlier, he ended up in Tashkent, working at a doll factory and living with his mother, "Aunt Riva" (my stepfather's first wife), and her husband, "Uncle Senya" Ziskind. Things did not work out with Ziskind, and at fifteen Mark made up his mind to leave. He tried out for Air Force school, but got into the Navy instead, and that decided his life.

The school was in Samarkand, with no sea in sight. They trained on dry land. Rowing was done on sand. Between classes they were assigned to unloading freight cars. Once Mark fell under the cement being poured off the car. At the last minute, someone pulled him out by his leg and saved his life.

I remember sharing a bed with him as a child, in a narrow kitchen without windows, next to the sink and the stove. He was twelve then.

We lived in a basement on Passage Descent in downtown Kharkov. Aunt Riva, who had left her husband a few years earlier, lived with Uncle Semyon around the corner and pretty much ignored her son. His father — my stepfather — didn't spend time with him, either. It fell to my mother to take care of him, from his clothes to his school and, most importantly, his health. He had some problems. My mother did not trust our socialized clinic doctors and sought out a private specialist, Doctor Bronstein, who actually brought Mark back to health.

Theirs was very much a mother-and-son relationship. One winter Mark fell skiing and broke his arm. My mother dropped everything, including me, to take care of him. She helped him get around in a cast, she worried about his X-rays, she stayed late at his bedside.

Mark and I became friends, too. He walked me to preschool — Salamander Kindergarten on Sumskaya Street — in the morning; he took me skiing and protected me from street bullies.

Just before Gena's birth in March 1941, Mark moved back in with his mother, who by now had one-year-old Mìlya, too. My mother had to agree, though Mark was still spending most of his time with us, teaching me to ride a bike. He complained he was feeling out of place in his family. His mother was absorbed with the baby. His stepfather and Mark could not stand each other. Mother begged my stepfather to take Mark back, never mind the crowding. But then the war broke out, and Mark was evacuated with his mother.

In '44 he graduated from Samarkand Navy School at the top of his class and was sent on to continue his studies in Baku. He excelled there, too, and went on to Superior Naval Engineering School in Leningrad. Once again at the top of his class, he was assigned to the Arctic Navy, where he stayed through his career.

I have always been proud that the name of Mark Berkovich is etched on a special marble plaque mounted in the lobby of the famous Admiralty building in St. Petersburg among outstanding graduates for the last two centuries.

His visit in Chimkent started a tradition for Mark. He alternated between my mother and his own on his vacations. This went on for twenty years until my mother died.

Return

In the late summer of 1944 we came back to the liberated Kharkov. The marks of war were everywhere: freestanding building walls with holes for windows, the bridge supports with the span gone, streets pockmarked with shells, broken trees, and streetcar tracks blown out of the ground. The streets were empty. A rare passerby covered his face with his coatsleeve as he fought the famous

The author's stepbrother, Mark Berkovich, as a Navy cadet, 1947.

Kharkov dust, multiplied by the ruins. The holes in the surviving buildings were not boarded, reeking of rot and mildew. All over we saw signs: "Checked — No Mines — Sergeant Yegòrov." This was our home town.

At first we were sheltered by our father's longtime friend "Uncle Pìnya," whose family had returned a little earlier. We stayed with them for two or three months and then we moved three blocks farther, to Goryàinovsky Lane, in the city center.

I was friends with Uncle Pìnya's daughter Anya from before the war. I remember how — only four years earlier — both of us rode the train to the summer camp, how we waved goodbye to our parents and then shared strawberries with sugar from the same jar. The smell and the taste of those strawberries stayed with me for the entire war.

Now Anya snubbed me and my friends, especially our games with the broken power meter. All the contacts were exposed, and we kept picking at them with a broken kitchen knife, getting hit by the current. It was standard European current of 220 volts — quite a hit. Whoever touched more times won. Anya didn't care for it and told the adults. The meter was boarded up. And we would not talk to each other anymore.

I enjoyed wandering around the ruins, where you could find all sorts of tasty bits — sunflowers, tomatoes, and even melons. No one planted them; somehow they just grew on their own. However, getting around piles of broken bricks and cement was no simple matter. It was easy to get hurt by exposed iron bars, or fall through a hole hidden in the garbage, or step into a pile of excrement.

One thing I learned while playing in the ruins with friends was not to fear heights. Sometimes I had to walk on top of the freestanding wall, two or three floors tall. Or jump over a hole at the same "altitude." For me, always

Dzerzhinsky Square in Kharkov, Ukraine, at the Revolution Day, 1954.

the smallest in our gang, it was a special challenge, since I had to jump even where others could simply take a step. It was scary. But being mocked for cowardice was even worse.

I didn't tell of this exploration at home, since it was strictly forbidden by my mother — but there was no other entertainment.

On the other hand, my first home library goes back to the pickings among the ruins. Some of the stuff I picked up was genuinely valuable, like bound issues of *Global Searcher* and *Around the World* illustrated magazines, which went back to before the revolution and had become rarities. And the books I found! James Fenimore Cooper, Jules Verne, Alexandre Dumas-*père*. Once I ran into a deluxe edition of a book called *The Chelùskin Epic*, about Soviet polar explorers. I was quite impressed by the drawings by Fedor Reshètnikov. I wished I could draw that well.

Other trophies included remnants of stamp collections, which we traded eagerly, unaware of their true value. A few years later, the father of my school-mate Natasha Multànova, a well-known Kharkov percussionist and stamp collector (who once traded a stamp album for a car!), found a few valuable stamps in my album: some 1901 Russian issues with value shown in Turkish currency, some Soviet stamps circa 1918, and a stamp showing an airplane upside down. I developed quite a taste for stamp collecting and later on missed my first album with the valuable stamps, sold by my brother Gena while I was doing my Navy service.

I was going to the third grade, at School No. 95, which was fifteen minutes away, a nondescript six-floor building, with the principal and caretaker's rooms on the ground floor.

In the winter the school was heated by a stove fashioned out of a small iron barrel. For a flue, it used an old rusty drainpipe, the kind that abounded in the ruins.

Every student was supposed to bring in some fuel every day. Anything you could find, anything that would burn would do: chair and table legs, pieces of window frames, staircase banisters. Sometimes we could steal a few lumps of coal in a boiler room. Anthracite took a while to catch fire, but then burned much longer than wood, providing heat through the end of the class.

The air was filled with smoke, causing us to squint. Sometimes there was not enough fuel or none at all. On those days we kept our coats and hats and sometimes even gloves on. On those days there was no writing in class.

Every day on the way to school I passed the burned-down building of the Central Restaurant on the corner of Rosa Luxemburg Square and Armenian Lane. I always found time to wander through its ruins and pick up something seemingly worthless: a shard of a mirror, a broken decorative tile, a toilet chain. Once I picked up a broken electrical transformer and extracted a roll of very thin wire. Later on I managed to trade it for something equally worthless. Some of my friends chipped away pieces of iron radiators, and I tried to follow suit.

We used these pieces as weights in making *lyàmbas*— a piece of fur with a glued-on weight that you had to kick as many times as you could before it hit the ground.

The game was highly popular among kids, though for some reason teachers hated it and categorically forbade it — you could even get expelled for it. In order to steer us away from it, they spread the rumor that the game had been invented by the Nazis to ruin Soviet children's health.

My friends were once again playing war. Now the game was less innocuous than three years ago. The ruins were a good source for both weapons and explosives.

A popular amusement consisted of pouring powder out of an unexploded shell and tossing it into a fire. This caused many accidents, with kids losing their eyes or fingers or hands — and sometimes lives.

A handgun was easily obtainable for food or a grenade. German handguns were "in." I got hold of a revolver once. It was heavy; I could barely hold it up. A friend of mine called Genrikh and I decided to re-enact a duel — just like the one where Pushkin was killed, according to the picture in the literature textbook. To be on the safe side, I spun the drum and emptied it of cartridges. Genrikh took out the magazine from his handgun, period. Then we counted ten steps away from each other and took aim. Genrikh fired first. After he pulled the trigger, it was my turn.

I was about to pull mine, too, when for some reason I remembered the words our military teacher at school never tired of repeating: Even an unloaded weapon fires once in its lifetime. I spun the drum again, and a cartridge fell out. It seemed to hide opposite the barrel. I realized I had almost killed my friend.

We were scared pretty badly. I still get shivers when I think about it.

Sometime in late April of '45 we had a guest — a friend of my mother's called Aunt Bùzya. She and her son came back to the city about the same time we did. Her husband Abram was in the army, and already somewhere outside Berlin. Aunt Bùzya wondered when this goddamn war was going to be over and promised two cakes to whoever would correctly predict the date. Without thinking, I burst out, "May eighth!"

Aunt Bùzya was as good as her word. On May 8 the war was over, and Gena — already four years old — and I were drinking tea with real, honest-to-God éclairs.

The end of the war was the sweetest day of my childhood.

3

Music Years

Kharkov

The City of Kharkov emerged in the mid-seventeenth century as a small wooden fortress built on the hill at the confluence of three rivers — the Kharkov, Lòpan, and Nètech. The first one gave its name to the city. It so happened that I spent my childhood and youth on the small plot of land where the fortress had once been.

These were my landmarks: the old Kharkov University, founded in early nineteenth century; small Uspènsky Cathedral, with a huge bell tower, built to mark the victory over Napoleon and visible from anywhere in the city; and Pokrov Monastery, founded together with the fortress. These names still sound sweet in my nostalgic memory: University Hill, University Street, Passage and Bursàk Descents (renamed Khaltùrin and Library respectively), and Goryàinov and Shlyàpny Lanes.

A famous Civil War tank (used by foreign "invaders") stood opposite the Historical Museum ruins' entrance. It was located at the bottom of the University Hill, next to a wide staircase that resembled the famous Potemkin one in Odessa (that's the one with the falling baby stroller). In Kharkov, this pompous esplanade ran into the blind rear of the university building built in the '20s (where the first Soviet "heavy water" was developed in the late '30s). I played there and roamed the ruins often.

Both the tank and the museum ruins are gone. Now there is a park, as in many other places in the city. There is a huge terraced park descending along Khaltùrin Descent where Old Passage once was. Another one replaced Red Army House, kitty-corner from Uspènsky Belltower. The old Nobility Assembly house became Young Pioneer Palace (once named after Bolshevik chieftain Pòstyshev who was executed by the KGB in the late '30s) and then was replaced by another park. City fathers used these parks to replace the city's rich architectural past.

In the summer of 1945, we lived in Goryàinov Lane—a short passage two blocks long in the center, behind the Uspènsky Cathedral. We lived in the first floor of the annex to the six-floor building burned in the war. The annex was in the courtyard, next door to a large, pre-revolutionary residential complex known as the Labor Palace.

We had a relatively large room with three small windows, big enough for our metal beds and a dinner table. Besides, we had a generously sized walk-through kitchen with a window, three steps wide, and a lobby with a sizable closet. The outhouse was not far away, and so was the water pump in the courtyard.

Above us was a similar apartment with an outside staircase.

It was a sunny Sunday. My stepfather was at work. I was playing in the courtyard. My mother, already pregnant, was doing the laundry. She called on my stepbrother Mark—who was enjoying the last days of his holidays—to help her carry the laundry basket outside.

The moment they crossed the threshold, an incredible racket came from inside. Broken glass and streams of thick dust flew through the windows. My mother's face was splattered with blood. A glass sliver struck her on the head and slashed her eyebrow. Mark grabbed her and, protecting her with his body, pulled her away from the house, while she fought back, screaming "Genaaaaaa!" for my four-year-old brother. Fortunately, he was outside.

Mark skillfully bandaged her head and ran back inside. A few moments later he re-emerged covered with black dust. He told us that the upstairs apartment had crashed in on top of us. The neighbors were unlikely to be hurt—he didn't see any bodies—but their apartment was gone. So was ours.

Mark took mother to the hospital where she had her wound stitched. Then, piece by piece, he retrieved pieces of our beds, a piece of table, and a chair from the ruins.

By the time our stepfather came back from work, we had firmly settled in the courtyard.

The Monastery

After our outbuilding collapsed, our family lived under an open sky for a few days. Then we were assigned to a place in one-floor, barrack-type building on University Street, a two-minute walk from our previous location.

Originally that apartment housed an elderly couple with an adult daughter. Now, over their protests, the government moved us into one of their tiny rooms. There was also a tiny hallway and a tiny kitchen. This kitchen had a small, coal-fed brick stove with two burners, a miniature table, a stool, and a garbage bucket with a washstand on the wall. The rooms also had built-in, coal-fed, stucco brick stoves. The apartment had no running water or indoor plumbing, to say nothing of a telephone.

This was the only time — fortunately short — when I lived in a "communal" apartment. This type of residence is a Soviet innovation that is important for historians. The future researchers of Soviet psychology will have to divide all of us into two categories: those whose consciousness was formed in communal apartments — and the rest.

The building stood in the courtyard of the Pokrov Monastery. A part of the monastery structure was assigned to a local natural history museum, which I visited daily. It was where I first saw a wax apple. It looked so natural that I simply had to try to bite it when there was no one around. I almost broke a tooth.

In the courtyard was a museum exhibit of trophy weapons: cannons, anti-aircraft guns, and even a German tank. All the children loved playing in it, spinning the heavy turret and turning other various handles. Yet soon we discovered that, as in so many other open-air Soviet museums, due to the absence of public toilets, the tank was used for other purposes.

Another exhibit was devoted to the Nazis' evil deeds. It was an actual *Gazenwagen*, or a van with the exhaust pipe leading to its windowless, air-proof compartment. Jews packed into it suffocated to death en route. I spent a lot of time inside, trying to imagine the experience of live people dying. I would never forget it.

Another monastery annex housed a bakery. Bread was still available with ration cards only, close to a pound a day per person — but you had to stand in line for hours. In our family, this was my responsibility. There were cards for other foodstuffs — salt, sugar, flour, butter, cereal — but they were seldom available.

Amazingly, the bakery made pastries, too; those were for the Party District Committee and for some other people who had access to those products. But that was not for us. And we knew our place.

Along with other kids, I spent hours sniffing the delicious smells that emanated from the bakery. Sometimes we were asked to run an errand — chop some firewood or bring water from a standpipe. The bakery had no running water either. Among the kids such errands were eagerly sought. They were paid for in kind — with tiny leftovers of biscuits or honey cakes, or sometimes just a handful of small tasty crumbs. Those were the days I hated the Germans and the war worse than usual.

The monastery was actually functioning — a rarity in the USSR. The church was almost always open. I liked sneaking in during services. On the one hand, I realized that God did not exist and that religion was an "opiate for the people." On the other hand, I had no idea what an opiate was. It seemed like it might be something sweet and tasty. When I learned that it

The GOSPROM complex at Dzerzhinsky Square. Kharkov, Ukraine, 1954.

was smoked, I thought it was burned as incense in our church. I liked the smell, the procedure of waving the censer, and the whole setting. Besides me and the other kids, the only other people were a bevy of old grannies. They eyed us distrustfully but did not chase us away.

Along with other boys, I would come to gawk at the baptisms. In those days it was not the babies that were baptized, but rather older children, about five or six, or even fourteen or sixteen. They were mostly girls. They were forced naked into the water-filled, stone tub. The room was not heated, and by their reaction I could tell that for them the ceremony was no fun. My mother angrily said they could get pneumonia easily. They had my sympathy. Also, it was kind of a striptease for us boys, although we did not think in those terms.

As for preaching, I didn't care much for it. It was hard to understand anyhow.

In January, my mother gave birth to a girl named Yanna. My younger brother Gena and I put on an improvised puppet show. We hid behind a few chairs, covered with a blanket. I made three puppets out of cloth — mother, father, and baby Yanna. The mother puppet was a happy one, repeating, "I have a daughter," and, "Finally I have a girl." The father puppet was skeptical, whereas she had to demonstrate with the baby and point at the place that made the difference. The show was a hit. The audience — friends and family — gave a standing ovation and asked for encores.

In the spring, Gena and I walked our sister in a stroller around the monastery courtyard. The weather was balmy, with trees in blossom. Suddenly she fell sick. She refused her mother's breast. She was losing weight, and kept sobbing like an adult. My mother was lost, and so were the doctors. Everybody gave up on Yanna. And Professor Bronstein, to whom my mother would refer frequently, was not back from evacuation yet.

The author's mother Maria Schneider with his sister Yanna. Kharkov, Ukraine, 1947.

One day we were sadly pushing our stroller. A nun approached. They lived in a two-storied building nearby. She lifted the edge of the blanket and eyed Yanna closely. "Your little sister is sick?" We nodded. "Go get your mom."

When Mom came, the nun removed something from her own neck and gave it to her. "Put it on the child and keep it there. I'll pray for her."

The next day my sister began to recover, and a week or two later she was once again a regular bouncing baby.

17 Tevelev Square

After nine months of life with hostile neighbors in a communal apartment, we moved from the environs of the Orthodox Christian monastery to an Orthodox synagogue (the only one in Kharkov), a hundred yards to the east, at 17 Tevelev Square.

To be precise, we did not move into the synagogue proper. The synagogue was located in the semi-basement of an old four-floor apartment building. We lived on the fourth floor. Yet when I was asked where I lived, I just said "at the synagogue," just as before I said, "at the monastery." In either case, this sufficed.

There was a pawnshop between us and the monastery, where my mother, to tide us over, often took our belongings when they were out of season. Next to the pawnshop was a firehouse. There was a paved courtyard, hemmed in by our house, the pawnshop, and the firehouse, where we played ball. A slightly sloping metal fire escape led to the roof of our building. We used its steps — thick metal rods — as horizontal bars for chin-ups. And we fashioned a wire basket into a basketball ring and attached it to the escape.

There was another rather small structure, a former barn or warehouse, which opened on our court. It housed the synagogue's shòychet, or ritual butcher, and before Jewish holidays elderly women lined up in front with chickens in their hands.

The entrance to the synagogue proper was from another courtyard, next to a squalid, smelly outhouse.

Compared to the church in the monastery, the synagogue did not look good. The Orthodox church was spacious, with sunshine coming though the light, sweet-smelling smoke from the censer. The synagogue was a dark, gloomy space, windowless and airless. With a capacity of about fifty, it had over a hundred visitors who had to go down a few steps to enter. Jews pray in a really shabby place, I thought.

The visitors were white-bearded, elderly men who somehow resembled my late Grandpa. They stared into their books and gloomily swayed to the prayer, casting angry glances at the kids. Out of mischief, we used to remove our hats when we entered. The rabbi did not like it, and with his helper constantly tried to chase us out. As they ran after us around the room, they bumped into benches and noisily overturned them. In the summer, I merely stood in the doorway and watched the service with curiosity.

The author's sister Yanna Berkovich. Kharkov, Ukraine, 1962.

When Grandpa died in Chimkent, I was dispatched to the local synagogue, and it was large and spacious. It was kept by Bukhara Jews who spoke Tajik. But, like their Kharkov brethren, they conducted services in Hebrew.

For some reason, I especially resented that part. At least in the Christian church you could make out the words: "Our Lord who art in heaven...." That made some kind of sense. And I understood Yiddish, too. But what was "Baruch ata adonai, alekheinu"? Utter obscurantism, I thought, using the school-learned terminology.

Now I was more critical of religion than when we lived at the monastery. I held the visitors in utter contempt. I knew from my teachers that the whole of mankind was inexorably progressing towards complete internationalism. This meant that these people and their rabbi were impeding progress. The rabbi especially should have been ashamed of himself. He had to know there was no God. Religion was dying out, and the sooner the better. Once these old men died, there would be no religion, and no Jewish nationalism, either. And then there would be no cause for anti–Semitism.

I was surprised and irritated that my mother believed in God. She did not visit the synagogue, of course. But she often referred to God as an existing and omniscient being. Moreover, she claimed something nonsensical: that the Christians' Jesus was a Jew. This did not explain anti–Semitism — people could not hate their own God.

I noted that this was only one of my mother's odd thoughts. For example, she thought genetics was a science, while everyone knew that it was an anti-scientific plot by western pseudoscientists, followers of Jews named Morgan and Mendel. I heard it on the radio speaker, after all.

But the most inexplicable, thing was this: why, several times a year, did thousands of Kharkov Jews go crazy and crowd outside our building?

About forty years later, in the winter of '86, we were vacationing in Boca Raton with Galya and Volodya Zilbersteins, our old Moscow friends. We saw an ad in the local paper: a cantor named Mikhail Aleksandròvich was singing in a synagogue in Fort Lauderdale.

The name was very popular in the Soviet Union. In our house, it was treated with awe. To us, he was a famous opera singer; a performer of various lyrical songs, including Jewish ones; and a decorated artist and Stalin Prize winner. During the war he traveled to the front lines to sing for the soldiers. We listened to him on the radio and to his records. Imagine my shock when I learned, still in my youth, that he was moonlighting as a cantor in a synagogue. The Soviet propaganda machine would never mention that this was his chosen calling and the repertoire he enjoyed the most. When he emigrated in 1971, the KGB was so angry as to spread impossible rumors about him. One was that allegedly he had been exiled to Siberia because the airport customs found diamonds hidden in his electric chandelier.

From left are the author's friends Galina and Vladimir Zilberstein, famous USSR singer/cantor Mikhail Aleksandròvich, and the author and his wife Marina. Fort Lauderdale, Florida, 1985.

We unanimously decided to go hear him. We arrived half an hour before the evening service and settled in the rear. The synagogue where he sang was nothing special: a comfortable, spacious, well-lit, air-conditioned auditorium for about six or seven hundred people. It was filling slowly with elderly Floridians, many of them representing three generations.

Observing their quiet, dignified air brought back the memories of my childhood in post-war Kharkov. It was hard to say how many Jews out of sixty thousand then in Kharkov were religious. But on High Holidays the entire courtyard of our house and the one before it and the pocket park on Tevelev Square were jammed — several thousand people, easily.

A microphone was placed inside the synagogue, and the service was broadcast via loudspeakers. As a convinced atheist, I pestered the rabbi: "Doesn't religion deny scientific progress? Really? How can you use radio then?"

The rabbi eyed me with pity and reproof. He would not argue back. That might land him in trouble with the KGB for "religious propaganda" (though what else was he supposed to do as a rabbi — carry bricks?) and get him exiled to Siberia.

Once the Jewish crowd overflowed both our courtyards and the park on the square. The crowd jammed nearby University Street and the two adjacent streets, too. I couldn't even get home.

"So what do you expect," my mother said. "First of all, it is Yom Kippur, and second of all, Mikhail Aleksandròvich himself will sing."

The synagogue was shut down in 1951. There were rumors spread that the Jews were caught in some legal violation: either the synagogues' chairman did something illegal to the rabbi, or vice versa, or both to each other — or maybe just one shul for Kharkov was too many.

The now-vacant basement was handed to a family of gypsies with four kids, including gorgeous, 16-year-old Galya. She was my age, and I liked her very much. Throughout the two years of our innocent "romance" my mother was in torment: she was sure that the gypsies would stab me to death.

(I survived. When I came back from the Navy, I had a hard time recognizing Galya in a pregnant, blowsy woman with two screaming, runny-nosed babies in her arms.)

Soon after the gypsies moved in, it turned out there were about thirty of them actually living in the old synagogue. Some gypsies would beg on the streets but did not make enough money to survive. Additional income would come on Sundays when around 6 A.M., rain or shine, the whole bunch of them, with babies and toddlers, went to the Blagoveschensky Market. They would come back in the late afternoon, carrying huge bags of food, sufficient to last the rest of the week.

Weather allowing, Darya, the mother of the family, sold sunflower seeds nearby on Rỳmarsky Street. That was a violation. One day a cop started pestering her. She poured him a couple of glasses (that was how the seeds were measured on the street). Yet he was drunk and would not go away. Unfortunately, Darya's oldest son Nikolay happened to come by — the only one in the family with a job, at a local factory. He took his mother's side, and the cop shot him.

I suspect the entire gypsy community came to the funeral. Soon thereafter I witnessed a scene: the cop's wife on her knees begging Darya to forgive her husband. She offered money and jewelry. A month later the cop was found stabbed to death.

The investigation revealed that the former little synagogue basement housed twenty-five people without legal registration. They were taken away. But a couple of weeks later, one by one, they came back.

Our lodging was smack in the center of the city. Under the tsars, this huge, clumsy, five-floor building in the city center featured a "Rooms" sign. It could have been a hotel or a whorehouse or a combination of both. Now it was a Soviet residential building, and we occupied a hotel room on the fourth floor.

Partial view from the window at 17 Tevelev. Kharkov, Ukraine, 1952.

Hotel rooms were spacious. I calculated that ours had been about 300 square feet. Its two windows had a southern exposure, overlooking the ruins of the Pioneer Palace, before they were turned into a park. To the left was a beautiful view of the Conservatory, which at the time housed the city council. To the right was the magnificent bell tower of Uspenski Cathedral. I always savored the view.

Our space was divided into four parts with plywood partitions. Half of the area was our main room with both windows. It was used as a living/dining room and bedroom. One quarter, with a plastered brick stove, served as a kitchen. In the early years, besides cooking, the stove also served to heat the entire space. There were no cupboards or a sink or a fridge. In the winter, the perishables were stored in a bag that was hung outside the transom window. In the summer, we sometimes bought ice and put it with the food in a large pot with a lid, and then wrapped it with a blanket.

The makeshift entrance hall, two steps by two, had a washboard hanging next to the door, and two buckets with drinking water on the shelf. Under the shelf was the slop bucket with a cover, which served as a toilet.

Yet another compartment of our hotel room, slightly larger than the entrance hall and separated from it by a plywood partition, was a tiny bedroom, into which we jammed a bed that I shared with my brother Gena and a bedside-table. When we had overnight guests, they slept with me, and Gena slept on the floor in the main room.

We did not have ventilation or air conditioning. On hot days, mother

hung bed sheets over the windows and sprinkled water on the wooden floor-
boards. In the winter, the stove was stoked up with coal. Five years later, we
got central heating. Now the food was being cooked on the kerosene stove.
In another two years, we got gas. And finally, thirteen years later, a refrigerator. We did not have a bathroom or a toilet or running water or indoor
plumbing or a telephone. Instead, as was the rule in every Soviet apartment
at the time, we had a radio speaker — a disk of thick black cardboard — in the
corner under the ceiling. It stayed on round the clock. The broadcasts started
at quarter to six A.M. and ended at midnight. Under Stalin, a disconnected
radio speaker was punishable by up to a jail term.

Ultimately, by the standards of that day, our hotel room was very decent
housing for a family of five (six, if you include my cousin Maya who lived
with us for a few years).

The landing outside our front door opened into a huge, glass-roofed
atrium. On the other three sides it was flanked by three wide metal staircases,
with decorative designs and iron banisters. Each landing had six rooms. There
were four more that could be accessed through a short corridor. At the end
of the corridor were storage cubicles. Five or six years after we moved in,
indoor plumbing arrived, and the cubicles were converted into toilets. Each
was shared by three families and was padlocked. One day my sister absentmindedly locked in a neighbor. It was daytime, everybody was at work, and
he spent a few hours on the toilet. Another cubicle had a water tap with a
sink, and — finally — we no longer had to fetch water to the fourth floor from
the outside.

In those years almost all urban residential space belonged to the state,
with rent and utilities heavily subsidized and costing peanuts. But once a
family lucked out with a room, its members were tied to it through the rest
of their lives. Families grew with children and grandchildren, but they could
not get out of the tiny room received from the state generations ago. The
neighbors' lineup did not change, either. The eight years I spent at 17 Tevelev
were spent next to the same people — over thirty families. All knew one
another very well; all traded news and gossip and regularly got into fights.

Our janitor, named Varvara, lived in a tiny cubicle under the stairs. She
was of small stature, with a short nose, a limp in her right foot, and an expression of perennial discontent on her face. No one knew what her duties were
or who paid her or what she lived on. She was rumored to be from Polish
nobility. On official holidays she dressed up, spreading an odor of mothballs,
and put on lipstick. In all the years we lived there she was the same age —
around seventy. Once in a while she was visited by her son, who arrived on
a racing bike. This led the ever-watchful tenants to conclude he was a professional athlete.

Varvara cleaned the outhouse in the courtyard — a small space next to the steps that led to the synagogue, with two open stalls and a sink. Basically they were holes in the ground with slight elevations for footpads. The outhouse was used not just by the tenants but by anyone who knew of its existence. Sometimes there were long lines.

Once, Varvara made a scene. "Saboteurs!" she screamed. "Enemies of the people!"

It turned out she was protesting against daily publications of Stalin's picture in the newspaper. That was truly seditious, and many tenants became scared. Yet the outburst was rooted in something completely different. The newspapers were used in the toilet, and Varvara found a scrap with Stalin's picture — and more than once, she declared. Alas, the Great Leader had not deemed it necessary to invent toilet paper yet.

The main entrance from the square had been closed long ago. We used the entrance under the arch, which was meant for vehicles. The grand lobby was converted into an apartment, occupied by the Petrènko family with two small children.

Above them, at the first landing between the floors, where in the old times the janitor used to live, now resided the Weiners, an elderly couple, whose two sons had died in combat. Their one window opened under the arch, and the room was always gloomy. Weiner managed the Kommunist printing shop, a job fraught with emergencies — hence he was the first in the building to have a phone.

On the third floor below us lived a middle-aged couple: a Jew named Lev and his German wife named Elsa. This mixed marriage made my mother very upset. "How can he! After all they've done to us!"

In the building were about a dozen children my age to play with. Lisa and Zhènya Braginsky, two sisters, lived on the second floor, at the same landing as my friend Eddy Knyshòv and his sister Lucy, who was the same age as my sister Yanna. His father was the principal of a trade school. Around the corner I had Garik Goldfarb and his sister Lilya, also same age as Yanna. Their father was a professor at the medical school or, perhaps, the university. From day one, Garik knew he would go into science. Five years later, the Knyshòvs and the Goldfarbs became No. 2 and No. 3 to get their own phones

Eddy became a military officer in the border troops (which were technically under the KGB's jurisdiction), and Garik became an engineer. Fifty years later, the Braginsky sisters settled in Brooklyn.

Our next-door neighbors were two elderly seamstresses, Polya and Sonya. Polya had a husband named Yefim who died soon, and a redheaded daughter named Lisa, who was ten years older than I. Sonya's son died in combat, and her widowed daughter-in-law Lyuba, a druggist, and her daughter Klava, who was my brother Gena's age, lived with Sonya.

Another apartment at our landing was occupied by a Dr. Rappoport, who spent her whole life writing a thesis on fighting TB. Before her defense I helped her with preparing big folders with illustrations, drawing all sorts of unpleasant stuff. She obtained her degree and died soon thereafter.

A few years later, the Ostroùmov family moved in next door to Dr. Rappoport. The older Mr. Ostroùmov, of retirement age, with a short gray goatee, wore a professorial little hat, just like — or so Soviet cartoons told us — tsarist professors had done before the revolution. Indeed, he used to teach at the Polytechnic Institute. Now his hobby was repairing old books. He bound my whole collection of Ogonyòk illustrated weeklies. My mother and he got along famously. She respected the Ostroùmovs more than any other neighbors.

The rumors had it that the Ostroùmovs had owned a small mansion on Darwin Street. Then someone in the family was arrested as an "enemy of the people," the mansion was confiscated, and they were moved into our building. They were pleasant people who kept to themselves. Ten years later, their relative was found innocent posthumously "due to lack of criminal content." But the mansion was not returned.

Another two kids my age lived on the top floor. One was Vova Bazàrsky; his father was a bookkeeper and his mother a salesperson at a bookstore. It was from her that I learned — two days ahead of everybody else — of the former KGB chairman Lavrenty Beria's arrest. She came home for lunch and whispered to me on the stairs: "They just called to take Beria's pictures from the shelves. You know what that means? He's out!"

Zòya Fesènko lived on the same floor, too, though my mother was highly disapproving of our friendship, most likely because she was a shiksa. Zòya had a kid brother Vitalik, who was the same age as Gena.

Zòya and Vitalik's father was taken prisoner in the war. He came back in '46 — tall, handsome, and reserved. He was a radio engineer and promised to help me assemble a ham radio. I liked him a lot. One night he was arrested and, like many other POWs, was never heard from again.

Ilya Reifman, with whom we would become lifelong friends, and his mother moved a year after us into the former warehouse where the synagogue's shoychet used to live. They lived in Kiev before the war. His father was killed early in the war in the defense of the city. His mother worked as a seamstress; her employer helped her get the former shoychet's office.

There was a brief period in my life when, at eighteen, I was seriously addicted to drinking. Oddly enough, it was initiated by my own mother.

I was working as a draftsman at a design office and took classes at engineering college four nights a week. The remaining two evenings and the Sunday were spent in the library. I used to have a cup of tea before work, and a sandwich — reluctantly — on my lunch. In the evening I invariably turned down food for lack of appetite. My mother was completely lost: I was losing weight fast.

My mother's brother-in-law, Uncle Lev, suggested a folk remedy — pure medicinal alcohol, which he enjoyed daily. Holding my breath, I chased a tiny sip of alcohol with a glass of water and immediately had a bite. Gradually, in order to be able to eat the same amount, I had to triple the amount of alcohol. Five or six weeks later, I couldn't swallow any food without alcohol.

Yet I missed my chance to turn into a chronic alcoholic. I was drafted and was sent to a closed Navy base in Finland, where liquor was prohibited. My mother conceded to my begging in each letter, and eventually smuggled to me a half a liter of alcohol in a hot-water bottle. But by then I had learned to do without it.

Later in life, I more than once found myself in situation where vodka was used like water, and I dared not turn it down. But now my body categorically rejected all alcohol.

I knew the taste of liquor from childhood. It appeared on the table on holidays, though my stepfather "bent his elbow" on the side. Of course, mother protested when he offered a shotglass of wine to my three-year-old sister, but I was allowed a couple of those at the age of ten. There was no age limit on alcohol use in the Soviet Union.

In fact I had my first chance to become an alcoholic at twelve.

Our building had a basement — a warren of storage spaces, where tenants kept coal, firewood, and various household junk. Once in a while I had to go down to fetch a bin of coal or some firewood. I would have to open a heavy, slanted hatch door and then climb down a vertical, worn-out wooden ladder. Even after I grew up, the basement struck me as a grim and spooky place. Its rare, dim light bulbs barely lit its labyrinthine vaulted corridors and its earthen floor. Every time I would sigh with relief to be back aboveground.

In 1947, a part of the basement that was adjacent to Tevelev Square was made into a liquor store. A rather wide concrete area well with a stair was built to access it from the street. And in our courtyard, right next to the synagogue entrance, the workers dug a hole to lower wine and beer kegs into the store.

The store was popularly called The Booze Joint. My mother hated it with a passion.

On paydays, the first and the 15th of the month, the entrance to the store was crowded with women (sometimes including my mom) — the wives who tried to catch their husbands before they drank their paychecks away.

The place was never without a drunk lying outside, covered with caked dirt and vomit. Sometimes he would lie there all night and be picked up by the police in the morning.

The tenants tried to complain, though they could not quite figure out to whom they should complain and of what. They did complain to the housing office and the district Soviet. Two neighbors — Knyshov, the director of the trade school, and Weiner, who worked at the city paper — drafted a tenants' letter to the high authorities. A plainclothesman showed up and tried to find out who had authored it. The writers were not given up, and the store was not closed, either. The only difference was that the local policeman started showing up twice, rather than once, a day. And so we continued to live like this, flanked by the temple and the Booze Joint.

A year later someone at the BJ had a bright idea to make it easier to deliver the wine in the basement. One end of a rubber hose was inserted in a keg atop a flatbed truck, and the other one lowered to the basement. Then you sucked a few ounces of the liquid, stuck the other end in an empty keg in the store, and the liquid would flow down by itself.

Another idea was to use the kids at the yard — us — as labor. It was popular then to use cheap children's work: in the years immediately after the war the real labor force was scarce. For a half-glass of cheap port or a mug of beer we had long been helping them roll the kegs to the basement. Now it was even easier: you stuck a hose in the keg, gulped a little wine and stuck it in the empty keg. By the time we were done with the truckload, we were so inebriated we had to turn down the half a glass we were to be paid.

At the time we were as young as twelve to thirteen.

Our 17 Tevelev was a microcosm of Soviet society.

A Woman from Music School

No one printed school textbooks during or immediately after the war in the Soviet Union. They were not available in stores, either. You had to go to the bazaar to sell your old ones and use the money to buy textbooks for the next year.

The word for Kharkov bazaar is *tolkùchka*, which literally means "a place where everybody pushes" or "a crowded place" (literally, "where you push with your elbows"). Interestingly enough, both meanings applied. You pushed your stuff, and you had to use your elbows, too.

Kharkov's *tolkùchka* was close to the city center, not far from Blagovèschensky Cathedral. Schoolchildren would come on Sunday, spread old papers down on the ground, and stack their books on top. Sometimes the proceeds covered not only new textbooks, but stationery and pens and ink. In those days you could find everything at *tolkùchka* that I was interested in and that was not available in stores: from officers' field bags that we used instead of briefcases to pencils and photo paper.

Like any other private endeavor, buying and selling textbooks was illegal, and from time to time police raided the stalls, albeit in a typically lackadaisical

Southern manner. But they zeroed in on others — people who sold cups of water from a bucket or home-made ice cream in waffles — whom they regularly caught and took to the precinct. We were left alone — perhaps because cops had children, too? — and I don't remember that anyone was ever arrested for it.

I brought my old third-grade textbooks. I had known I would have to sell them and had been treating them with care: I had not made any marks or dog-eared them and even wrapped them in newspaper so as to keep the cover as fresh-looking as it looked when I bought them at the same *tolkùchka*.

Barely did I settle down when the first customer arrived — a young buxom woman, fashionably dressed in a short green skirt and a light-wool, rust-colored sweater that matched her hair color. She quickly went through my "goods" and declared that she would buy them all.

I was overjoyed. It was an extraordinary stroke of luck. Not to have to spend a whole day or possibly even the next couple of Sundays at the bazaar! Although she offered considerably less than what I had expected, I agreed immediately.

Afterwards my customer told me that if I gave her another discount, she would help me enroll in a music school.

There had never been a musician in our family. Or any musical instruments. Just the record player and a few records with popular pre-war Soviet recordings by Utesov and Lemeshev. True, at family gatherings relatives would sing in chorus, as Ukrainian Jews are wont to, and I joined in. But that about covered my relationship to music.

Detecting interest, my new acquaintance added that she was a member of the parents' council at the Kharkov Music School and, perhaps to sound more convincing, she introduced herself: Ms. Serebryànskaya.

She told me that the school was for gifted children — and I certainly qualified. (I liked that.) I needed to take an entrance exam, but for me that would be a formality. The school taught the same subjects that a regular school did, plus music. And students got two teaspoons of sugar a day with tea. (I liked that even more. At other Kharkov schools you didn't get any.) Finally, there would be financial assistance — three hundred rubles a month! For me, a ten-year-old, that sounded like the chance of a lifetime. I had to strike the iron while it was hot, I thought. I accepted whatever money she gave me, handed her the books and offered to carry them to her house.

En route Ms. Serebryànskaya told me more about that wonderful place. Students could borrow various musical instruments: violins, clarinets, accordions, and some other stuff with intriguing exotic names like oboes, saxophones, cellos, flutes, and the utterly mystifying xylophone.

She lived close to the school, in a large building close to the Kharkov Hotel on Sverdlov Street, which I knew well.

When an hour later we came to the music school, we learned that the office did not open till 1 P.M. — it was Sunday, after all. I stayed to wait. She left. That was our one and only meeting.

Embouchure

The music school entrance test was a snap. First the examiner played a tune on the piano, and I had to reproduce it by clapping hands. Then I had to sing another tune. Finally, they played a few notes with me standing with my back to the piano, and then I had to find the keys that had been played.

They told me on the spot that I was accepted. The school principal Nikolay Stepànovich talked to me personally. He inspected my hands, felt my fingers, and placed me in the cello class. "You don't have what we call a perfect pitch, but otherwise your natural talents are excellent."

In the evening I shared my joy with my parents. Until then I kept my musical-school plans secret. My father did not mind. Distrustfully, he asked again about the scholarship, which was comparable to his official salary. But my mother was delighted beyond belief, repeating how "my Garik will be a famous musician."

Yet when she found out the school's location across town, she became worried: I had to promise her I'd be careful and keep my eyes open, especially when crossing the streets with streetcar tracks — several routes had already been repaired in post-war Kharkov. She could not know that her son had long been competing with other boys, jumping on and off moving streetcars.

When classes started, I found out that the cello was just a huge violin, taller than I, and it had to be kept between my legs while seated. The school warehouse had two cellos, but neither one was in working condition. I had to wait for them to be repaired.

The boys in our courtyard were utterly envious of me.

A month later, the principal ran into me in the hall and asked about my progress. I told him I had no cello, and he got very angry. He told me to come by his office after classes.

Our conversation was brief. He had already reached a solution. "You, Berkovich, have an excellent embouchure for a flutist. We've got an extra flute at the warehouse. So take this paper to your parents and have them sign it."

I had no idea what embouchure was, but I was impressed and flattered. I informed my courtyard pals that from now I was a flutist. None of us knew what a flute was. After a long discussion we concluded that it was sort of like a clarinet — a metal instrument, curved like a question mark, with a mouthpiece at the tip. That one we knew very well from a recent British movie called *Let George Do It.*

The author's ID as a musical school student. Kharkov, Ukraine, 1946.

Prudently, I did not brag about my embouchure in the courtyard. That might have been going too far.

Leonid

At our school, the teachers held music classes at their own apartments. My mother was afraid that someone would steal the school flute on the way. For the first class, she asked my cousin Leonid to accompany me.

As a precaution, we took the dissembled flute out of the case. My mother wrapped each piece in a cloth and put the whole lot into the shopping bag. Thus disguised, I brought the flute to my first instructor Beylin, who played flute at Kharkov opera and lived on Rymarsky Street next to the Opera, ten minutes away.

Beylin intended to teach me how to extract sounds out of the flute. But he couldn't. Every time he saw my bag with the flute, he was overwhelmed with laughter.

My very tall schoolmate Alik Gamelyanov, who also took Beylin's classes, reminded me of this scene for years. Yet he attributed the laughter to something completely different and repeated: "So this was your cousin? *He* was about to defend you?"

Leonid was thin and feeble and shy, looking around all the time, as if expecting to be attacked. And he stuttered, too. Shortly before that he had been hired as a shoemaker's trainee and was now hiding his dirty hands, covered with wounds from misusing the tools. Yet he was proud of his mission, which implied he was considered strong enough to protect me. He remembered this episode through the rest of his life and never missed a chance to tell about it.

Leonid was not a complicated fellow and grew up to be a decent and considerate man. It so happened that I was more in touch with him than the rest of his family. In early '53 he went to visit his older sister Irena who lived in Kràsnogorsk outside Moscow, and never came back to Kharkov.

He found a job at a construction tower crane factory in Moscow as a welder, and this became his profession through the rest of his life.

In 1970, Leonid received an invitation from his brother Yuzik to visit him in Brazil. It was no longer forbidden to have relatives in capitalist countries. His sister had already visited Yuzik twice.

In order to visit his brother, Leonid had to go through a number of painful procedures. One of them was obtaining a character reference from the factory's Triangle: the Party Committee, Union Committee, and the Director's office.

Although Leonid was a worker in good standing, with his picture regularly on the Board of Honor, he was still nervous. During the Triangle's meeting, someone asked, seemingly as a joke, if he had plans to stay abroad. ("Like I would tell them!" he would comment later.) Upon the answer in the negative, the officials breathed a sigh of relief and told him that by the time he came back in a month, a new one-room apartment would await him. (Pure coincidence, of course). Leonid and his wife and child, who shared a tiny dorm room, had been waiting for the apartment for twelve years. (Needless to say, he traveled to Brazil alone. The family stayed behind — another way to assure he came back.)

Brazil stunned Leonid. The Soviets were right: it was not altogether a great idea to send Soviet blue-collar workers to visit their millionaire brothers.

When he came back, the airport customs abused him as much as they could and kept three suitcases out of his four — so much for carefully selected gifts for his family and friends. When he got home, he lay down on the couch, turned his face to the wall and stayed on the couch for a month. He never left the house or saw anyone.

His co-workers were afraid to inquire whether he was back.

When he finally showed up back at work, his boss cried with relief. He had signed the character reference and was now facing a possible expulsion from the Party.

The factory director was overjoyed. He invited Leonid to his office and told him he forgave his one-month "leave." Moreover, he would get paid for it. If Leonid had stayed in Brazil, the director would have had serious problems with the Party Committee.

The Union Committee pitched in and issued Leonid and his wife a free voucher for a stay in a factory sanatorium.

The apartment, however, was too much for the director.

After putting in thirty-five years at the factory, Leonid retired and then, in the early '90s, emigrated to Israel with his family.

The Band

After two classes with Bèylin I could play six notes on the flute — almost the entire first octave — and recognized them on music sheets. Suddenly I was summoned to see the director. "Berkovich! Why are you missing the band rehearsals?"

I did not even know the band existed and lied by saying the first thing that came to my head: "I was taking my shoes in for repair."

"Watch out! Another no-show — and you're out!"

I had already noted that at school, Nikolay Stepànovich was universally feared, even by teachers. He was tall and broad-shouldered and sported a short moustache under a meaty pimpled nose. With hair falling on his fore-head, he resembled Hitler cartoons. Sometimes I even wondered if Hitler was hiding in disguise as the director.

He was stern. Much later, in the winter, all of the boys in my fourth grade were called outside during class and lined against the wall, along with the other grades' boys. The director paced along, his hands behind his back, scrutinizing the students severely. Then he stopped and asked in a well-mod-ulated, music-teacher voice: "Who wrote fuck in the toilet?"

Thank God it wasn't me, I thought.

In the dead quiet, the director added: "You better confess nicely! I'm not letting you go until the bastard confesses!" Once again, he paced along the lineup, looking each boy in the eye. Once he reached the end of the line, he turned to face us. "I know who did it. But I want him to confess. Or else I'm kicking his ass out right now!"

Once again, I thought, "Isn't it great it's not me." We used to do this a lot in the old school. I even got caught once and threatened to be taken to see my mother. I barely managed to tear away.

"I'm counting till three," said the director. "One!"

All froze. The teachers' voices in the classrooms behind closed doors were heard clearly.

"Two!"

I knew it wasn't me, but I was still dying to go to the toilet. What's next, I wondered. He wouldn't keep us here till evening.

The next instant took forever. Finally, a tiny, third-grade piano player shyly raised his hand.

A few days later I came to the band rehearsal.

"Where's your instrument?" asked the director, who turned out to be the bandleader as well. It had never occurred to me to bring the flute. Clearly, I wasn't good enough for the band.

Two days later at the band rehearsal I was told: "Why is your flute in the case?"

The author as a musical school student. Kharkov, Ukraine, 1947.

Where else should it be? Not in the shopping bag.

"Get it out!" the director commanded. "Let's see how you learned your part!"

I didn't think I had come so far as to learn the flute part in the band.

"Come on, Berkovich, what are waiting you for?" he continued in his high notes. "Show us what you've learned!"

Later on I had chances to see what would happen when Nikolay Stepanovich really got mad at rehearsal. He could easily use his baton on someone's back. I got it a few times, too, later, when I played at the symphony orchestra with him.

For now, the only thing left to do was to put my flute to my mouth. The band grew quiet. I could not get lower than G in the one-line octave. I started with A and played everything I could — all nine notes.

"OK. Now go in reverse," the director ordered, smiling for some reason.

I had never tried that before, but I dared not talk back. I did the best I could. The rest of the band broke out in laughter, and a break was called.

The director was amused most of all. "I want you to play "Jaeger Marsch" by the next rehearsal. Is that clear?"

When I told Beylin, he was enraged. "This barracks bandleader is sabotaging my pedagogical process."

Nonetheless he helped me to play, though slowly, the first eight bars.

At the next rehearsal, I proudly assembled the flute and played — slowly, as if savoring every note.

At normal tempo, "Jaeger Marsch," though written in a minor scale, sounds bravura-like, almost merry, somewhat reminiscent of the Jewish dance "Freylekhs." But I couldn't play that fast yet. And the further I got playing slowly, the more our director raised his eyebrows and stared at me.

Finally, I got to the end of the passage that I had learned, quite happy with my performance. In the corner of my eye I saw the director and could not figure out his reaction. Especially at the end when, along with the band, he exploded in laughter.

The music school's marching band. Kharkov, Ukraine, 1946.

By playing slowly, I had turned the joyous march into mournful, funereal music.

Through the rest of my school years, I was asked from time to time to play this number for an encore.

Pianoforte Obbligato

Studying at the music school where I had landed by pure accident and out of childish rashness was no piece of cake. I enrolled in the fourth grade, in a class of thirty-five; by the seventh grade, only eighteen were left. The ten-year school program was done at an accelerated pace — in nine years. At the same time, musical training was going very seriously. In the tenth grade, students did nothing but music, training to enter the conservatory.

Music classes included, besides the major (flute in my case) a variety of subjects: solfeggio, musical theory, musical harmony, musical literature, wind and symphonic orchestras, ensemble (duet and later quartet), and, finally, piano (unless it was already a major).

The author (second from left in upper row) with music school classmates. Kharkov, Ukraine, 1947.

I had to go to piano classes at the teacher's house. Anastasia Sinèlnikova was a charming, relatively young woman, with dimples, just like my brother Gena. She was unmarried, like so many women in those days, and lived in a small communal apartment on Sumskàya Street near the park — a fifteen minute streetcar ride.

I was required to rehearse two hours a day. But we didn't have a piano. There were a few at school, but they were reserved for the students who majored in piano. I arrived at lessons unprepared and was looking at flunking the course.

Then I had a revelation. I glued together several sheets from my notebook and ruled them like a keyboard, with black keys where appropriate. It was a wonderful piano that I practiced every night on our table after supper — and silent, too, bothering no one. My mother was touched.

Sinèlnikova detected the change right away and soon asked me where I was rehearsing — did my parents buy me a piano? I proudly pulled my "keyboard" out of the bag and spread it on her table. She was delighted. We became close friends.

Like my flute teacher Bèylin, she believed in the classical training method: the first year was devoted to "training my hand properly." Then we learned scales and simple etudes.

Our neighbors on the floor above had a piano no one was using. It was a good piano, though considerably out of tune. By that time our finances had improved, and my mother decided to spend part of my scholarship on my training. She arranged for me to study at the neighbors' for one hour a day, three days a week. The pay was nominal, but for them, with the head of the family in the gulag, every bit helped. After a year, we bought the piano on time. We jammed it between the two windows and after three years paid it off.

At first, I enjoyed playing piano even more than the flute. But by the time when, according to my teacher, I could take on more interesting and complicated things, plus I could rehearse at home, I got bored with it. Yet I could not quit lest I be expelled from school.

I was a conscientious student. Anastasia liked me. I stayed at her house long after the class as she treated me to tea with preserves, showed me musical collections from her small library, and played music for me.

There was no sheet music for sale. I had to copy it, which was painstaking labor. I started with ruling five-line stuff on a blank sheet; then neatly and with pleasure I copied treble clef and bass clef and then, with some verve, after the key and time signatures, the rest of the notes. Gradually this turned into a hobby.

Once Sinèlnikova asked me to copy a musical work for her, two pages long. I put in my best effort. I even copied the line with the address of the publishing house — or it could have been the store. I still remember it: "*12 Neglinnaya Street, Moscow.*" Anastasia could not stop laughing, and that made me even happier.

Afterwards she found clients for me — to copy sheet music for money. It paid peanuts, and for some reason I was ashamed of it. I preferred to do it for free.

I spent a lot of time at my teacher's home, and we used it productively. We mastered Czerny's "Etudes" for beginners and then I started on Tchaikovsky's "Neapolitan Dance." Then suddenly our friendship began to crack. Moreover, she grew to fear me.

At twelve, I had a solid reputation for being a troublemaker that Aunt Shura had detected early. At school I was notorious for being a class clown — even before I was in the winds section and played a gleeful "Alter Jaegermarsch" as a funeral march. I cracked jokes in class right and left. I was expected to be game for anything, and caused laughter in advance. Sometimes they laughed at my jokes, but sometimes, I suspect, the joke was at my expense. In those days I could not tell the difference. I cracked a joke at Sinèlnikova's house, too, and it was a bad one — actually a dangerous one.

Once, when I was already at the door, with the next student already at the piano, Sinèlnikova reminded me that the next class was off on account of a state holiday called Constitution Day, or, as it was called then, Stalin's Constitution. I dropped casually: "Of course, Anastasia Yakovlevna. Stalin's — Prostitution ... right?"

Feygin

Soviet education was centralized, but individual programs varied. Every time I changed schools I had to play catch up. At music school, the general subjects were also taught in accelerated mode. When I arrived at the fourth grade, not only was I three years behind in musical subjects, but at least six months behind in general ones, too.

I didn't know which way to run. When I was called in front of the class in musical harmony, the question sounded as if it were in a foreign language. For example, the teacher would play a chord that I had to name. But I could not even hear it. Then I was supposed to solve a musical problem using this chord. I took a guess — sometimes a correct one, but more often I got Ds. There were no textbooks; we took notes. I listened to classmates' answers and tried to put the picture together. I developed a trial and error method (and kept it through the rest of my life). Ultimately, this helped develop intuitive thinking — though at the expense of logical thought.

I shared a desk with a boy who kept sniffling and kept his mouth open. His name was Valentin Fèygin, and his mother taught piano. He was constantly engrossed in his own thoughts, responded absentmindedly, and laughed where others didn't. And he kept buttoning his shirts the wrong way.

We became friends. Like everyone else, he was a year older. He saw that I didn't know the first thing about music and started to help me. He told me about octaves, scales, tonalities, and chords, and taught me how to write notes. With his help, I was able to catch up.

Valentin was a godsend. We studied at his house in the Cold Hill neighborhood, where his family lived in a tiny house with a tiny vegetable-and-fruit plot. The Cold Hill Bridge was not rebuilt yet, and we had to cross what seemed like hundreds of rail tracks to get there.

They had a huge grand piano, almost the size of the room. Valentin told me that he used to climb under the keyboard console. He would touch a key and try to figure out the note. Now his kid brother Grisha was doing the same. (Grigory Feygin would become a famous violinist and winner of many international competitions.) Both brothers had a perfect ear. I liked that idea. By now, Valentin was able to recognize and write down complicated chords.

His instrument was the cello. He was ahead of our class in musical subjects. When he performed in concert, everybody dropped everything to "listen to Feygin."

His Jewish father had spent the war on the front lines. His Russian mother and he lived through the German occupation. Somehow his mother was able to hide her "brunets" from the Nazis. And the neighbors did not betray them — an unheard-of story in Ukraine.

By the sixth grade, I no longer felt like an outsider at school. I played in the band and the symphony orchestra. I loved my flute. I took pleasure in learning new musical pieces and orchestra parts. I performed in concerts, though I was still shy when playing a solo.

At that time I was obsessed with composing. Melodies and whole compositions sounded in my head and sometimes even in my dreams, sometimes in orchestra arrangement. I started writing them down. At first I was doing it for flute; then for orchestra. Imitating Shostakovich, I put sax players in the symphony orchestra.

Valentin Feygin was the only person I shared my notes with. He didn't laugh, and patiently tried to make sense of what he called my "cacophony." He even praised a few things.

At a certain moment I decided I was going to be a composer. It turned out Valentin was thinking of that, too. One day he played some of his piano compositions to me. I could tell the difference; my spirits sagged. It occurred to me that the musical mastery that I was sweating so hard to acquire was something auxiliary — but I didn't seem to have the main thing.

Our last meeting took place in 1965 when I lived in Novosibirsk. I learned of his arrival from a huge poster: "Concert with Valentin Feygin, WINNER of the international competition in PARIS."

We had not seen each other for fifteen years. I knew he had graduated from conservatory and toured the country and abroad. From Tchaikovsky Conservatory posters I knew he had taken graduate classes from Mstislav Rostropovich (while I was attending the Architecture School).

The huge auditorium of Novosibirsk Opera Theater was jammed. Valentin was in top form. At the end of the first half he was performing a Bach fugue. Suddenly someone in the stalls section, not too far from me, snored loudly in a strange way. Then the snoring turned into wheezing and groaning. Valentin stopped playing.

I ran up to look. The elderly man who had been making these sounds was a well-known architect named Bobrov, recently retired, who had not missed a single symphony concert since '45.

Over his white shirt and colored tie his face took on a brown color. A doctor who happened to be sitting nearby unbuttoned his shirt and said tersely, "Heart attack." He died fifteen minutes later.

Ambulance medics covered him with a sheet and carried him outside. The orchestra struck up "Requiem."

I headed backstage. The musicians, agitated, argued whether the show should go on. I voiced my doubts. Valentin, looking as usual into space, dropped, "What a stroke of luck to die to music like that."

In the late '90s, I wanted to find Valentin. The online phone directories showed no entry for Valentin Feygin in Moscow. Could he have moved to Israel? I turned to Google: Professor of Moscow Conservatory Valentin Feygin (1934–1995).

Young Pioneer

A few weeks after I was enrolled in musical school, a boy from the seventh grade came up to me at the long recess. "You have a Young Pioneer assignment. Stop by the eighth-grade room after classes."

I was proud to be treated like a Young Pioneer and to be trusted with an important assignment (presumably, there was no other kind). Earlier, I read *Timur and His Team*, a classic Young Pioneer book. And now I would be like them.

I did not know that joining the Young Pioneers was not exactly a snap. You joined at a special solemn meeting of the YP organization. In the old school I would have joined in the fourth grade; but here all my classmates must have joined in the third.

In the eighth-grade classroom I saw a huge roll of paper on the floor with the words in capital letters: "Long Live the 28th Anniversary of the Great October Socialist Revolution!" An eighth-grader was kneeling next to the paper. From time to time he picked up a box with watercolors and spat in the red-paint section; then he stirred it with a hard brush and colored the letters. He was almost done: only "...alist Revolution" remained uncolored.

"Are you Berkovich?" He shook my hand. "You came — that's great. Get down to work. We've got to hang it up tomorrow. I'm off."

I had never done anything like this before. I wanted to ask him something, but he was already gone.

It took me a few hours to color the remaining word and a half. I ran out of saliva, and almost ran out of red paint, too.

Soon thereafter the same seventh-grader came up to me at the long recess and thanked me on the behalf of the Komsomòl (Party Youth) organization. He told me I clearly had artistic leanings. I knew how to handle watercolors. Hence my next assignment would be putting out the wall newspaper.

"Wall newspaper" was something no Soviet institution, from a police precinct to an alcohol rehab center, was complete without. It was only remotely related to a newspaper (newspaper offices had to put out their own wall newspapers, too) and its usefulness was dubious. The only comparable item in America is a "newspaper" you put up on the wall in the hall at a middle or high school. It is clearly designated as having an educational purpose. It can be argued that its Soviet analog had the same purpose, and the Party treated the entire population as a bunch of schoolchildren.

A regular newspaper is a fantastic human invention. It is universal. You could use it to wrap your textbooks and notebooks. Or you could use it to protect yourself from rain — or from a sunstroke. You could wrap herring in it, too, on those once-in-a-blue moon occasions when it was on sale. You could fold it into disposable vodka glasses for vodka to be consumed surreptitiously during the May Day or Revolution Day parade. Or if you fold a double page into a triangle, it could become a funnel — a universal container for hard bagels or salty fish or any old working-class chaser for vodka. A newspaper page could be torn into neat little portions that could be used as rolling paper. Or you could crumple them and use them as toilet paper. Truly, a newspaper has infinite uses.

By contrast, the Soviet invention called "wall newspaper" was good for nothing. Its hidden essence is mysterious and unfathomable.

Generally, it was a full-size sheet of thick white drawing paper that was filled with text and pictures and tacked to the wall. The header was on top or on the side in properly large letters — just like the real thing. The longer the header, the better; but even more importantly, the letters had to look good, and the name had to be ideologically sound.

Our fourth-grade wall newspaper had a rather primitive title, which was upsetting — the banal "Fourth-Grader." Others came up with somewhat more imaginative titles: "Lenin's Dawn," "Young Leninist," "Musical Leninist," "Leninist Musician," and even "To Communism with Music" in one of the senior grades.

I stayed the wall newspaper editor for the next four years. The duties took up a lot of time. But I didn't complain, since it was considered an important YP assignment, and I worked my butt off.

I ruled the entire sheet into five columns. Every issue had an editorial written by a teacher, and a humor section, which consisted of copying jokes and cartoons from *Krokodil* and *Peretz* satirical magazines. The rest of the content, which I had to copy by hand, came from my classmates. These were called "articles" and had to be begged from them for weeks. Like true pros, the authors delivered in the eleventh hour, forcing me to burn the midnight oil. Come to think of it, this timing was perhaps the sole aspect where our product earned the name "newspaper."

I did the layout on the dinner table at home. I made a special cover from a newspaper and attached it to the lampshade so as to keep the light away from everyone sleeping in that room: my parents, sister Yanna and cousin Maya, who was living with us. Sometimes I stayed up all night. Lateness was not an option. The production of wall newspapers was watched closely and delays were punished. Conversely, the winners of the best newspaper contest were showered with praise.

The papers were mostly timed to national holidays: the Revolution Day, the New Year, Lenin's death anniversary, the Red Army Day, International Women's Day, and May Day.

Besides individual class papers, there was also a school wall newspaper, where I also participated. I also painted banners for Revolution Day and May Day. But it never occurred to me to use a water jar instead of saliva, and no one would tell me. Later, when I painted on cloth stretched on a frame, I used toothpowder mixed with water instead of white paint.

Eventually I became the school painter, known as Bera the Gloomy Painter. *Bera* stood for "Berkovich," but *gloomy* in school slang meant "slightly touched in the head," which was a standard name for all flutists. The *painter* part forced me to live up to the nickname. I copied pictures from textbooks; then started drawing from reality. My first drawing showed Ionic columns from the district Best Workers board. Odd choice, perhaps — but I just liked them.

At first the older boys would let me do the most primitive things. Later, when I trained my hand, I started copying famous cartoonists from Pravda. Once, I really got too big for my britches and painted Lenin. My Komsomòl bosses panicked and told me to take it out: "Don't you understand we'll get punished for this? You have to be a professional painter to be allowed to do Lenin."

For years, I would be asking myself the same question: "When exactly does one become an artist? Is it the day you get your graduation degree from an art school?"

Besides the wall newspaper and banners, I had to do other social work. I visited sick teachers and classmates, I tutored students who lagged behind, I went to collect scrap metal and paper, and I helped at the voting precinct. As a child, I turned out to be the epitome of responsibility. Whatever activity the *Young Pioneer Pravda* encouraged, I charged ahead. I was noticed, and given more assignments. I took pleasure in doing them.

Amazingly, my touching loyalty to the Party cause did not make me less of a troublemaker. From time to time my mother was called to school and once she even had to plead to save me from expulsion. I called our solfège teacher, my school friend Sergei's mother, Ms. Klebanova, a whore in front of the class. She left her husband — composer Dmitry Klebanov, who was being pilloried by the critics for his Holocaust-themed symphony *Baby Yar* — for another composer, Yuli Meitus, who just had composed the properly ideological opera *Young Guards,* and was awarded Stalin Prize for it. Fortunately, I merely called her a "whore" with no hidden political motive. My childish maximalism was a lesser sin.

At the end of the seventh grade I was approached by the same student who got me into social work three years earlier. Now Garik Gelfand was in the tenth grade, the secretary of the local Komsomòl unit, and a pianist known all over the country before long. He suggested that I apply for Komsomòl membership. "The minimal age is fourteen, but I believe they'll make an exception for you at the district committee. Come on, fill in the application."

Misha

In the spring of 1950, Aunt Bronyà's older son Misha showed up in Kharkov. He came by for a short while to say goodbye to his mother, while waiting for an exit visa.

Misha was born out of wedlock in 1917 in the Ukrainian city of Uman. The next year Brònya married Josif Zamel, a Polish-Jewish butcher who adopted Misha and took them to Pyatrakov in Poland, where Brònya gave birth to seven more children, while competing — with some success — in local beauty contests.

Misha was his stepfather's favorite son, with every whim catered to. One of these almost ended in tragedy. Misha told me that in 1937 he and a friend tried to smuggle his girlfriend's Jewish relatives out of Germany. They successfully crossed the German border, but were caught in the very first village. The friend escaped back to Poland, and Misha found himself in Dachau. He had his share of suffering until his stepfather found the right contacts in Warsaw and bought him out — in January 1938, a year and a half before the Germans invaded Poland.

In 1940, Aunt Brònya's family fled the Nazis occupying Poland and settled in Uman. Misha got married. A year later, it was time to flee the Germans again. With a great deal of difficulty he managed to bring his pregnant wife Dora to the town of Fergana, in Uzbekistan. In 1942 he enrolled in the Jewish brigade of the Polish Army, led by General Anders. Soon, following the orders of the Polish government in exile in London, Anders led his army through Iran to the Middle East to fight "under the Queen's colors." And this is how 25-year-old Misha found himself in Palestine.

When Misha found out that they were being redeployed in Africa to fight Rommel, he changed his mind and joined the Jewish underground, where he fought side by side with the future Israeli prime minister, Menachem Begin, against British occupation. Soon, he got tired of that, too, and he returned to the British army. He landed with the Allies in Sicily, marched north, and settled in Holland.

He met a woman and was about to marry her. But then he had the brilliant idea to go to the USSR and see his mother — and while he was at it, find his wife and son and bring them to the West. I noted that Aunt Brònya's family was never short on ideas.

The Soviet consulate in Holland assured him that everything was legit and he would have no problems in the USSR. He was promised help and even provided with the address of his family, who by then had returned to Uman.

I remembered his visit well. He told us about his life in the West, his fighting ("drove his jeep through all of Italy"), and his Dutch fiancée. He even showed me, a fifteen-year-old, her picture. Lowering his voice, he intimated that he had been a Young Zionist in Poland ("just like Young Pioneers here").

Misha spent two months in Uman, waiting for an exit visa for his family. Instead, one night plainclothesmen knocked on his door and gave him one hour to pack up. Then they put him into a cattle car and took him to Turukhànsk, deep in the heart of Siberia — coincidentally, where Stalin had been sent in exile, too. Turukhànsk's second claim to fame was "the pole of cold," the coldest place in the Siberia. Without trial or investigation, Misha was sent there for "eternal settlement."

At thirty-three, Misha now trained as a house painter. Like the rest of the exiles, he had to register with local police regularly. Yet after Hitler's Dachau, the Jewish underground in Palestine, and the British Army, Misha remained an optimist. He claimed that every time he came to see the police, he tried to convince them that the words "eternal settlement" were nonsensical, since nothing is eternal in the world. It took the police agent three years to see Misha's point — when Stalin died. In the summer of '53, Misha went to the police office for the last time, this time to learn he was free and could settle anywhere he wanted. He chose Moscow.

Misha tried to settle in Moscow and even found a job. Yet soon, due to a treaty between Khrushchev and Gomulka — then Poland's ruler — he got a legal chance to move to Poland, and that's what he did.

Misha didn't stay in Poland for long, and soon moved to Brazil. Two years later he came back with his family (now with two sons). "It's not good in Brazil — they don't have cherries." He missed cherries.

Yet he didn't have the chance to settle in his homeland. Jewish luck, it was then that Gomulka decided to purge Poland of Jews. In the early '60s, Misha and his family and a couple of other Polish Jews found themselves in Malmö in Sweden.

As a skilled housepainter, Misha got a good job at the shipyards. But then suddenly his wife Dora died.

Already fifty, Misha mourned for some time and then married an Army widow with the similar name Dorit. A few years later she died of cancer, too. In the early '70s, Misha left his sons in Sweden and went to Brazil, where he married the widow of his brother Yuzik, by the name of Dorinia.

But Misha and Dorinia didn't get along. Two or three years later he divorced her and moved to Canada, where, showing an incredible consistency in choosing women — or, rather, women with certain names — he became engaged to a woman named Dorina, the widow of a wealthy contractor.

Dorina and Misha visited us in Des Plaines outside Chicago in 1981. Then in '86 we met in Florida, where they wintered in Dorina's condo. Misha complained that he was still young (at sixty-nine) and wanted to go out dancing and have fun, while Dorina, just over fifty, preferred to stay in front of

the TV and "was not very interested in sex." She also had diabetes and needed regular insulin shots. A couple of years later he divorced her, and a few years after that she died.

Misha stayed a bachelor. He had a girlfriend — naturally, a widow named Dorinet — twenty-five or thirty years younger. They met two or three times a week and went to Majorca together. Misha became fond of Majorca in his Swedish days and went there every year. He was known there and greeted in every hotel. At eighty, he did not complain of poor health.

Suddenly, a year later, he abruptly started losing his memory. At eighty-two he went to visit Israel for the last time, and then he went to Sweden, where his sons placed him in a nursing home. He died in 2006 at the age of 89.

In retirement, Misha was well provided for. He got a pension in Sweden based on his employment record; in England, as a war veteran; in Israel, ditto (this time, a war on the British);

The author's cousin Mikhail Zamel in exile. Turukhansk, Siberia, 1950.

in Germany, as a victim of Nazism; and finally in Canada, on the basis of his age.

Misha spoke his two native languages, Polish and Yiddish, plus German, Russian, Ukrainian, Hebrew, English, Dutch, Swedish, Portuguese, and, from his Siberian exile, the Russian cursing language.

At sixty-eight, he wrote a memoir in Polish under the English title, *History of My Life*. I saw the manuscript with a number of unique pictures and asked him for a copy. Unexpectedly, a year before he left for Sweden, I got it in the mail. To read it, I had to study Polish.

Rabinovich

One night I found a strange guest in our place — an old, bearded, short Jew wearing glasses. He was discussing something very serious with my stepfather.

The guest was from out of town and seemed preoccupied with something very grave. The next day my stepfather told me that he was a distant relative of ours named Rabinovich.

I couldn't help letting out a laugh. Rabinovich was the name of a character used in all the Jewish jokes. It was nothing that I was considered an anti–Semite in our family.

According to my stepfather, our Rabinovich was in trouble, caused by his brother's emigration to America, never mind that it had happened forty or fifty years ago.

It occurred to me that since Rabinovich was a relative, that made his brother one, too. Which in turn meant that we could be in trouble as well.

"We could," my stepfather confirmed. "And that's not the only reason. A few of my brothers and sisters left for America, too. By the way, Rabinovich brought me a letter from my sister Tuba, who lives in New York."

I was taken aback. That's all I needed — a Soviet Young Pioneer like me having capitalist relatives!

"So how are we related to your Rabinovich?" I asked.

"My nephew Izzy married his niece," he said, and gave me a meaningful look. "Idiots," he added. I understood whom he was referring to. "Rabinovich's brother died over thirty years ago. We have a street in Kharkov named after him. And now Rabinovich is in trouble."

I had a hard time imagining a Rabinovich Street in a Soviet city like Kharkov.

"There isn't," my stepfather said. "It's called Sholom Aleichem Street — that's the name he used. And Izzy is a writer, too. But you have to keep quiet. Or else they'll start working on us as well. God willing, he'll get out of it," he said, referring to our guest.

Soon Sholom Aleichem Street was renamed to Lavrènty Beria Street, then, quite simply, to Rỳbnaya, or Fish Street and later — to Kooperatìvnaya. Then the place where we lived, the Tevèlev Square, was renamed, too. Although Comrade Tevelev was a decorated Bolshevik and a Civil War hero, his Jewish name no longer looked good on a street sign.

My stepfather kept from me that Yitzhak Dov Berkovich, a Jewish writer and his nephew — and Sholom Aleichem's son-in-law — was living in Tel Aviv. Many years later I would learn that he is treasured in Israel as one of the founders of modern Hebrew literature, and Tel Aviv has a Berkovich Street named after him. I suspect this was the kind of notoriety he was afraid of even more. The late 1940s was not very good time to be a Jew in the Soviet Union.

4

Trade School

The House Painter

In 1949, at fourteen, I entered Kharkov Construction Trade School.

Just like my previous school vacations, I spent the entire summer of 1951 working as a housepainter. I was already sixteen. At first I undertook to paint the library at the trade school I attended — for free, since I was a friend of the librarian named Felicia. After that a classmate named Tòlik Mìtin arranged for me to join a housepainter crew where he had been working since early summer.

They were fixing the dormitory of the Party school affiliated with the regional Party Committee. The foreman, Vassily, did not really care whether I had experience. "You'll be getting four hundred rubles a week."

This was a fabulous sum, more than twice my father's formal salary, not counting his moonlighting. Generally I brought in three hundred rubles a month, my school scholarship, and it was considered big money. Now I would be getting four hundred a week! My mother did not believe me. She thought I was a trusting fool. We agreed that I must have misheard, and the pay was four hundred a *month*. But I never asked Vassily again.

My main duty was to make the paint — dissolve the painting powder in a bucket of water — and then carry the bucket up the stairs to the seventh floor. When I had time left, I was trusted with a brush and painting proper. I had already developed some skill, and my work met approval.

Two weeks later the whole crew took a streetcar to the outskirts to get paid. En route I was warned: whatever the amount I receive, don't be surprised. "Just sign your name and get going."

I was upset. My mother must have been right. I was about to get ripped off and receive much less than what I had been promised. Yet the paymaster actually paid me twice as much — sixteen hundred rubles. I had never seen this kind of money in my life! Yet, forewarned, I remained calm.

The Kharkov Construction Trade School building. Kharkov, Ukraine, 1953.

Then the entire crew walked to the park, where the foreman was waiting on the bench. Like everybody else, I surrendered my pay. Then he looked me up in his little pocketbook and paid me off— eight hundred, as promised. "That's it for now," he said. "No more work. When I need you, I'll find you."

After Vassily paid everybody off, he stuck the bills in his pockets and took us to a booze joint nearby — to treat us to "a few glasses."

I had never had a good stomach for booze, even as an adult. That night I had to be brought home and handed over to my mother. Yet I was happy, and in the morning I solemnly handed her my pay. For some reason, she was less than overjoyed.

Sasha Frishman, my closest friend, treated my stories of fabulous pay with a grain of salt. Yet he could not argue the facts and asked me to bring him along the next time.

A few days later I found some of my crewmates, who by then had already formed a crew of their own and had found a job painting the dormitory of the local police authority. They were willing to take me aboard, and Sasha, too.

The police dorm was in the former synagogue on Kotlòv Street. Sasha and I were entrusted with painting the huge vaulted hall, which had two-tier metal cots, always taken by sleeping off-duty policemen.

We started with the ceiling. For that we had to move some of the cots aside from time to time and put up a jury-rigged scaffolding, about twenty feet tall. We put a couple of long boards on top, somehow climbed up, and, balancing on these boards like acrobats, painted the ceiling. It was scary, but we tried not to look down.

On the second day, just before we were to leave, my new foreman Peter told me he had to split right away. He handed me a large bag and asked that I take it when I left. To my surprise, later on he was waiting around the corner to pick it up.

Next day, the same errand; except this time he asked me to bring the bag to Blagoveshchensk Market. Now Sasha was getting similar errands, too. We figured out that we were being used as mules to smuggle out the paint that belonged to the police authority.

"I don't think my father would like this," Sasha said. He feared his father. Well, my parents wouldn't approve as well.

We didn't like it either. But we dared not say no.

Peter was a Communist and often proudly displayed the member card he always carried in his breast pocket. He was also fond of telling us how he had joined the Party in the lull in the fighting during the war.

According to the Communist ideals proclaimed on every corner, a Communist could not be a crook. Yet our foreman and his buddies most certainly were.

I have to admit that we were not treated unfairly and were soon considered full-fledged partners in crime. The proceeds from the stolen paint were spent on daily boozing after work — and we were expected to participate.

At that time, mother's older sister was visiting. My mother was very proud of me and invited Aunt Shura over to see what a nice boy I had turned into.

It was my bad luck that that was a night when our crew was "celebrating." Once again, I was carried home, dying of alcohol intoxication. Frightened, my mother called an ambulance. Paramedics forced a three-gallon bucket of potassium permanganate in my mouth — at the time, a standard way of cleaning the stomach. I vomited. Aunt Shura arrived in the middle of this show — paramedics and all.

Mom's proverbial Jewish luck truly held that night. Soon after Aunt Shura's arrival, we were joined by my friend Sasha. His face was something from a horror movie, covered with razor cuts and bleeding all over.

Unlike me, he had made it home on his own. But then he thought he would go to the Shevchenko Park to have fun and decided to shave himself. Like me and everybody else, he was using a straight razor, unsafe even when sober. Now he came over, the results of shaving on his face, to invite me to join him on his outing.

"Looking like this, you'd fit right in," my mother said. Then she gave Aunt Shura a sad look and broke into tears.

House painting had always been part of general repairs. We had to plaster and adjust moldings, which at the time were very popular. Besides, since our crew was also fixing the Builders Club, we had to do some decoration work, which was considered a superior skill. We cut out and made stencils for decorative painting. It was simple: you drew on the cardboard and then pierced the contour with a nail. Then you pounced on the drawing with a special soft pad doused in dry paint. Then the contour was traced with a brush. We liked this routine.

A month went by, then another. Little by little we were getting used to theft and boozing. We enjoyed the work, but we were not getting paid. We made hints, but Peter deftly changed the subject.

Then something happened.

We were working again at the police dormitory at the former synagogue. Once, as Sasha stood under the vault of the central nave, he became so caught up in his work that he did not notice he moved to the cantilevered edge of the board atop the scaffolding. At first the board yielded and then it bounced him in the air, the brush in the one hand and the paint bucket in the other. He flew twenty feet and dropped sideways on the floor. I was downstairs, too. The whole thing took not more than two seconds.

The noise was far from deafening, yet it was enough to awaken some of the policemen who were asleep and now erupted in curses. I broke out in a cold sweat.

Unexpectedly, Sasha got to his feet very calmly and unhurriedly. He shook the paint off; then, without looking at anyone, picked up the bucket, and climbed back on top. I was still in a state of shock when, a few minutes later, he came back down, pale, with his knees buckling. "That's it," he said. "I'm not working here anymore."

And we left, unpaid.

Field Work

In the summer of '52 along with some of my classmates from our Trade School, I was sent for field work training at YuzhSpetzStròy (YSS), a firm that specialized in construction finishing work. The YSS HQ was in Rostov-Don, but upon arrival we learned they were not doing any work in Rostov, and we were sent around various departments in different towns.

My friend Sasha Frishman and I found ourselves in a suburb of a place called Novocherkassk, a mere twenty-five miles away from Rostov. Sasha's girlfriend Zhènya got the best assignment and was sent to Sochi — the Soviet

The Rostov-Don Theater. Still in ruins. Rostov-Don, Russia, 1952.

number one Black Sea resort. Sochi was rumored to have a few more vacant spots any day, and, hoping to get them, we hitchhiked to Rostov's office every Saturday. We stayed overnight at the office. We bunked on the floor, wrapping ourselves in floor rugs, since the nights were cool — and spent Sundays in the city.

Rostov was still recovering from the war damage. The downtown was one big ruin of a burnt-down government complex on Engels Street. We heard that the architect had been executed early in the war for "sabotage." Allegedly, he had built the complex in the form of a swastika, so that the Germans could easily recognize it and bombard it from above. The ruins of a theater designed by Soviet architects Tschukò and Gelfrèich were especially magnificent. Sasha and I spent hours inside, running around concrete structures and, when we splurged on a camera, shooting a whole roll of film.

I'll never forget the long walks we took under the lindens of Kirov Boulevard. And on the whole, I fell in love with Rostov. Somehow it reminded me of Kiev. I still believe the two were the most beautiful cities in the European part of the Soviet Union.

After a Sunday in Rostov, we would thumb a ride to Novocherkassk with a passing truck. The latter was a small, verdant town, the capital of Don's

Cossacks, with a large Russian Orthodox cathedral and a monument to Yermàk, a Cossack chieftain who conquered Siberia.

The local YSS department operated in a nearby settlement named Molotov, four or five miles away. It grew next to the construction site of a huge chemical factory, whose first stage of operation had already started. It had been disassembled in Germany seven years earlier and transported to Russia in an unexplainable hurry, as if it was loot. At the time the future factory site had not been picked yet. Therefore, immediately after crossing the border back to the USSR, metal elements of buildings and equipment were dropped off the train platforms and left there to rust until the construction started. The Soviets took an immeasurable number of factories like this out of Germany, and the area at the border sprouted huge cemeteries of steel carcasses.

While we were in Molotov, they were delivering materials for the second stage of construction — deformed, rusted, and ultimately unusable. Right from the station it was taken to a scrapyard in nearby Budyonny for melting down. Even the few usable pieces often became trophies for quick-thinking Russians who took them from the construction site to the metal scrapyard. One truckload was good for three or four vodka bottles.

The Molotov settlement where we were assigned cots in the dormitory had a population of about twenty thousand — mostly ex-convicts who for a few years were not allowed to settle within thirty miles of large cities. Vodka was the food item of choice, and it was a rare week without a drunken fight including a murder.

Two middle-class seventeen year olds like us were very uncomfortable among this populace. We tried hard not to stand out. We learned to curse. We gave up washing and shaving. We never turned down a glass of vodka, however sick we felt. And yet the locals had no trouble spotting us.

The bath house in the settlement was open two days a week — one day for men and one for women. It consisted of two rooms, each with cold and hot water taps and concrete benches. The rooms were connected by a wicket-gate made of decrepit wood boards.

Once Sasha and I came on a so-called unisex day, and the gate was closed. There were few people — just us and another guy lying on the bench face down.

Suddenly someone called from the women's half: "Hey, Ivan, you need to get your back scratched?"

The gate swung open, and two maids showed up wearing nothing but their tattoos. Sasha and I were taken aback as the guests set about rubbing and massaging their friend, laughing and cracking dirty jokes. They paid no attention to us, covering ourselves with our washbowls in the corner. At a certain point we heard, "Whoa, girls — not with the boys around." And the trio retired to the other half.

Our YSS department specialized in tin metal work, glazing, roofing, flooring and painting. When we showed up, our bosses had no idea what to do with us. We were appointed foremen assistants and dispatched to count parquet floor pieces piled up in a huge warehouse. We were told to sort them out by size and put them in neat stacks. Our first impression was that this assignment could last us through the rest of our field work. Perhaps that was our bosses' hope, too.

Yet we so despaired of the prospect of spending all this time in a dusty, hot, windowless warehouse that we decided to put in twelve- to fourteen-hour shifts instead of eight-hour ones. We left the warehouse only for a quick run to the canteen on lunch break — and then back to work. A week later we presented the results.

After that we were assigned to work with roofers who were just beginning to lay "flat roofing." First they glued two layers of tar paper, and topped them with roof felt attached with special mastic. The mastic came by horse-driven cart in the form of thirty-kilo bricks that were then dropped in a large metal vat heated by a bonfire. The boiling mastic was extracted from the vat and passed to the roof; then the workers used sticks wrapped with rags to spread the mastic before putting the rolls of cover on top.

The slanted roof started at a height of about sixty feet. Mastic was delivered by means of a primitive rope with two wheels, one on top and one on bottom. The lower one was brought into motion by an electric engine and made the rest of the system work. The buckets with hot mastic were supposed to be suspended from the ropes — except there weren't any available.

The bosses wondered how much we knew about tin metal work. We decided that, since we were almost fourth-year students, we could not admit we knew absolutely nothing. And thus we were assigned to bucket production ASAP.

We were issued tools and tin metal at the warehouse. We made the workbench ourselves. Our first buckets were positively unusable; they spilled even sand. By the time Sasha and I finally produced a bucket that could hold liquid we had wasted all the material. The leftover was good for three buckets — and the mastic lifeline was working!

Once Sasha stayed by the vat to keep the fire going, while I took the cart to get the next shipment of mastic bricks. As a city boy, I never rode a horse. I saw one from the distance and in the movies and could not guess it required special skills. With my luck, on the way back I did not notice an electric cable on the ground, brought down by a crane that had passed earlier. The poor horse stepped on the cable and was electrocuted instantly. I ran to the office, anticipating a reprimand and punishment. Yet for some reason the news was met with open joy. The horse was taken away. The carcass was instantly cut and cooked, and the hide was sold, actually traded, for vodka. All the work stopped. There was a feast, and everyone got formidably drunk.

Sasha and I stayed away and retired to the dorm.

We had another roommate. Although a former inmate, Yerofèy did not drink vodka every night like the others and instead took notes in a thick notebook. It turned out he was writing a novel about buoy keepers.

His family had been buoy keepers on the Yenisèy River in Siberia for generations, and he was planning to do the same. Unfortunately for him, the times were hard. At seventeen, he went to the collective farm field to dig up from under the snow some tiny, rotten and frozen potatoes. He was arrested and got five years for theft.

He let me read his manuscript, and I liked it a lot. I was put off by the curse words in the dialogue, but he assured me that buoy keepers talked exactly like that.

He had a girlfriend in the women's dorm named Galya (for some reason, most girls in the settlement were named Galya). She would visit in our absence, or sometimes we would pointedly step out for a couple of hours. One day they told us they were moving into his friend's room. He had a vacant cot and they had to hurry before the director moved in someone else. The friend also had a steady girlfriend.

They planned to live in this tiny room as a foursome, on three cots, periodically swapping partners—"in order not to go crazy from boredom," the future writer explained. He offered to introduce us to "nice girls," too.

The plan failed after less than two weeks. On a payday, the settlement was in its usual state of mass inebriation, and his friend was knifed to death. No one else had been moved into our room yet, and so he returned.

The work went on. Once, a bucket with hot mastic dropped off the rope. Luckily, there was no one below. But the bosses were concerned, and we were instructed to improve work safety. The dangerous area was to be fenced. Since part of the rope passed over a road, we were to make warning signs and place them there.

We made up texts like "Don't be a Dope/Don't Stand under the Rope" and wrote them in block letters on plywood sheets. The bosses loved them, and we were promoted—to the roof, to spread hot mastic and glue felt and tar paper.

Then there was a setback in glazier work. All three glaziers went on a binge. The month was at its end, and we had to put at least some glass somewhere in order to meet the monthly quota, especially since we were expecting an inspection from Moscow, and one of the inspectors was rumored to be a teetotaler—a recipe for disaster in Russia.

The building was lighted with a "shed roof"—a special skylight construction on the roof. Naturally, we broke a lot of glass, but not all of it. We managed to install some glass before the inspection. After that, we were taken off the roof and dispatched to painting work.

The painters were relatively young female ex-convicts. Some of them were even allowed to leave and settle in the city, but for unknown reasons chose to stay. Perhaps they liked the familiar environment or simply had no other place to go. As a foreman assistant, I didn't have to do any painting myself, but merely had to "help and organize." But I knew painting, and enjoyed doing it myself.

The girls were quick to notice me blushing at their racy language. That prompted them to use it even more and get a kick out of watching me turning beet-red. It was not that I was unfamiliar with this lexicon in Kharkov, but there was something particularly off-putting in hearing it from young women.

One day after lunch and a few drinks, my co-workers embarked upon the memories of their camp life. In particular, with many colorful details, interrupting one another, they recalled the times when they raped men — one of them to death. Warmed up with vodka and pleasant memories, one of the girls nodded at me —"why not the boy here?"

At first I thought they were joking. But in an instant they were all over me, locking the door and undressing me and wrestling me down on the floor. I fought back and yelled, which seemed to inflame them even further.

Someone overheard us and banged on the door.

At the meeting the next morning the painter foreman Galya whispered to me: "Don't you snitch on us."

Indeed, a complaint was fraught with a visit to the parole officer and possibly going back to jail.

"They were just kidding," she added. And then, as we walked to the site, she said, "What were you afraid of? Five broads — big deal!"

I still don't know whether they were joking.

In a final report of our work at YSS we had to submit — as everywhere in the Soviet Union — the number of inventions we generated and implemented. In my work with painters I came up with one invention only: by tying three brushes together, I could cover a greater area with one stroke. My co-workers were not happy about it. A bunch of brushes with paint on them turned out to be too heavy. Yet the management got bonuses for implementing inventions. And my crew was miserable.

But in the aftermath of the rape episode, I found it hard to feel sorry for them.

Izzy Fridenthal

In the fall of 1949 the country celebrated the writer Nikolay Gogol's 140th anniversary, but another date was approaching, even more epochal: the

**The author (left) with his friend Sasha Frishman working on the Nikolay Gogol'
140th anniversary poster. Kharkov, Ukraine, 1949.**

70th birthday of "our leader and teacher, the leader of all progressive mankind,
Generalissimo Stalin."

Kharkov Construction Trade School was working on a deluxe illustrated
edition of articles by teachers and the best students, dedicated to Comrade
Stalin's life and achievements. Our year was represented by Sasha Frishman,
Nikolay Deynichenko, and me. The design was assigned to Izzy Fridenthal
from an older year, along with his best pal, Vadim Bogdànov, called
"Bogdànchik" for his diminutive stature.

Izzy outlined the general plan of illustrations and distributed them among
us (I was assigned a picture of Stalin at fifteen). He took the toughest part
upon himself, and everything worked out fine. Our work won a prize at the
student competition of Stalin's anniversary works.

Naturally, we all became friends, and remained friends through the rest
of our studies.

A year later, Izzy and Vadim went to a mountain-climbing camp in the
Caucasus and upon their return organized a mountaineering club at school,
which Sasha and I joined. Izzy organized climbing training. In the absence
of mountains locally, we used the ruins of the burned-down crematorium.
He also got us into swimming, since mountaineers are supposed to have well-

developed lungs. We went day-hiking in a park at Pomèrki, outside Kharkov. And wherever Izzy went, his "Bogdanchik" followed.

Nationwide, there was a great shortage of construction engineers. In 1952, Kharkov Engineering College opened an accelerated two-year program to admit people with work experience or a trade-school certificate. And trade-school graduates cum laude did not need to spend three years working or to take exams. This

The author as a student at the Construction Trade School. Kharkov, Ukraine, 1950.

meant getting a college degree in two years (instead of four) and being exempted from the draft at the same time. Most importantly, (especially atypically for the Ukraine) there were no Jewish quotas.

Both Izzy and Vadim graduated cum laude and enrolled in the program. Izzy spent a lot of time trying to persuade Sasha Frishman and me "not to behave foolishly and use a chance to beat the draft."

Sasha did not have a chance of graduating cum laude and thus was looking at the draft upon graduation. I was hoping to make the top 5 percent of A-students who were given special status that entitled them to enter college without having to work for three years. I was dreaming of Moscow School of Architecture; but the two-year program in Kharkov Engineering College looked like a decent fallback position. Having a college degree at twenty was a tempting idea.

As Sasha and I discussed our future, we doubted whether it made sense to become an engineer at such an early age before acquiring life experience. Then again, engineering school provided you with construction-designer skills — and what about architecture? This was something we would have to learn on our own. And in any event you would be treated as, a second-sort — an architect without an architectural diploma. On top of that, was dodging the draft doing the right thing? Real men didn't do that. And most importantly, it would provide fodder for anti–Semites who would always remind you that Jews used college to beat the draft.

It is painful to remember these arguments now. But at the time they appeared well-founded, especially the one about reproaches.

Izzy heard us out and shook his head. I suspect he no longer respected us.

Six months later I ran into him — and Vadim was no longer at his side.

At the Kharkov City sign during the mountaineering club's running exercise. From left are an unidentified person, Vadim Bogdànov, the author and Izzy Fridenthal. Kharkov, Ukraine 1952.

It turned out that their friendship was over, and Izzy would not even hear about Vadim.

A month earlier the local paper ran another article about Zionist intrigues in the city. Articles like this came out at the rate of several a day. Those were the days of the famous "Doctors' Case," of the "murderers in white robes" who aimed to "poison the international proletariat's leaders." This time the newspaper exposed the Zionist intrigues in the area of services. Izzy's father, a hairdresser, was cited as one evildoer who was "abusing public trust." He was caught taking tips, thus "bringing shame to the entire hairdressing profession." Moreover, he was foisting "Zionist haircuts," whatever those were, on unsuspecting clients. Do these "internal political émigrés" belong in the Socialist society, the article's author wondered.

Izzy's best friend Bogdanchik brought this publication to school. He read it aloud in front of sympathetic students and then insisted that Izzy, as a

One of the presentation boards of the author's diploma thesis at the Kharkov Construction Trade School: Mountanview Tourist Center. Kharkov, Ukraine, 1953.

Komsomòl (Communist Youth) member, publicly denounce his "Zionist" father. Izzy barely avoided expulsion from school. And he broke up with the newfangled anti–Semite who then enrolled in a military academy and became an Army officer.

Izzy stayed in architecture and proved that the degree was not the most important thing. In fact, a design of his even became the subject of a Soviet postage stamp. He worked at many design offices and then became city architect at the town of Kislovodsk in the Caucasus, where we met again twenty years later.

Climbing

In the fall of 1951, I became devoted to mountain climbing and did it seriously for three years. In the summer of 1952, my friend Sasha Frishman and I went to a climbing camp. The place was run Army-style. Our instructors emphasized they were training future mountain troops. Many of them had spent the war in the Caucasus and liked talking about how the skills acquired during climbing before the war saved their lives.

I had the good fortune to meet some of the Soviet climbing legends still alive then, such as Abalàkov, Pogrebètzky, Malèinov and others, and hear their stories by the fire.

Sasha Frishman saved one of the letters I wrote him at the camp while he was already in the Army. It conveys well the atmosphere of the mountain scene in those years.

09/19/54. Ìskra Climbing Camp

I'm leaving tomorrow, two days early. During this stay I did [climbed] a 2-B, a 2-A, and a 1-B, unassisted [as a group leader], plus a 1-B pass. [Difficulty is measured from 1-A, the easiest, to 5-B, the hardest.] As you see, I didn't manage to do a 3.

With the camp management we had, thanks at least for that. Getting on a climb is a big deal here. First they don't let you, then it is bad weather, then you register the route and re-do it a few times. Then the doctor went off to Pyatigòrsk and there's no one to confirm your fitness. Finally, you got all the signatures, but by then it started to rain.

People say thank God if they get to do one or two peaks in a shift.

I already qualified for Third Athletic Degree and already have two B-2s to qualify for the second one. I really wanted to do 3 (A or B) this year. Although I didn't, I'm still happy. I went on a 2-B which until last year was classified as 3-B. I'm talking about South Mongolian Peak. You might recall its three shape peaks sticking out when you drive down Baksàn Gorge past Adỳr-Su.

This route is generally done in 2 or 3 days. We did it almost in one. Our group consisted of four people. You know the leader — Jòsif Kahiàni [a legendary alpinist from Svanetia in Georgia]. You may remember the time he got hit with a fireball at the Shakhtèr Camp, and Lìta Taràsova smothered him in Vaseline.

We were going at a very brisk pace. We were supposed to start out in the morning and pass Lokomotìv, Spartak, Shakhtèr, and Jan-Tugàn camps. At that point the road takes a sharp turn left and up the grass slopes and then along the

In winter time, members of the mountaineering club swam and skied: a climber needed good lungs. The picture shows the author's swimming-pool pass, with a separate page for STD examination checks. The picture on the pass is not typical for such documents. Kharkov, Ukraine, 1952.

Mountaineering: at a halt. The author is third from right. Caucasus, 1952.

slides to the Union Pass. We would break for the night on the pass; in the morning we would do the peak and then come down — at best.

We left all the extra items slightly above Jan-Tugàn and reached the pass and the peak the same day and came back by 11 P.M. You can imagine the pace.

The Union Pass is much, much nastier than the two we did together at the

Top: The author (left) next to a friend, Sasha Frishman, during training on a glacier. Sasha is sipping glacier water. In the background on the left is Mt. Elbrus, the highest peak in Europe. Caucasus, 1952. *Bottom:* Mountaineering Sasha Frishman is third from left, the author is second from right. Caucasus, 1952.

Shakhtèr Camp. Even at a slower pace it is so draining that people want to pitch tents right away and lie down to rest. Everybody got fatigued in our group, even Kakhiàni. I did, too, though I felt better than I did when we did the Kurmà Pass, remember?

After a snack at the pass we started the descent to the foot of the peak. This is the third 2-B for me, but technically much tougher than the first two. First we climbed on small and large slides. Then it was tilted plates. Then we proceeded to rocks of medium difficulty, like the ones you and I climbed roped at Locomotive. We approached on these rocks to the wall that we scaled on the tilted ledge and a chimney. We belayed with a nailed hook and a crab. Then we arrived at the bridge on the crest, where we finished our chocolate. [In 1954 it was a hard-to-get expensive food.]

The crest was very sharp. We used it for climbing the next section. We arrived at the rock wall a hundred feet high. I have encountered walls like these in our rock-climbing classes, but much lower. We could find footholds, but it was a lot of work. And before that we had to do a frontal climb of a *gendarme* [a buttress with a smooth face]—a pretty tough one as well.

We drove in a few hooks on the wall, which gave us a good belay. Kakhiàni led under the lower belay. [The leader drives the hooks in the rock in the course of the climb, hangs the crabs, and puts his rope through them. In case of an accident, he would fly to the last hook he put in.]

After the wall we found ourselves on a snowed platform. Then we followed a sharp crest, though with enough footholds to get to the peak. It was so sharp that only one person could stand there comfortably! While Kakhiàni wrote the

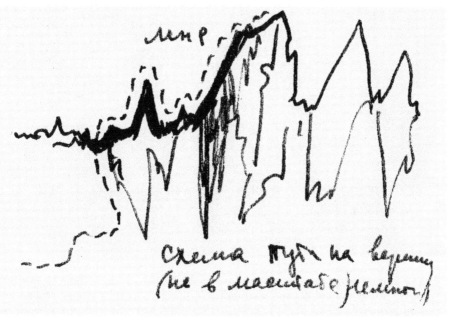

Picture from the letter to Sasha Fishman. The South Mongolian Peak climbing route schematics. Caucasus, 1954.

The author in the mountains. Descending by Dulfersitz, rappelling "atop the rope," where the uphill rope is straddled by the climber then looped around a hip, across the chest, over the opposite shoulder, and held with the downhill hand to adjust the shoulder friction. One wrist controls the direction, and the other, the speed of descent. Caucasus, 1952.

The view of the Mongolian peaks from the Baksàn Gorge. Caucasus, 1954.

note [which is left on the peak or on the pass as proof of the climb], we were hanging on the crest just below him.

The moment we approached the pass the weather went bad — wind and fog, snow and sleet. Thus we climbed the peak hardly seeing one another — and climbed down the same way. We barely avoided having a "cold sleepover." [Sleeping in the mountains without a tent or sleeping bag at freezing temperature.]

On our way back we had to descend by Dulfersitz rappels. [Dulfersitz is the kind of rappelling "atop the rope," where the uphill rope is straddled by the climber then looped around a hip, across the chest, over the opposite shoulder, and held with the downhill hand to adjust the shoulder friction. One wrist controls the direction, and the other, the speed of descent. Descent by a Dulfersitz is by fastening two ropes and dropping the main one, using the auxiliary one for belaying.] One was at 30 meters, and the other at 25 meters. That's it.

[I omitted in the letter a rather curious episode of this rappelling. Kakhiàni sent me first, and to save time, decided to ignore the belay, which was an open violation. I looked down the gorge and saw in the fog that the end of the rope was a couple of meters short of the slippery rock shelf that, as it were, I was supposed to jump on. My knees went weak, and, as a diligent climber, I refused to break the rules. Kakhiàni had to hit me with an ice pick to get me going.]

I had a lot of fun doing this climb.

When you get here you should climb the South Mongol, which I consider real climbing. Many instructors were envious, since they wanted to do it for a long time. You might remember Gusàk (he climbed with Abalakov a lot). He envied us, too.

When we passed Jan-Tugan on the way back, they turned on a march on the loudspeaker. The camp commander invited us in and treated us to watermelon. Everybody congratulated us — Maleinov, Beletsky, Markridin, and others whose named I didn't remember.

I'll write you about other peaks, too, if you are interested. But this one was the most exciting. If the pictures come out, I'll send you some.

I made many sketches in the camp. I'll send you my albums when I get to Kharkov.

Once again — don't forget to write.

Garik

English

In my Kharkov Construction Trade School, I started studying English.

The instructor's name was Lìdiya Petròvna. She was in her early twenties, but at fourteen she looked very adult to me: a petite reddish blonde, always elegant, always in fashionable short dresses.

I liked my teacher and worked hard. She took note. I was called to recite homework more often than others. She benevolently corrected my mistakes. Soon, my English took off. Mostly we were translating texts from English into Russian from our textbook, designed for college correspondence courses. After about a month we had reached an article on the Soviet biologist Michùrin: "We cannot beg nature for alms. To seize them — is our task."

To impress Lìdiya, I memorized the whole two pages. I suspect that, with a little effort, I could recite it in Russian even now, word for word. To my regret, this was to be the high point of my progress in English. For sometimes, small events set in motion unforeseen larger ones.

I loved everything about Lìdiya. Except perhaps one thing: why did she have to use lipstick? She was so pretty to begin with. Somehow I mentioned this to my classmates.

"She does that to hook a guy," Engels Orlòv said with a leer. He was tall, with red cheeks, and a full, blonde head of hair. A plain Russian fellow named after one of the founders of Marxism.

Like several others in our class, as a teenager during World War II, he had been drafted and sent straight to the front lines. Now they had returned: cynical, twenty-five-year-old, seen-it-all survivors. They treated us youngsters condescendingly, practically ignoring us — yet envious of us, too. They told us obscene Army jokes, in which an abundance of four-letter words passed for humor, bragged of their romantic adventures and invited us, fourteen- and fifteen-year-olds, to participate.

"Actually, she is a nice-looking broad," remarked Engels, and started to describe in vivid terms how he would "drag her to his *hut*."

Left: The author at the Kharkov Construction Trade School. Kharkov, Ukraine, 1951. *Right:* The author at the October Day demonstration. Kharkov, Ukraine, 1951.

I got upset, flustered and very unhappy — why on earth had I mentioned her? It was painful to listen to all this. Such talk about *my* Lìdiya? There was nothing there to stir up filth. She was — *different.* Was it really her fault that she was single? Guys of her age had not come back from the war....

"Why are you blushing, kid?" Engels mocked me. "In the meantime, I will order her to give you A's." Then, amid the laughter of the entire company, he said: "Do you want to bet? Will you give me a week?"

Several days later, Orlov saw me watching as he was waiting for my

The author as a graduate of the Kharkov Construction Trade School. Kharkov, Ukraine, 1953.

Top: The author's student ID. Kharkov, Ukraine, 1949. *Bottom:* The teachers of the Construction Trade School at the May Day demonstration. From left are an unidentified Ukrainian language teacher; Yakov Grichevsky, the construction structures teacher; Fruma Aronson, the chemistry teacher; Fedor Rosenthal, the Marxism teacher; Peter Lastochkin, electrical mechanics teacher; and Lìdiya Stroy, the English teacher. At right with a flute is the author. Kharkov, Ukraine, 1951.

teacher outside on his German trophy motorcycle. And I saw them drive off.

The next week Lìdiya, as always, called me to the blackboard. I answered somewhat worse than usual. But nevertheless I got an A. I noticed that she stared me in the eye strangely. I avoided her gaze and turned away.

Many times later I saw her on Engels's motorcycle, gripping him from behind and pressing her entire body against him. I felt an inexplicable frustration. Everything in me was stirred up — as if I had been cheated. Engels never missed a chance to brag about his "conquest" and to describe their relations in intimate detail.

Somehow all this cooled my zeal. I still wanted to learn English, but soon I stopped studying for Lìdiya's classes entirely. If she still gave me an A — OK, I'd catch up in a week. But then something more important would appear. There were so many other subjects and chores — my self-discipline was limited. Meanwhile Lìdiya behaved as if she were taking revenge upon me and stubbornly continued to give me high grades. Even — perhaps especially — after Engels stopped driving her around on his motorcycle.

Thus my first attempt to learn English fell through, unexpectedly and ignominiously.

Seven years later I was to take college entrance exams. Among them — English. The requirement was to read aloud several paragraphs, translate the entire text into Russian, and analyze the grammar of one sentence. My relative, an English instructor, after testing me concluded that I needed at least two years to prepare. This was out of the question, and I went to the exam.

Not without trembling, I entered the auditorium. Cards with questions were laid out face down on a long table. I picked one, and with trepidation read the title of the article I was to translate from one of the books lying nearby — an old, long-forgotten college textbook for correspondence students: "We cannot beg nature for alms. To seize them — is our task."

5

On the Way

Comrades in Arms

The first year of my military service in the Soviet Navy in the early 1950s I spent in Finland, in the rocky woods of Porkkala-Udd Peninsula. The remaining two years were in Estonia. We had to shiver in freezing winds that blew through our summer tents while building our own quarters on the shore of the cold Baltic's Khàru Làkhta Bay.

Our detachment was a part of the "Legendary Red Banner Baltic Fleet." That's how pompously it was referred to. The name of my unit sounded rather modest: Construction battalion, *Stroibàt*, for short in Russian.

Later on a very accurate account of our *Stroibàt* existence showed up in *One Day of Ivan Denisovich*, Solzhenitsyn's famous gulag novel. The same barracks with wooden, double-bunk beds. Pre-dawn reveille and marches. Breakfasts of lukewarm tea and a slice of frozen black bread that had to be thawed in your armpits. Six to seven roll calls a day. Waiting in lines at a medical unit hoping to get a release from work. The forced labor. No vacations outside the camp during the entire three-year service. The gibes of commanders (I almost said "guards").

Our job was to build various structures: fortifications, roads, engineering utilities, single or multi-storied barracks, industrial and cultural buildings, runways for military planes.

There was no privacy in our life, not even in the toilet, a large dark shed with holes in the floor one could easily fall into, especially in the icy winter night. Which happened to some soldiers who, to add insult to injury, were punished for that.

However, we had our own fun: a film called "Chapàyev" that played twice a month, and a visit to the bathhouse before the show. When I served in Estonia, the closest bathhouse was in the town of Lòksa, ten kilometers away. We marched there singing, in a column formation. It took about two hours one way, unless rain or a blizzard slowed us down.

124

The positions of power and privilege — clerks, librarians, bread cutters and cooks — were reserved for "whites," Russians and Ukrainians. Many of them were former convicts with habits and attitudes bred in penal institutions. They didn't march to the bath but rode there on tractors and trailers. That was business as usual and we didn't protest.

Most of our soldiers hailed from Soviet Central Asia and the Caucasus — Uzbeks, Turkmen, Tadjiks, Kazakhs, Azeries, Armenians, Georgians. The "white" minority called them *choochmèks* or simply "darks" or "blacks." These people were the main labor force and a constant target of mockery and derision.

They were punished for not knowing military rules, which they could not master because they did not understand Russian well, which was one of the reasons, along with the low level of their education, they landed in *Stroibàt*. The Muslims among them were forced to eat pork, and commanders made spectacles out of that. And then they were required to sing marching Russian songs alien to them.

Walking without a formation was strictly forbidden, as was marching in formation without a song. Our commanders could turn us around and march us a few more times. We had to sing:

> We are the Guards, we know no fear,
> The Party taught us to fight and obey.
> We shall follow to death dear Stalin's orders,
> And stand fast on our victory way.

Toward the end of my service "dear Stalin" was officially changed to "beloved Motherland." Then, instead of "our victory way," I taught my *choochmèk* friends to sing "our dinner way." Imagine a column of the Soviet Armed Forces, several hundred men, schlepping ankle-deep in mud, wearing scuffed high boots and torn cotton jackets, and singing a melancholy tune:

> Vee shall fallo b-la-aved Mudr-land odors
> An stand fass on our dinnr vey.

That was the refrain. Also, they had to suffer through the main stanzas:

> Our cannons shine in the sunlight,
> Our bugle men sound reveille,
> We have to prepare for a combat,
> Our cruisers are ready to sail!

The shiny cannons, the cruisers, the bugle men — all these glorious details of the Navy invented for this song by the most talented Soviet bards — didn't quite reflect the morose stupidity of our life in the swamps of Finland and Estonia. Fortunately, my fellow *choochmèks* didn't understand the meaning of the song. To them it meant only one thing: don't let a sergeant order another march through the rain.

With friends-in-arms, "choochmèks" at lunch. The author is fourth from the right. Khàru-Làkhta Bay, Estonia, 1956.

The Requital

My platoon commander in the Soviet Navy construction battalion in the 1950s was Lieutenant Prytkòv. He had a reputation for being dapper — always sharply dressed, high boots shined, smelling of alcohol and aftershave. And he embellished his speech with expletives, considering himself a dandy. A teenager from the outskirts of Leningrad during World War II he went to the front in 1941 and worked his way up from a private to an artillery sergeant. After the war he became an officer and remained in the Navy, for lack of a civilian trade.

As soon as I landed in his platoon, Prytkòv decided to give me an "education." "A rotten fucking intellectual, you know!" he used to say about me to his friends. And he spread false rumors about my protesting "the hack swinging," i. e. taking common assignments. "The only Jew in the battalion, you know!" he said, as if quoting me. "Got to take care of him!" I do not know where he got the idea, but he was convinced that I had it in mind. Brought up with the ideals of internationalism, I couldn't say that to him.

Once a week, on Sundays, from 2 to 5 P.M., we had so-called personal time. During these three hours we could write letters, rest, or even take a nap. High on booze, Prytkòv would come to my barrack and would summon me to the clerk's office for a "chat" — thus wasting these precious hours.

On those occasions, sometimes he forced me to play chess with him. I didn't dare refuse; I just sat there and moved the pieces, trying to think something pleasant like letters to my mother. Prytkòv played chess rather well, much better than I. After beating me he always caressed his neat mustache and mumbled: "You are a Jew, but I beat you in chess." I didn't even suspect that without much effort or thought I had helped him realize his innermost dream of beating a Jew in chess!

Typical photo-card from the author's time in the Navy. Porkkala-Udd, Finland, 1954.

With friends-in arms. From left are Sasha Butuzov, the author, and Boris Boret-sky. Khàru-Làkhta Bay, Estonia, 1956.

At times, Prytkòv didn't want to play chess, preferring an actual "chat." He wouldn't invite me to sit down, and the Navy rules didn't allow it, either. So I stood for hours, dizzy from the smell of his cheap cigarettes, and listened to his endless alcoholic blabbering.

He opened with a preamble. "Here you are, a Jew, and you think you are smarter than most people? But in chess, you see, I can always give you a start." The preamble took usually about 15–20 minutes. Then, as in a classical musical composition, the main theme was gradually introduced. It was intertwined and complicated with different variations summarized in a masterful, paranoid *idée fixe*: Jews think way too highly of themselves, but Russians are something!

Gradually Prytkòv's favorite passages, repeated over and over, made me recall other similar episodes from my life. And as time went on, I developed a logical sequence of thoughts that clicked together. I was suffering because I was Jewish. According to my trusted theory of internationalism, the distinction should vanish if I tried hard enough. But it didn't, and what's worse, "they" didn't notice my efforts. On the other hand, belonging to the "smartest" (as "they" said) people on earth was not so bad. Something worth suffering for. All nations were equal but if "they" could be proud of being "great Russian people" then it was not such a terrible crime to be proud of being a Jew.

I used to simply dismiss such thoughts, especially since state ideologues created a burning brand for that sort of thinking: "Jewish nationalism." That led to "fascist Zionism" together with the very scary term of "international cosmopolitism."

But suddenly those horrible ghosts began to retreat. Excited and confused, I wondered at the changes. The fruits of the long-cultivated, stupefying propaganda were turning into mirages in front of my eyes. And Prytkòv was an unwitting actor in that show. Along with these chimeras, my own learned "anti–Semitism" that my family had painfully noticed long ago, melted away. This process dragged on for many years; alas, unforgivably long.

Meanwhile, the Prytkòv Show went on. The next act was an ever-present burp and a sermon: "You're an architect, an educated guy, but look at yourself. You can't even wear the uniform properly. You are a hopeless civilian, Berkovich." My "hopeless civility" Prytkòv attributed to my Jewishness. He meant to say that Jews were no warriors and generally a cowardly nation. Arguing with superiors was forbidden: "Keep silent when a commander is speaking!"

"You are under my command!" he threatened. "If I choose, you will never get a break from the roster of duties!" And he did so every time he felt like expressing himself.

Prytkòv carried on these "chats" weekly, month after month, driving me crazy. In his words he "taught me to love freedom," a well-known Russian camp guards' taunt. I was completely powerless in the face of these offenses — and that was most infuriating. I had to listen to all that drivel and derision silently, daring not to risk potentially serious troubles. Yet I could not avoid even the small ones such as out-of-turn duties.

Prytkòv "taught" me not only during my "personal time" on Sundays but on any possible occasion that happened daily or even hourly. He was never tired of "whacking" me "to remember him by," as he put it.

Hard to say how it would all end but about a year later a small but significant event slightly changed our routine.

At a construction site on a very cold, snowy day, I came into a tiny, five-by-six-foot security cabin to get warm. Twenty men huddled there around a wood-burning metal stove. The air was warm, thick and full of smoke. Among others there was Prytkòv's friend, another platoon commander who took part in my "education" too. When I showed up, he had probably just finished telling some anti–Semitic joke because they stopped talking and all heads turned to me. The commander, obviously continuing the prior conversation, asked slyly: "Hey, Berkovich! Come in, come in. Could you, dear friend, explain the difference between a Jew and a Kike?"

The author at the construction site. Khàru-Làkhta Bay, Estonia, 1956.

Suddenly, a lump stuck in my throat and fire flashed inside me. I lost my usual patience and exploded, blurting insultingly: "It's like between you and a doorknob!" The cabin cracked up, roaring with laughter. I left and heard his reply from outside: "You'll hear from me yet, just you wait!"

Only then did I realize what I'd done, and I got scared. I had offended an officer in front of his subordinates. All day I tried to think of a possible defense. My friends who had witnessed the incident agreed, this was serious business, and some sort of investigation would follow. Finally, we decided that I'd go see the political officer (*Zampolìt*, in Russian) and tell him my story first.

Our logic was simple: ethnic strife undermines the armed forces and thus plays into the hands of enemies, such as the American imperialists. And that would be easy enough to explain.

The argument worked. The *Zampolìt* was pleased with me and said that he was outraged by "the officer's actions" even more than I. Still, the outcome of the investigation was unexpected. That pathetic anti–Semite was discharged from the Navy.

I found out about it a few days later. Prytkòv summoned me to his office and introduced a young woman — the wife of the unfortunate lieutenant. When we were left alone she literally fell on her knees and begged me to forgive her husband, to help him remain in the Navy. She said that without a civilian skill he wouldn't survive outside the military and their family, including a small child, would have to beg for living.

Next day I went to the *Zampolìt* and asked him to pardon the officer. The *Zampolìt* didn't like it. "How dare you, Berkovich, undermine the international unity of our armed forces! That officer does not belong in our midst. He should face a tribunal! He not only ruined his unit's discipline, and we warned him, but now this incident — enough is enough! And why are you defending him, anyway? I don't want to hear from you about this case again! Dismissed!"

That was the first time in my life I inadvertently used the contradictions of the Soviet system. Later on, with every hard beating, I discovered more discrepancies in it, and used them to defend myself, as did most of us in the USSR.

After that episode my commander became more cagey and careful with me. He still summoned me for the conversations, but not as often. My "education" was relegated to the sergeant, who became especially strict with me.

Shortly before my discharge, Prytkòv was "sent to the reserve." By that time my pain and anger were so intense that I decided to find him one day and beat the living daylight out of him. My friends contorted in laughter when they heard that idea — they knew I didn't like fighting and didn't know how to fight.

At first, I also could hardly imagine how to take my revenge, but gradually I devised a plan. I'd come to Prytkòv with a bottle of vodka and in the course of drinking I would remind him of his offenses. He wouldn't like it, and would start fighting and I'd beat him as much as I could. I'd be hurt, too, but the payback would worth it.

A year and half later I visited Leningrad and found Prytkòv's address. Fortified with a bottle of vodka I went to a multi-story building on Litèiny Prospect where he lived with his wife in a tiny compartment under the stair.

When he saw me at his door he froze in an apoplectic fit, his mouth agape. Then he screamed at the top of his voice: "Holy shit! Berkovich! Nàstya! Come here right away! Look who's come here! Goddamn! Berkovich, my friend! You didn't forget me, ha!" Then again to his wife: "Nastya, bitch, run to the store, buy something for the table, damn!" Then back to me: "Oh, you brought a bottle, good for you!" Then to her: "Nastya, get another bottle, fuck it, and some wine, too! Excuse us, pal, we haven't got squat at home. But what a jerk am I! Standing in the door like a whore! Come in, dear! Let me kiss you! Son of a bitch!"

Our former dapper boy had mysteriously changed, as if a butterfly had suddenly turned back to a caterpillar. His shoulders sagged, his dress was sloppy, his hair unkempt, his face unshaven, his mustache hung down like shoe laces.

Civilian life must be hard on him, I thought. He taught me "to love freedom" but now he had learned that lesson himself. Maybe he loved Jews now, too?

Within half an hour, after a few shots of vodka, I forgot the purpose of my visit. But even if I had not, Prytkòv's joy was so genuine that revenge was simply out of the question.

Afterwards he went to see me off. We walked hugging each other in the middle of Liteiny Prospect, empty at night, heading toward the Neva River, singing our hearts out. Suddenly, a street car screeched to a stop next to us, and a voice from inside screamed "Prytkòv!" and then joyously, "Berkovich!" Prytkòv wasn't surprised. He turned his head lazily in the direction of the voice and mumbled in a staccato, barely controlling his lips: "That's K-nì-ga, mama's dick, the str-r-reet car numb-r-r f-r-r-teen."

A small man, almost a midget, descended from the car. "That f-faggot always s-s-stops here when he s-s-sees me," continued Prytkòv catatonically.

I recognized the driver — our battalion's deputy commander for cultural education and enlightenment and librarian, appropriately named Captain Kniga (his name meaning "book" in Russian). Someone joked that Kniga "never learned anything from his book." Or from any other book, I thought.

Prytkòv pulled the unfinished bottle of vodka from his pocket, flipped off the cork with one finger and offered it to Kniga. Some sleepy passengers in the streetcar woke up and grumbled. Kniga cheered up and barked at them. He clearly didn't feel like saying goodbye.

The next streetcar stopped behind and started ringing. "The th-h-irty s-s-second f-f-fucking line," said Prytkòv slowly and indifferently, glancing aside like a standup comedian after a joke.

The author during his military service. Khàru-Làkhta Bay, Estonia, 1956.

Kniga reluctantly handed the bottle to the driver of the next streetcar, gave me a hug — he barely reached to my waist — climbed back into his seat and drove off.

Prytkòv turned around and pushed off home without saying goodbye.

Abram

In the late '40s and early '50s, my stepfather's Kiev nephew Abram Berkovich often came to visit. He was the son of his half-brother Michael and was about seven or eight years older than my stepfather. He got his education before the revolution, when the family's powerful grandfather, Mark, was still alive. Abram graduated from Kiev's High Commerce College, which at the time was an elite school. He was an all-around cultured person, who spoke several languages and was fond of classical music and poetry. He read and recited Goethe in German. And he was interested in Jewish history.

He came to Kharkov on business. He worked as chief inspector at Ukraine's Meat and Dairy Ministry. Each visit was followed by a newspaper article about someone at Kharkov's meat-packing house or the local dairy factory having been indicted for theft. I considered his job a dangerous one and was afraid for him.

A functionary at his level would not have trouble getting a hotel bed, but Abram chose to stay with us, and we were always glad to see him.

Each visit we spent a lot of time talking. Abram told me about Jewish traditions and the Bible and episodes from Jewish history. He tried to "enlighten" me. This was a thankless task. As an internationalist, thoroughly brainwashed by textbooks and media, I argued back, with a fifteen-year-old's conviction that brooks no argument, and termed his stories "nationalist propaganda."

Abram heard me out patiently, and calmly tried to explain himself. But his hands were tied: he could not tell me the whole story out of fear — fear for me, I would realize much later.

I remember our argument about assimilation. I thought this to be the only right path. Nations were an atavism. There would be none under Communism. My mother couldn't take it anymore: "My Garik will marry a shiksa? Perish the thought!"

Abram would calm her down. I'd grow up, I'd sort things out. I was outraged: what was there to sort out? It was all crystal clear.

Abram and his wife Klara had a daughter named Nina. Unmarried at thirty, she was considered a candidate for spinsterhood, and had her parents worried. There was a lot of talk about it. Finally one day we learned she had found a husband.

From left: Abram Berkovich; Klara Berkovich, Abram's wife; Roza Berkovich, Abram's sister; Aron Berkovich; unidentified; Maria Schneider, the author's mother; Larissa Bogdànova, daughter of Roza Berkovich; the author's sister Yanna on her mother's lap; Mark Berkovich, the author's step-brother; unidentified; and Nina Berkovich, daughter of Abram and Klara Berkovich. Kiev, Ukraine, 1951.

My step-brother Mark, a Navy officer who served in the far North, took a vacation especially to attend the wedding in Kiev. He showed up in the middle of the feast. Right in the doorway, amid numerous relatives and strangers, he bumped into his former Navy buddy Nikolay Parey. Small world, Mark wondered.

Nikolay was from the Altai Mountains, a straight arrow, and an ethnic Russian. They served on the same destroyer. My brother was in charge of engines, and Nikolay was a political officer. Only a few months earlier, they had celebrated Nikolay's departure for the Ministry of Defense's Political Academy in Kiev. And now such a pleasant surprise!

They hugged and stepped out for a smoke. Mark asked his buddy: How come...?

Nikolay broke out laughing: "I'm the groom here!"

In 1952, the Meat-and-Dairy Ministry changed bosses, and the new broom swept Abram out of the office. In those years Jews were swept out of all sorts of offices — and worse. In 1948, Solomon Michoels, a famed Jewish actor and a public figure, had been murdered in a staged car accident and posthumously declared a British spy. Also in 1952 a group of Jewish cultural figures was arrested on trumped-up charges and executed. The country was abuzz with rumors of the coming Jewish relocation to the Far East.

The minister personally signed the decision to "dismiss Abram Berkovich for gross negligence." Abram sued. Grounds: a bold lie, a violation of the Labor Code, and a demeaning wording of the decision. He would not hire a lawyer. Considering the current situation, the family trembled, expecting the worst. Klara filled a bag with a change of underwear and dried bread (Russian prison food). Yet for some reason, no arrest came.

The lawsuit went on for over a year. A "highly vital" nationwide discussion on Stalin's articles on linguistics came and went. The Jewish doctors were arrested and, after considerable torture, released. Stalin died. The Korean War ended. Finally, Beria was executed.

Abram won the case. He told us that the minister apologized in writing, had him reinstalled in his job, and paid the salary for the eighteen months involuntarily missed. After that my cousin declared he was not working for "them" anymore — and retired.

In 1972, I visited Kiev for the national architects' conference. I went to visit Abram, who twenty years later still lived on Zhadonovsky Street near the railroad terminal. The evening was a sad one. Klara, who never got over her daughter's marriage to a goy, had died long ago. Nikolay Parey had retired. His wife Nina, who had gained weight and turned into a copy of her mother, was busy in the kitchen. Their daughter Anya — Abram's granddaughter — was studying for her college exams and did not pay us any attention. As for Abram, he had just got back home after yet another police detention.

In the last years of his life, Abram turned into a "Zionist." He regularly attended unsanctioned Jewish demonstrations in Baby Yar, in remembrance of the Kiev Jews executed there in 1941. This led to repeated arrests. He was still tall, though stooped, and, after eighty years of age, turned taciturn and distrustful to the point of paranoia.

I wanted to talk to him so badly. I wanted to hear his intelligent reasoning once again. I wanted to tell him I had realized he had been right all along. I just wanted to chat with him about things Jewish.

But he did not acknowledge me and largely stayed out of the conversation. Only at one point, clearly responding to my former devotion to communist ideas of twenty years ago and some inner thoughts of his own, he remarked: "That's not a good religion that you picked for yourself, son."

I Am a Jew Now

I didn't become a Jew right away. Never mind the circumcision.

I was six when I first heard about Jews from my grandfather. The only thing I remembered was that I was a Jew and "God punishes those who hurt the Jews." I learned the word "synagogue" when I was eight. My grandfather died, and I was sent to this place to order a memorial service.

A little later I learned the word "Yid." We came back to Kharkov from evacuation and I heard this word a lot, especially addressed to me. It turned out that being a Jew was a shameful thing. But I had a hard time hiding it, with my facial features, last name and a characteristic rolling "r."

At about the same time something happened to me that subconsciously started me on my way to Jewishness. We were playing soccer on one of many sandlots with which the city abounded. After the game my soccer pals — some of whom I had considered real friends — suddenly forced me on the ground and pulled down my pants. All they wanted to do was to see what a certain part of a Jewish boy's body looks like, and they let me go.

That's all. I was not physically harmed. Yet I could not forget their hands on me and my powerlessness and helplessness. I could not figure out why they had to use violence. If they had asked, I would have shown it. It took me many years to realize that violence applied to a "Yid" was especially exciting.

While I was at high school and trade school, I was successfully brainwashed into believing that anti–Semitism came from Jewish nationalism. I was a trusting child and I believed this story. Moreover, I kept arguing with my family that this nationalism was the evil. Whatever the stories about anti–Jewish discrimination, I always managed to come up with a convenient Soviet explanation. If a Jew was refused entrance to college, it was because he got poor grades on exams; if he was fired from a job, he hadn't performed well; if he was denied a job, there was no real vacancy. I considered street anti–Semitism as an uncultured phenomenon we had inherited from Czarism, something that was bound to vanish as we approached Communism.

My family was amazed by what they termed my "anti–Semitism" and intoned: "You wait, you wait — you'll get it, too, and you'll sing a different song."

My first encounter with official anti–Semitism goes back to the time I was turned down at Chugùyev Flying School.

The admissions chairman explained to me that my high school graduation had been filled out improperly. It was done on the letterhead of a ten-year music school, rather than a regular seven-year school.

At the time I swallowed the explanation and did not get upset. I didn't really want to become a military pilot — it was my mother's passing fancy — and I took my papers to the architecture-and-construction trade school, where they were accepted without a hitch. Many years later I wondered at the disproportionate representation of the Jews of my generation in construction, and someone told me that at the time this was the professional area most accessible to Jews. I had certainly hit the bull's eye.

The top 5 percent of the graduation class of the trade school won special treatment: they could skip the obligatory three-year job "on assignment" and enter any college without exams.

I was not included in the Five Percent Group, and that made me really wonder.

I had wanted to become an architect — badly — since I was fourteen or fifteen. At the time there were several architecture departments in engineering and art schools, but there was only one real school — the Moscow School of Architecture. I dreamed of studying there.

There were certain rules for getting in the Five Percent Group. First of all, you had to have A's in at least 95 percent of your courses through your four years of study. I had 98 percent. Next, you had to participate in extracurricular activities. I was a Komsomòl (Party Youth organization) activist and I was on the school committee, I was on the mountain-climbing team, and I played in the band (which rated even above athletics). Finally, I delivered papers at students' science conferences and my projects were exhibited at national student shows in Moscow. I had no doubt I was Candidate Number One. I was wrong.

Aha, said my family.

I did not budge yet. A misunderstanding, I said.

But I was terribly upset. My mother comforted me the best she could, and then wrote a letter to Voroshilov, then the national president.

"Dear Comrade Voroshilov, I am the sister of Yakushevsky, your Civil War combat friend. Please help his nephew who has become a victim of an injustice —"

A month later we had a messenger from my trade school. "Comrade Putìlin" — the school director — wished to see me.

Putìlin knew me well, and seemed to respect me.

"What are you doing to me?" he said without greeting me. "You know I treat you well. We love you and we support you in everything. You are the pride of our school."

Even then I could tell I was being BS'ed.

"And here you are, writing complaints — to the president himself."

I tried to counter, but he would not let me.

"Here is your slanderous complaint. It has been returned to me. Investigate. Now, you judge. You are not a kid any more. You should understand the politics of today." It was July of 1953. Stalin had died already, four months before. But this kind of talk I heard twenty years later, too.

"Do you think the Party district committee will reward me if I put you in the Five Percent? Look, I have a family and children to support. You are young, you have drive, you have a good head on your shoulders. I bet you are going to make it to that school with or without my piece of paper. So — don't do it to me."

Five years later, I came home from the Navy, and finally entered the Moscow School of Architecture. As luck would have it, I ran into Putìlin outside the school, which shared a courtyard with the Higher Education Ministry, where he had come on business.

Putìlin saw me and cried out in triumph: "See? I was right after all!"

So he was. Yet I had gone through a shift: I was no longer uncomfortable being Jewish. Moreover, I was proud. And now I confronted anti–Semitism as a full-fledged Jew — as one of us.

6

~

Studies

The Gambit

In late 1957 after doing my Navy service I came back to Kharkov, Ukraine, and found a job at a design office. Simultaneously I was taking evening classes towards a bachelor's in construction engineering. I was young and gung-ho. My body ignored the stress of working six days a week and putting in four hours of classes five days a week with Saturday nights and Sundays spent on homework. Incredibly, I even found time to be social (important at a Soviet workplace) and play flute in the band with my workmates.

What I really wanted to do was architecture. So did my friend Sasha.

Sasha and I were inseparable: we took evening classes and studied for tests together, and, weather permitting, ran a couple of miles or more each morning before work. Our Sunday morning run was a real basic-training, full combat gear exercise. Loaded with easels, tiny portable chairs, pads of paper, paint, brushes, and flasks of water, we would race each other to a designated spot to do watercolor sketching. We deemed it an important skill for future architects.

Since Kharkov did not have an architectural school, we decided to take a different route. To make up in part for the lack of architectural education, we would get a degree in engineering at first — that's three more years — and then enroll in the local Art Institute. And given that the Art Institute did not teach architectural subjects either, we decided to master them on our own, in our own free time, whatever that meant. We began with art history. By spring of the next year we had mastered Babylon and ancient Egypt. But the idea of graduating from two schools lost some of its appeal. The back-breaking fatigue suggested there was something wrong with it.

And then my girlfriend Ada Landman came up with a brilliant thought: to live out our cherished dream of studying architecture we should drop everything and go to Moscow. The only architectural school in the Soviet Union was in Moscow. I decided to give it a try.

When I shared the plan with my mother, she nodded understanding and said she had been worried about my strenuous lifestyle for quite some time. Clearly, here was a definite sign of mental strain. She pleaded with me to go to a psychiatrist.

At work, the reaction was similar.

While I was in the Navy, my boss moved to *Yuzh*, the huge design office, to join his big-shot friends. When I came back he brought me on board, too. We had always had an excellent, friendly relationship, and now his friends were my friends, too. From a mere technician I had been promoted to an engineer's position. In short, I was valued — a regular boss's pet — and as such was assigned an apartment in an almost completed building smack in the city center. For a single guy this was nothing short of a miracle. Other lucky ones settled for rooms in communal apartments, and the rest were not considered at all.

And now I was about to piss it all away. Why don't you at least wait till you get the apartment, people at work said. You don't get a chance like this every day. You have to be an idiot to give it up.

In late June I took a vacation and headed for Moscow. My goal was to get a transfer from the third year of engineering school to the second year of architecture school.

I stayed with my Aunt Shura. She listened to my plan and managed to find something positive in it. Specifically, I had four whole weeks of vacation, and I was spending it in Moscow. She figured it was enough to find me a nice Jewish girl. A marriage would bring me a Moscow stamp in my internal passport, which would enable me to stay there. It would be like getting a green card, or even more than that — like instant citizenship for a foreigner in the U.S.

After all, no one was waiting for me with open arms. For a Jew, getting into a Moscow school was no small feat, even with a bribe. Without one, it was "banging your head against the wall," and Aunt Shura felt sorry for me and my wasted time. She took stock of my stubbornness and concluded that her sister was right: "You need to see a good doctor." There was no stigma attached: "It could happen to anyone."

When I saw Comrade Koziàtko, the rector of the School of Architecture, he seemed to think along the same lines. Yet he diplomatically kept it to himself and referred me to the Ministry of Higher Education. The minister, Comrade Krasnòv, would not give me the time of the day. NO TRANSFERS. Period.

It took me four days to have my plans smashed to smithereens. Now I could go back to Kharkov with my conscience assuaged. At least I had given my dream a shot.

The next day I stopped by to say farewell to the School of Architecture, and at the reception office I ran into a guy who had just managed exactly the kind of transfer I had requested. Moreover, he came from something called the Fisheries Industry School, which had nothing to do with architecture or construction. Why was he so special? (As I found out later, his father was deputy minister of the Fisheries Industry.)

I went back to Comrade Krasnòv. How come the fish guy got his wish and I didn't? Were some students more equal than others? Aha, a new reason: I didn't have a Moscow residence permit. And what would Comrade Krasnòv do if I was Mikhail Lomonosov, who allegedly in 1730 walked to Moscow from a northern village and later came to found Moscow University? How did Comrade Krasnòv know I was different?

He did not have to know. Moscow didn't need another university, as far as Comrade Krasnòv was concerned; and it certainly didn't need another Jewish upstart like me. He told his secretary never to let me in again. And if I persisted, to call the cops.

Five years earlier, I had had a similar unsuccessful experience of the ministerial runaround in Kiev. Then I had tried to win my place in college on the grounds that I was eligible for the 5 percent quota as an honors graduate from a trade school. Of course the Navy had changed me. I felt I had done my "duty for the Motherland," and then some. Now they owed *me*. Yet Aunt Shura had a point. Against a wall like this, I could definitely smash my head.

Before leaving I went to see my Navy buddy Volòdya Gerasimov. He lived in the Cherkìzovo neighborhood and worked as a loader at a food warehouse. After we split a bottle of vodka, he heard out my sob story and suddenly came up with an incredible gambit.

His recently deceased father was an old Bolshevik who had joined the Party about the time Lenin did, if not earlier. Since his fighting days in the Civil War he had been friends with Yemelyàn Budyònny.

There were three Budyònny brothers. The eldest one, Semyòn, was a legendary Red Army cavalry general, Stalin's best friend, and an all-round Soviet icon. The youngest brother Leonid was an obscure architect. And the middle Yemelyàn, also a Civil War commander, had served out his years before retirement as the Kremlin's commandant.

"There's nothing Yemèl'ka can't do," Volodya told me. "If something goes wrong, he'll call his brother Semyon. And that one can really do *anything*."

Calling a Civil War hero Yemèl'ka, a somewhat pejorative-sounding nickname? He must have inherited that from his father.

The next day, two half-liter vodka bottles under our arms, we went to Yemèl'ka's apartment on Kutuzov Avenue — next door to Brezhnev's. The military guards were already expecting us.

Yemèl'ka's place stunned me. The size, the trimmings, the furniture, the odors — everything about it evoked the pre-revolutionary country abode of a well-to-do Cossack. A huge saber with a belt graced one wall. Much of the wall space was covered with framed, blown-up pictures of deceased relatives, both singly and in groups, and all in full Cossack regalia. The rest of the space was taken by mammoth sentimental oils of waterfowl, the favorite of Russian country fairs. Gigantic iron-sided chests, some with embroidered throw pillows, lined the walls.

We were led to a vast room, with a table and chairs that seemed to have been made to order by a village carpenter. A colossal bed with headboards made of nickel tubes decorated with numerous shiny nickel balls. The wardrobes were massive and enormous, the chandeliers sparkled, the wall mirrors had fancy molding, the rugs…. The old lady who served food was straight from central casting for a Don Cossack movie.

A few rounds of vodka served to unleash a flood of memories. The former Kremlin governor narrated the Civil War Battle of Samàra with Volodya's father at his side, the Whites being saber-slashed from here to here (with that same saber on the wall, my imagination suggested vividly). Suddenly, his face fell as he went on to complain of his famous older brother Semyon who was now "too big for his britches" and had committed the seemingly unpardonable sin of having his memoirs ghost-written.

A few more rounds followed, and I still had no idea if Yemèl'ka understood what my problem was or what I was doing in his apartment — except providing drinking companionship. Actually, that made two of us, because I, too, had a hard time figuring out what I, a Berkovich, was doing at this make-belief Cossack farmstead.

Yemèl'ka summed it up himself. He was happy to help out a pal, "even though not one of us." He would get a Moscow registration stamp for my internal passport tomorrow. That's easy as Cossack pie. Then he was told it was not about registration, and that put him into a shock so great it sobered him up instantly.

"What? They don't want to transfer you? Those White bourgeois sonuvabitches!" Tomorrow he'd show them.

The thought terrified me, but I just had to close my eyes and grab at the only straw I had. The next day, with a by now customary half a liter under my arm, I brought Yemèl'ka to the School of Architecture.

I don't know if I will ever rid myself of the shame that overwhelms me every time I think back to the scene at the rector's office.

Rector Koziàtko remained on his feet throughout, with his legs slightly bent, and leaning with the tips of his fingers against the desk. Yet from the moment Yemèl'ka crashed the defense line — the rector's assistant Valentina and a disabled graduate student — until he withdrew, Koziàtko got out only one phrase. "I don't decide anything here. It's up to the ministry."

"You fucking red tape bastards!" Yemèl'ka roared on his way out. "I'll slash you to shreds!"

At the minister's office, the pickings were slim, too. The minister was out. The scene at Deputy Minister Rumyàntzev's office was identical to the one at the rector's — though with a twist. Rumyantzev suggested that we leave a request in writing. He would render his verdict a few days later: "The Ministry approves of a transfer to any college or university except for those in Moscow and Leningrad." A most elegant solution, considering there were no schools of architecture anywhere else.

I took the weary Yemèl'ka to the nearest greasy spoon, where we polished off the half-liter. Mostly he did, of course. As a farewell, he said, "I don't understand how the Jews' minds work. Why bother with those sumbitches. Come by in the morning, I'll get you a residence stamp, and that's it."

I thanked him and explained I didn't need it. I wanted to become an architect and go back to my hometown of Kharkov.

"Well, it's your call." He was genuinely upset by my foolishness. I never saw him again.

The next day I was about to go home, but at Aunt Shura's suggestion I went to see Rector Koziàtko, ostensibly to apologize. According to my aunt, the scandal the day before could have scared him into changing his mind. I didn't believe it, but who knew? She was local, and she knew their ways better.

The moment I stepped inside the reception office, the ever-graceful Valentina greeted me with a smile. "The rector isn't in, but his deputy Comrade Lukàyev would like to see you."

Soon Lukàyev himself came out to the reception area and invited me in. After he sat me down, he settled in his own chair under Stalin's portrait and began stuffing his pipe with aromatic Java tobacco — slowly and languorously. Finally, he lit up, took a few puffs, and spoke with a thick trans–Caucasian accent, enunciating every word that was longer than one syllable, as if to make really sure I got it: "I like you, Berkovich. So *per-si-stent*, you know." After a pause he added: "Who was that man yesterday? *Ay-ay-ay*, so much noise he made. A relative of Marshal Budyonny? Your relative, too, eh?"

"A friend of the family," I lied. I liked the opening.

While Lukàyev kept toying with the pipe that kept going out, I was trying to remember of whom he reminded me. He looked so familiar. I also reflected on the ways I could turn this twist of fate to my advantage. How should I ask him for help without seeming too forward?

"We can help you," he said, enveloping me in the tobacco aroma. "Of course it is *prac-ti-cally im-possible* to do a transfer." He took another drag and fell silent. "I think, "he started.

And then I realized it. He was just like character of the portrait above his head — the moustache, the accent. An ominous resemblance.

He puffed out more smoke. "— you need to take *en-trance* exams. As any *can-di-date*."

I had thought about this earlier. But then with fourteen applicants per vacancy, I would have to compete in two weeks with boys and girls straight from high school. And I would have to start in first year and thus lose another year. Most importantly, the law proscribed admitting students who were already enrolled in another college. My trade school certificate rested in a file cabinet at Kharkov Engineering School's personnel department. Without it, on what basis would they allow me to take exams?

Lukàyev read my thoughts. "You take your *cer-ti-fi-cate*, tell them you just *bor-row* it to make a copy. And we look the other way that you are their student. You *nevvver* told us any*thing*." He leaned back, very happy with his own inventiveness. As if on cue, the pipe went off full blast.

"If you have *problems*, don't be shy — come by, *we'll help* you," my new and unexpected guardian angel told me. With an air so fascinatingly conspiratorial, I started wishing for a problem to bring and drop in his lap.

What a wonderful benefactor Life has sent me, I thought, without wondering about Life's motivation. I wasn't surprised, though. Miracles have their own ways.

I couldn't have known then that I was being groomed by Mephisto himself— the school's KGB rep.

Transfer

Finally, I was allowed to take entrance exams at the architecture school. I fell into deep thought. I had two weeks left. There were six exams: drawing, draftsmanship, Russian literature, math, physics, and a foreign language. It had been five years since I graduated from trade school. I had to revive my knowledge fast, and I didn't have enough time. I remembered a joke: if you wanted to work twenty-six hours a day, you had to get up two hours earlier. I could do that — even three hours! Difficulties were nothing new to me.

I had to push myself. And I did. I passed the exams, beat the competition, and was admitted as a freshman. Aunt Shura summed up, with respect: "You were truly born with a silver spoon in your mouth. You bought a lottery ticket, and it's worth a million." And she added: "I want you to come home early tomorrow. I want you to meet a very beautiful girl from Novo-Girèyevo. You never heard of it, but it's only forty-five minutes away by subway. For you, this means a Moscow stamp in your passport, a car, and a co-op apartment. Garik! Don't say no! Don't be a schmuck!"

I chose to be a schmuck.

After two weeks of studies I was called to the deputy rector's office. Lazar

Lukàyev received me in a friendly manner: Was I happy with the dorm? Did I get along with the other students? Wasn't I bored to be taking the courses I had already taken in Kharkov Engineering School all over again? He remarked in passing that perhaps I should visit a few chairs. Who knew, some of my Kharkov grades could be confirmed.

Then — as if it had just dawned on him — he wondered if I liked the idea of being promoted to second year. I could take tests in the courses I had not taken in Kharkov — preferably in my first semester, of course.

To be doing second-year studies and at the same time taking tests for my first year? But that was my original plan! I agreed right away. Of course I never wondered why Lukàyev kept helping me and why he was being so friendly.

In part, he told me this himself. I thought he just spilled it out. Perhaps this "spill" had some back-handed intention to it. I didn't see it. According to Lukàyev, he needed the transfer more than I did.

The transfer freed up a slot in the first year (there was always more space in the senior years due to dropouts) for the son of an architect couple, well-known in Moscow, and winners of Stalin Prizes. Actually, I came to know the boy later, and he turned out to be a decent guy. Forty-five years later he became a big wheel at the Russian Architect Union. But in those days he flunked an entrance exam in Russian language and literature. Yet with my help he did get in, albeit through the back door.

I didn't know how Lukàyev got around the law. The admissions committee had already been disbanded. Most likely, the fortunate son's grade was forged. All I know is that no one caught Lukàyev — at least not that time — accepting a bribe.

It was out of the question to accept a candidate who had scored not high enough — but not flunked an exam outright. This candidate could have turned out to be Jewish. And plenty of our kind had already been taken in, filling out the entire (unspoken) quota.

In retrospect, I believe that Lukàyev had planned this combination all along; even as he advised me to take the entrance exams, he was already thinking of transferring me to the second year. There were plenty of candidates to employ his services to gain the first-year slot.

One way or another he was doing me a favor. He won my trust, gratitude, and a feeling that I owed him one. It took me quite some time to figure out why.

Group

And so my dream came true. I was a sophomore at the Moscow School of Architecture, and my coat lapel proudly featured an MSA pin.

During the fall semester I was to pass a bunch of exams for the first year, as if the second course load were not enough. Fortunately, a few general and construction-related grades were allowed to be transferred.

Math was the easiest. My instructor Nikolay Fomìn remembered me from entrance exams, when I solved a problem with the help of integrals, which were not taught in college until the second year. I explained to Fomin that I had already completed the second year of engineering college after Navy service. That was another surprise for him: my name was not in the list of ex-servicemen on his desk (who would be treated less severely). Just an innocent "oversight" on the part of admissions, and math was my last exam.

Now, when I asked Fomin to approve the transfer of my first-year grade in his course, he asked me to solve a few simple problems. For him this was enough to release me from math for the second year as well. This made my life considerably easier and provided me with more time for other labor-intensive subjects like art and architecture history, descriptive geometry, and introduction to architectural design. I attacked them with the zeal and relish of a true workaholic. The first semester flashed by in an instant.

I was placed in the Màmontovo Dorm along Yaroslàvl Railroad outside Moscow. This was a tiny ramshackle structure without heat or running water. Seniors recalled that when they were freshmen, they were told by the seniors of their time that when they entered school they had been promised that a well-appointed dorm would be built in Moscow. When we became seniors, we passed that tale along, too.

The Màmontovo Dorm was never heated, and the water in the sink, delivered from outside, was always cold. To get to school we had to take a suburban train and then the subway. The village of Màmontovo had no paved sidewalks, the fall was rainy, and the mud was up to our ankles. I had to put on construction boots again, which made me feel slightly yokel-like at school. But none of this got in the way of my bliss at attending the school I had dreamed of all my life.

Architecture is a magic word; it sounds prestigious and attracts a wide variety of people. Few actually understand what this profession entails, except for architects themselves and their families.

During the entrance exams, applicants had to show their drawing skills. Thus there were some highly capable artists among the students.

Students with a more distinct artistic bent were concentrated at the industrial architecture department. They misunderstood the connection between architecture and art. They perceived architecture as a field of emerging shapes and expected to have a wider berth for this activity at industrial architecture. Yet they found it only in their school projects; eventually these people left architecture.

At first I walked around the school in a daze. Little by little I became settled and got to know my classmates. Most of them came straight from high school, both Muscovites and out-of-towners. There was no one from the countryside. I doubt there were any in Moscow schools, even in the agricultural one. While they were given every break in admissions, the village schools just didn't give the proper level of education.

Our group was international — Vu Thuòc and Nguyen Chic Luen from Vietnam; Sasha Karvovsky, formerly of France; Lev Kozlov, formerly of Iran; and Yan Dautovsky from Macedonia. Genderwise, we had seven girls — one quarter of the whole.

Among the teenagers straight from high school a few gifted ones in our group really stood out — Dima Radýgin, Lev Netzvetàyev, and Igor Ivanov.

Igor was one of the most capable students of my year. I can still see his remarkable wash of the façade of the Guggenheim Museum in New York (one of the first western buildings included in our curriculum). We grew close in the summer of '59 while traveling in the Northwest.

In the third year, his father died. Our group was going out of our minds trying to help him. But Igor shut himself off to the world for a long time. Sometimes he would bring his etchings, reminiscent of Lithuanian painter Ciurlionis. Vast black-and-purple meadows, spotted with ominously oversized dandelions. For a while, we had serious misgivings about his psychological condition.

A year later, Dima and I did a contest design for a theater for remote areas. Igor helped us with a clay mockup and a group of nifty Eskimos with a deer sled.

After graduation he joined the KGB, which puzzled me to no end. A decent, talented guy went to work for an outfit that evoked nothing but disgust in everyone I knew.

Right now I would not judge him by my standards. True, the KGB is a repellent place, but their salaries were double those elsewhere. Plus they got a supplement for a military rank. The Committee was truly the dispenser of the Soviet cornucopia. It was hard to resist the temptation.

A few years later I asked Igor a nasty question. How many concentration camps had he designed? None, he said; just a few resorts for personnel. We'll never know what he really did. The oath of silence is part of the KGB package. He did receive a state award, though.

There were a few older students in my class, including me. We felt we were a separate group and at first regarded the "schoolkids" condescendingly. We realized that we came there to learn and tried not to waste time. Yury Konovàlov and Lev Kozlov were the most diligent ones. Yury was appointed the group leader. He was very proud of it and tried to set an example in everything he did. Lev's inborn industriousness deserves a separate book. Tòlik Lukyànov came from a cadet school, was a gymnast, and had an Army-serious

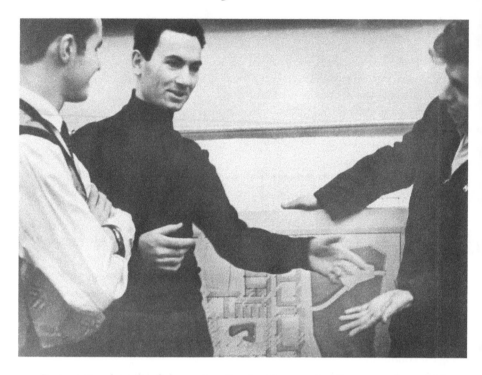

Presentation boards of the project for the Community Center on the corridor walls at school. From left are Dima Radỳgin, the author and Igor Ivanov. Moscow, 1960.

attitude to studies. Fedor Gazhèvsky had already graduated from a construction trade school in Petrozavòdsk, and his structural decisions never lacked in gravity. Sasha Karvovsky's forte was in the art of presentation. Sasha Batàlov, rather shortish, with legs wide apart and large glasses, was a perfect target for cartoons.

We were in close contact in college and the dorm and indirectly influenced one another's creative growth. I could feel it more as time went by.

A few students in our group formed a group of their own — the children of the Moscow elite. I did not use the word "elite" then and called them "the Sons," as the phrase *du jour* went. My mind was still polluted with leftovers of faith in Socialist ideals. I was well behind my classmates in discovering certain basic truths and was late to see the precise class stratification of our student body.

The stratification of Soviet society was based upon different methods that the state employed to motivate its subjects' loyalty. Rank-and-file citizenry was motivated by promotions and pay raises and free vacation vouchers to resorts and summer camps for their children. In addition, high-placed officials and prominent scientists and artists had access to special food and a goods distribution network, special health care, special resorts, and foreign trips, all at the state's expense. The lower classes fought to get closer to this trough, and the upper classes fought to hold them back. Movement from below was realized by seizing positions in the Party and the Komsomòl. At the end of the twentieth century the upper classes were unable to ward off the assault, and Russia had a revolution. Although the system officially turned capitalist, the stratification never went away — waiting the next explosion.

The parents of The Sons in my school were members of the government, highly-placed officials, and architects who had fought their way to the eagerly sought trough of the Socialist state. Any change in the power hierarchy, the slightest change of political course, meant another round of war for positions for their parents. The parents realized that their offspring would not make it by themselves and were worried about the clan's cohesion. Part of the solution was sending the offspring to prestigious schools like ours.

After The Sons, the next rung on the hierarchy ladder was taken by regular Muscovites — teenagers who graduated from Moscow high schools and received additional training at art schools and in private lessons. They had Moscow residential registration, with all its entailing privileges. The more popular benefit distribution points were innumerable creative unions — the writers', artists', actors', journalists', architects' — all paid for by the state.

The Muscovites were followed by Regional Sons — children of directors and chief engineers and other powers-that-be from the provinces. These looked forward to the easy life of the provincial elite — not bad, especially if you came from the ethnic elite.

At the very bottom of the ladder were people like me — the hoi polloi. Yet not all of us were content to stay at the bottom, and were prepared to fight.

Among the sophomores, our Sons were in fact led by a Daughter, Yelena Tarànova, who was puny and nondescript, but older and more energetic than the rest. When she was eight, her parents, both Stalin Prize winners, got her a leading part in a movie called "First Grader." This left Yelena with a notion of herself as a movie star for the rest of her life, and little to back it up with. Her apartment was where her group would hang out. The crowd included the children of deputy ministers for construction and agriculture, a popular stage director, and an ex-rector of our school.

They were late for classes together, they spent recess together, they went home together, and they spent vacations together at the Architects' Union Sukhanovo resort. They befriended their ilk in the other years, too. They were not interested in studies and — what enraged me the most — in the subject of architecture, that had by then become my obsession.

As a provincial and a recent marine in rough construction boots, I was irritated by these elite boys and girls — "golden youth," as they were called. There was also a feeling of rancor. I had wasted so many years to get here. They got it for free. No wonder they were studying without enthusiasm, merely going through the motions, without any love of architecture. I despised them, and the feeling never went away.

The offspring of the Soviet architectural elite brought to school the biases of the Stalinist era. I once mentioned the name of Nikolay Kòlli, a well-known Constructivist. The same Yelena recited, with a great deal of aplomb — as befits a film star — a silly ditty about "a collie making a better architect than Kòlli."

I had no doubt that this was about all she knew of Kòlli's work — a man who had worked with Le Corbusier, incidentally. She must have heard the ditty from her parents, whose socialist-realist talents were barely enough for a Stalin Prize.

It took me a few years to get above my Kharkov outlook and realize that things were not so black-and-white. In time, The Sons changed, too, and so did our relations. On the one hand, they mocked my clothing, my cheap haircuts, and my poorly articulated speech. On the other hand, despite their own infantilism, they took note of my industriousness, my greed for knowledge, my fast progress in drawing and watercolors. That made them think, too.

Not until graduation did I figure out how uneven the playing field was in our allegedly classless society — and I still didn't want to accept the rules of the game.

In time, we got over our personal differences and became friends. But the class differences did not go away.

One of The Sons, Alexey Shcheglòv, became a hard-working student, and late in life penned a brilliant book about my favorite actress Faìna Ranèvskaya. He is teaching at our school now. (So does Sasha Batàlov.) The beautiful Natasha Chaldymova married a diplomat — as expected — and spent most of her life abroad. I heard that someone asked her son Misha what he wanted to become when he grew up. "A foreigner," Misha said.

Nguyen went back to Vietnam and became the head of the local architect union. Yan Dautovsky went back to Macedonia and worked as urban architect in Skopje. Fedor Gazhèvsky spent his life working in architect Belopòlsky's studio and designed a few interesting projects, including a monument to Yury Gagarin. He died of cancer in 2000. Dima Radygin has his own successful firm in Moscow, as does Igor Ivanov.

Not everyone stayed in architecture. I heard that Lev Kozlov works as an interpreter in the Iranian Embassy in Kiev. Misha Katòk is a sculptor in New York. Lev Netzvetàyev is a poet and a painter in his home town of Simbìrsk.

The May Day demonstration. At left in the hat is professor of political science Isaak Aisenberg. Behind him, with the banner in his hand is Nguyen Chik Luen. Front and center is the author. Behind the author at right is Vu Thuòk. Moscow, 1960.

Sasha Karvovsky was a poet and a translator till his death in a car accident in 2003. Nonna Selipanova, who, despite her petite size, had a strong drawing hand, became a successful jewelry designer and moved to the United States in the '90s. And Volodya Antòshkin sings in a Moscow church choir.

I often think about my school and classmates. Our personal contacts and friendship are what I treasure most about attending the Moscow School of Architecture.

Kozlov

Lev Kozlov and I met and became friends almost on the first day of school, when we became roommates. Lev told me that in the early '30s, when the Volga area was struck by famine, his grandfather took their whole family via the Caucasus to Iran. In 1958 they came back.

Lev was born in Isfahan. Persian was his first language. Yet he learned Russian, too, both from his family and at Sunday school in church. He spoke an odd kind of Russian, with singsong eastern intonations and certain expressions from an earlier century.

Lev completed two years of architecture school in Tehran University, and he was admitted to his second year in Moscow without exams. Unlike me, he didn't have to jump through hoops. And no one asked him for a Moscow registration either.

He made me admire foreign standards of teaching languages. After two years of university, he spoke fluent English. When he came to the foreign languages chair with a request to transfer his English credits, they wondered if they should invite him to teach it. Of course he was released from English classes.

Once he found out I was studying English, he offered to help me practice it. He needed practice, too. Our practice was over after one morning I told Lev that "I washed my voice," meaning "face," of course. Lev realized we couldn't really talk and called it off. He would be mocking me for years as the guy who "washes his voice in the morning."

With his foreigner's naivety he could never figure out why for years we were taught to deduce formulas of structural calculations. In Tehran they had been taught to understand structures and their elements. Of course, an architect should be able to calculate them, but why learn to deduce formulas? Lev wondered. Besides, if you need to do calculations, you could always hire a specialist.

Lev was a diligent student, met every deadline, and was sincerely taken aback by the happy-go-lucky attitude that is dominant in a Soviet college. As he put it, "We in Teh-ra-a-an don't —"

In the spring of 1959 he was visited by his father, who had just been repatriated. His father refused to go back to the USSR with his family and hid somewhere in the boonies of Iran. Eventually, he was picked up by the authorities and delivered to the Soviet border. Kozlov Sr. shared our meal at the student cafeteria and was astounded that "one person could get two rations."

A year ended, Batàlov moved out, and the rest grew closer and moved from dorm to dorm with the same group — until Lev moved out to marry Tanya Shàdrina. A huge Komsomòl wedding was celebrated in the dorm.

In the morning we beset Lev with questions about his first wedding night. "You kno-o-ow, guys," he said in his usual singsong, "kissing is better."

Dima

In February of 1959, Lev Kozlov and I were assigned to share a room with Dima Radỳgin and Lev Netzvetàyev at the Dorogomìlovo Dorm behind Kiev Railroad Terminal.

Dorogomìlovo was built in the early '30s. It was about a dozen six-floor buildings with well-lit staircases and wide hallways, each with common use rooms, washrooms, and bathrooms. Each floor had a large study room. Compared to the misery of Màmontovo, we were in heaven.

During the war, many rooms were taken by families in collapsing houses nearby who never moved out. Thus there was a pleasant, family-like mix of these families and the student crowd.

On the very first morning, Kozlov and I rushed off to class. Our roommates were sound asleep and showed up in class an hour or two later. Good sleep, they explained, is more important than any knowledge.

Soon Dima had a visit from his father Fèdor, a colonel who taught at a military school in Orenburg. He called me outside and gave me a scolding. How could I, the oldest one in the room, recently de-mobbed, fail to discipline two teenage boys? He ordered me to take Dima under my wing.

From now on, Lev Kozlov and I woke them up every morning and forced them to make it to the first class. Naturally, the two were not happy, especially Lev Netzvetàyev, who was in a sense "collateral damage" from Dima's father's visit.

And then there were five of us, after Sasha Batàlov was assigned to the room too. He had been a sergeant in the service and had no problem maintaining discipline. Now all four of us had to tow the line.

In time Dima, Lev Netzvetàyev and I grew close. They were only five years younger, which at this age is a great difference. We belonged to different generations. This turned out to be mutually helpful.

At twenty-three I considered myself a Marxist and a Materialist. My mother's definition was more precise: "an inflexible idealist."

Nothing could shake my positive attitude towards the regime and its ideology. Nothing could make me doubt the correctness of my convictions — neither encounters with anti–Semitism, nor events in the country and abroad, nor discussions with relatives and friends.

During our very first conversation, Dima exclaimed: "Garik, you can't really believe all this junk! Come on! You're putting us on." His generation could not conceive of such conformism.

We spent many an evening in the dorm in these discussions. Dima marveled at my convictions. I was wondering about the problems of my worldview.

College introduced me to a great many people. Yet Dima's arguments seemed the most convincing. They helped me begin looking around me in an unbiased manner and ridding myself of dogmatic preconceptions that took root in my head in early adolescence.

According to Dima, in his childhood and adolescence his favorite pastime was reading the encyclopedia. This gave him a strikingly sensible picture of the world. Besides, he was the only one among us who had read the Bible. With his fine memory he quoted it often and appropriately, evoking my admiration.

With classmates at the Moscow School of Architecture. From left are Dima Radỳgin, Lev Netsvetayev, Sasha Batàlov, the author and Fedor Gagèvsky. Moscow, 1961.

I was also impressed by Dima's passion for drawing anything that moved, from cars to choppers, which he drew from the most improbable angles and in loving detail. Like his watercolors, his drawings were easily recognizable.

In the fall of 1960 we were moved to different rooms. And the next spring all four of us moved back together at Alexèyevski Dorm, a temporary wooden 1937 barrack for construction workers who built the Agricultural Exhibition.

Six months later we were assigned a freshman, Sasha Kiselèv, and we were five again.

Sasha quickly befriended the girls from the cafeteria of the Higher Education Ministry in the school's basement. Some of them visited our room, staying overnight in Sasha's bed. He offered to hook us up, too, but we didn't care for it. We were already inconvenienced in the morning when we were in our underwear with the girls around.

On the plus side, in the cafeteria you had to buy a separate coupon for

During a seminar on the strength of materials. At the blackboard to the right is the author. Moscow, 1960.

every dish, which you redeemed at the counter. We would buy a cabbage salad for a few kopecks. Sasha's girlfriends would coolly accept the coupon and bring us instead a double portion of lamb goulash, worth perhaps ten times more. At first I thought they had made a mistake, but then I got used to it. Dima was uncomfortable with this fraud and tried to avoid it.

We spent our days at the school, running from a lecture auditorium to a seminar to the library to the drafting board. We would come back to the dorm about 9 or 10 in the evening.

Sometimes in the evening we made up our own architectural mini-contests with the kinds of projects our Socialist teachers would never think of suggesting: a jail, a castle, a villa.... Dima and I really went for it.

Lev Kozlov went to see his girlfriend Tanya.

The other Lev — Netzvetàyev — would be drawing, often a self-portrait, which is something we were all fond of. It was a subject that did not need to be coaxed into posing. Netsvetayev was also fond of reading a French dictionary out loud, relishing the music of the language. He adored Pushkin and was a devotee of Mikhail Vrùbel, a Russian painter of the turn of the century.

The chalk caricature on the blackboard depicts (from left) Nonna Selipanova, Dima Radýgin, Lev Netsvetàyev, and the teacher Peter Sipin. Moscow, 1960.

Once he pinned a small pencil drawing over his dorm cot. The manner of the drawing was clearly reminiscent of Vrubel. Lev had bought it for peanuts at a used-book store and claimed it was an authentic Vrubel. We made fun of him throughout the semester. When we had guests, we made a big show of demonstrating a "genuine Vrubel" over Lev's cot.

Before the summer break, Lev unpinned the drawing and took it to the Tretyakòv Gallery, the prime Russian art collection. They were in shock. It turned out to be a work Vrubel had done just before his death. It was known to experts and was considered lost. But buying it? They simply didn't have the resources.

Lev gave it to the museum as a gift. They were so touched they gave him a year's pass to their warehouse, where the "prohibited" works were kept. They also made a few reproductions of the drawing for him for free. He signed one of them for me on the occasion of my 25th birthday.

I often talked my friends into participating in open architectural contests.

The student project for the War Hero Monument, the first architectural competition at the Moscow School of Architecture. The authors were Dima Radỳgin, Lev Netsvetàyev and Gary Berkovich. Moscow, 1958.

The first one we did was a monument to Zòya Kosmodemyànskaya, a World War II underground heroine. We went to show our sketches to my friends, graduate students at the Construction and Architecture Academy who lived in a dismal basement of the famous arc-shaped Tschùsev building on Rostov Quay.

Finally, we submitted a few versions. Lev Netsvetàyev drew a gorgeous night perspective for one of them. The exercise did a lot for our architectural mastery — more than our standard school projects ever did.

Another extracurricular project was a mobile theater for remote areas. That was an international student contest, and our school was assigned two slots. One of them came my way due to my presidency of the Student Science Society, and my "sponsor" Lukàyev's patronage.

Our Levs were not interested, and it was Dima and I who went for it, with Igor Ivanov helping out a lot at the end.

We started out with Dima's idea: an inflatable theater frame would be transported to the location with a special helicopter (Dima was very much into choppers then). Then I improved on his idea. I proposed that we design

The contest project for a mobile theater for remote areas. The contest's program called for the design of a theater to serve hard-to-reach areas above the Polar Circle, where roads are nonexistent. The specially designed helicopter was to inflate and expand its flexible tail to form an auditorium for 100 people. The authors were Dima Radỳgin, Igor Ivanov and Gary Berkovich. Moscow, 1961.

a special helicopter as a flying theater. The inflatable frame of the auditorium would serve as the tail stabilizer in flight.

We were not sure that the machine we designed would take off and fly. We went to see the deputy rector for Science Professor Tùpolev, who was the nephew of the famous aircraft designer of the same name. He called his uncle for help. A few days later the consultant arrived. He confirmed that the flying theater/chopper was quite real and functional. We were immensely proud.

I don't know the subsequent fate of our project. I don't think it made it to the contest. Remember, it was an international contest, and this design was unlikely to be let out of the country. Who knows. A theater designed on the base of a brand-new Soviet military helicopter? Why would the Architects Union take such a risk? What if it was a military secret?

In the dorm we constantly discussed our school projects. We argued about architecture, of course. Where it is like art and where it is not, or whether it *is* a variety of art. Whether the concept of science applies to architecture.

Opposite: The author's design for the First Man in Space Museum. The museum was conceived as a monument to mankind's achievements in space exploration. One of its features — the light beacon — symbolizes our infinite quest for knowledge, extended to other civilizations. Moscow, 1967.

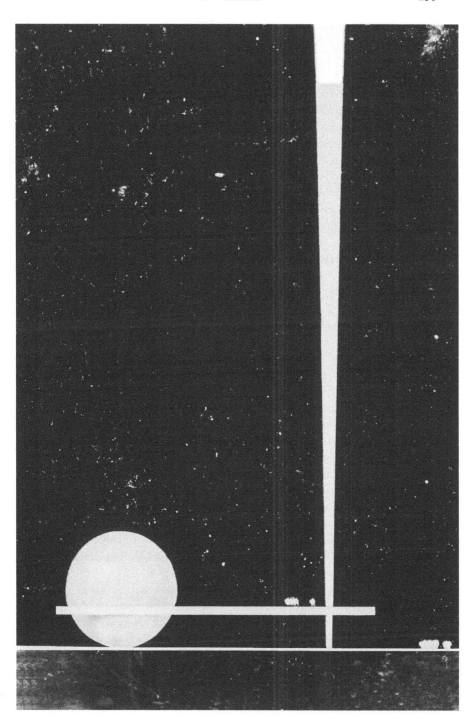

What is the relation between architecture and sculpture, or architecture and construction.... Our arguments often came to the point of fisticuffs.

At one time, I suggested that each narrate his position on paper. Dima instantly grasped the idea. He wrote well, in a fine cultured style. His arguments had impeccable logic. We used this kind of polemics later more than once. Alas, none of this has been preserved.

Lev Kozlov quickly got tired of this. "We-e-elllll, guys, I'm off to hit the sack." And we went off to continue in the rec room, which in Alexeyevka was in a different barrack and had a piano. Dima got at the piano and played decent Beethoven.

As in any dorm in the world, there was plenty of booze. There were never any age limitations on alcohol sales in the USSR. It was not considered a sin to be drunk in your free time. Only bad conduct while drunk was reprimanded. Otherwise, you could drink as much as you wanted — and off to bed!

Once Dima stayed out very late. At night, when we were deep asleep, around 2 or 3 A.M., there was a noise outside. There were two policemen at the door. "You have a Rumanian student named Rumunescu living here?" Without thinking, I nodded. "Well, you can have him." And they pushed Dima — horrendously drunk — inside.

In the morning we learned that Dima had been drinking heartily past the subway closing hour. He had to walk home and was spotted by the cops. Fortunately, he thought fast and pretended he was a foreigner. Otherwise, he would have been put in a drunk tank — which would lead to trouble at the school.

In the early summer of 1960, Dima Radýgin and Lev Netzvetàyev were sent for post-study field work at a construction site in Moscow. Upon completion, a report and a character reference were to be submitted to the school. Nobody at the construction place was eager to waste his time on writing this. The routine was that a student wrote it and the site manager signed. The understanding was that no one would be reading it.

For variety's sake, Dima and Lev wrote character references for each other. The contractor named Goldman signed them. He overlooked a phrase Dima wrote in his paper on Lev: "Comrade Netzvetàyev is very disciplined, except for one time when he showed up at the site in his beard but without underwear."

It was my friends' bad luck that someone read their essays at the construction production chair. A scandal broke out. Both were on the verge of expulsion. I went to see Lukàyev. Somehow the whole thing was swept under the rug. But the vacations started off under a cloud.

That summer Dima, our friend Pasha Kovalèv and I were about to visit Kizhì and Solovets Islands in the far North. I went on the trip earlier, and we agreed to meet at the Solovets. Tired of waiting for them there, I left for Kem on the mainland.

I arrived there aboard the *Karelia* cruise ship. For a while we stayed in the harbor. A drizzle turned into a nasty cold shower. No one was allowed on deck. We were waiting for someone to come pick us up. Finally, a motor boat arrived and moored five minutes later.

The waters were choppy. The boat was thrown sideways. The small engine was sputtering. The passengers yelled at one another. A rope ladder about twenty feet long was lowered from the *Karelia*, dangling along the side. No takers. The passengers were scared.

I pulled up the backpack and my track pants and started my descent. Halfway down the ladder I stepped on someone's hand. I looked down: it was Dima trying to use the same ladder to climb aboard.

In 1961, Dima Radỳgin, Sasha Karvovsky, and I were "caught" after we sent what I thought to be a rather innocent letter to *Komsomòlskaya Pravda* newspaper.

At the time, the authorities were considering holding an Expo in Moscow. To that end, a dozen design proposals were exhibited at Architect House. They were for the most part mediocre, except for one, done by our professor, Yakov Belopòlsky. It was completely ignored by the architecture writers. They praised the ugliest one, by Chechùlin, formerly Moscow's chief architect and a former member of Stalin's infamous VOPRA architectural association.

We wrote in our letter that it was unfair that the most interesting project had been overlooked. We did not know that the exhibition had been visited by Prime Minister Kosỳgin, who passed the presentation indifferently and paused in front of Chechùlin's. The media got the hint. Or, rather, they got instructions.

As for our threesome, we immediately got flunked in a course called Marxist Leninist aesthetics (this was the middle of mid-year exams). One by one, we were summoned to the rector's office to find out who had authored the letter.

Six years later I learned that a close family friend was a journalist who worked at *Komsomòl Pravda*. In violation of the rules, she hid similar dangerous letters and took them home, saving the authors from persecution and, at a risk to herself, warning their authors of consequences. But our letter landed on someone else's desk.

Although Khrushchev gave up the Expo idea, this was not the end of our story.

We were forced to take the Marxist Leninist aesthetics test again. The course was taught by a notorious character named Mozhniagùn. Girls complained that during the oral exam he would put his hand on their knees; if the student protested, he would flunk her. He had a torn nostril. Despite his claims of this being a war wound, rumors said someone had bit it off after drinking too much.

The class of architectural design. From left are Professor Ismail Gaynutdìnov (glasses), Aleksey Shcheglòv, the author, Dima Radỳgin (white shirt), Avraam Urbakh (the instructor), and Professor Michail Sinyàvsky. Directly behind Radỳgin is Lev Kozlov. Moscow, 1961.

After one attempt to get by Mozhniagùn, Dima came to the chair and refused to take his test with him. In an unusual twist of events, a special commission was made up instead.

The Marxism Leninism chair was the most influential at school. We had to take several courses: party history, philosophy history, dialectical materialism, political economy, scientific Communism and Marxist Leninist aesthetics.

Students were to read Marxist classic works and decisions by party congresses and the Central Committee. We needed to present proof we had actually studied all that. To that effect, we took brief notes and submitted them to the chair, where they were duly recorded.

Note-taking on Marxist works was about as much fun as watching paint dry. Dima Radỳgin, as usual, trying to get a little kick, rhymed his in classic hexameter and topped it off by using pre-revolutionary spelling and usage. If discovered, this could have been found subversive — but no one ever read those notes.

I loved Dima like a kid brother and I still do, while forgiving him many things that I still don't find acceptable, especially his newfound conformism. His projects that I recently saw at his Web site are not worthy of his talent.

Surely the creation of an architectural masterpiece requires not merely a gifted architect but also a sophisticated client. Frank Lloyd Wright might not have built his classic Guggenheim Museum without the Guggenheim family.

Close school friends: (from left) Lev Netsvetàyev, Dima Radỳgin and the author. Moscow, 1960.

Who can imagine Fallingwater without Kaufman, and Robbie House without Frederick Robbie. Like many Soviet architects of his day, Dima was unlucky twice. He was born and trained as an architect under the burden of Soviet ideology, and then he had to work in Russia where there are no clients of the kind Wright had. Dima might not have been discovered by a sophisticated client in the U.S., but he would still have had a chance.

It's a shame that Dima was to sell his considerable talent short, whether consciously or not.

Destinies

My schoolmate Sasha Karvovsky was born in Paris. His father, a Russian painter, immigrated to France in the early '20s. Ten years later he married a Russian actress who was touring with her theater — and she stayed with him in France.

In 1955 they came back to Moscow with their two children, Sasha included. Like other returnees of that wave, they were given jobs and apartments out of turn. Soon Sasha married a girl who was his fiancée back in Paris. Her Russian family repatriated too.

A month later he was drafted and sent to serve with tank troops in the Caucasus, on the Turkish border. Soon Sasha's commanders grew apprehensive about his Parisian origins. They were afraid to familiarize the "Frenchman" with the "latest secret achievements of Soviet tank engineering." Sasha was sent away to serve as a clerk in HQ in Tbilisi. Apparently, serving in HQ did not expose Sasha to any secrets.

As an HQ clerk, Sasha was released from the hated barracks routine, like marching, guard duty, and lineups. He could walk around the city in relative freedom, and could even have an occasional meal at the officers' canteen.

One day he stayed after the meal to read a letter from his wife. Naturally, it was in French. He heard someone wheezing behind his back. To his surprise it was one of the waitresses — a plain Russian woman in her fifties, with rough hands, undone hair, and a face that reflected long-time liquor consumption.

She was taken aback when discovered reading over his shoulder. Then she said in unaccented French: "I'm so sorry sir, I just could not hold back. It is not very common to see a Soviet solder reading a letter in French."

Sasha was surprised no less. A Frenchwoman working as a waitress at an officer canteen in Tbilisi?

During the 1917 revolution, her noble-born parents fled to France with their two daughters. The money did not last; the parents soon died in poverty. The two girls survived by working as prostitutes. After ten years, the older one opened her own business in Paris, and the other one (the one Sasha met) went to seek her fortune in Algiers. A few years later she came back, robbed by her lover, and worked at her sister's establishment.

After World War II they decided to return to Russia. They were counting on help from their uncle, a well-known painter and Arts Academy member called Lancerè. But he would not acknowledge them, possibly out of fear.

Stalin treated the first wave of returnees rather cruelly. The two sisters were exiled to the Karaganda Region in Kazakhstan to die. They could not possibly practice the only trade they knew: it was illegal, no one around had any money, and their age was advanced, too. They were starving until a Parisian friend in Tbilisi heard of their troubles, invited them over, and helped them find jobs. Now her older sister was already retired, while she needed to work for another year or two.

She helped Sasha meet and befriend others from Tbilisi's Parisian community, thus making his isolation more tolerable.

Five years later Sasha and I spent a few days in Tbilisi. The sisters were very sweet, coquettish elderly women. They received us very warmly, and I was impressed by their extraordinary affability and zest for life.

Karvovsky

Sasha Karvovsky and I became friends in the summer of 1959 after we traveled together to Pskov, Novgorod, and the Baltics.

This was my first student vacation. I wanted to learn about old Russian architecture—to do a few sketches and watercolors, and to take a few pictures.

In those days I was regularly in touch with my "patron," the college rector's deputy Lukàyev. He often invited me to his office to talk about my successes and routine problems. He was also eager to hear about the dorm and students' opinions. I shared my summer plans with him, and he liked the idea of traveling. He talked to the head bookkeeper, and I was issued funds to buy tickets for five people.

The word spread around the department, and eleven more people joined. The group more than tripled—though the money didn't.

The route became more ambitious, too. Besides Novgorod and Pskov, we decided to visit Nàrva, Tallinn, and Riga. Naturally, we stopped by Ostrov, Izborsk, and other old Russian towns—and picked up Minsk and Vilna on the way back.

In the Soviet Union of '59, we didn't have travel agencies, charter buses, and group rates, but we were young, and travel was fun. We took buses and boats (on Pskov and Chud lakes) and hitched rides from truckers. We slept wherever we could: student dorms and high schools (on the floor between desks) and in haylofts in villages. We ate in cafeterias and had a lot of small adventures. We became friends for the rest of our student years.

I had fallen in love with Tallinn back in my Navy days. Now we went to see Professor Ederberg of the local art school. I brought a letter of recommendation from our own Professor Brunov, one of the most famous architecture historians in the USSR.

Ederberg was an aficionado and a connoisseur of his city. He set aside his chores to spend a few days with us, and thanks to him we visited places that tourists and even locals didn't know about. He showed us residential and public buildings and warehouses and medieval towers. We were fascinated by his stories and explanations, but most of all, we were stunned by the comparisons he made to the world's architecture and by the stories of places he had visited.

Astonished, I dropped, "How did you manage to see so much?"

"That was in the days of Republic of Estonia," he said proudly.

Just before we left I borrowed the institute's 16-mm film camera and, with Lukàyev's help, got hold of rolls and rolls of film. I made a film of our trip and cut it upon our return. I called it *Kolyvan*, which is Tallinn's original name.

Lunchtime during summer travels around the northwest part of the USSR (Pskov, Novgorod and the Baltics). In the foreground are (left) Igor Ivanov, and (right) Dima Radýgin. Pskov, Russia, 1959.

The film became the center-piece of our "creative account" of the trip, along with the watercolors, graphics, and still photo that we mounted at the Red Assembly Hall at our school.

I had long admired Sasha's drawings and paintings, but I had not seen his photos before, and I was overwhelmed. I had been a shutterbug since childhood, and had used a similar Soviet camera, but I could not dream of achieving such quality. I still have and enjoy some of his work.

I was just as impressed by his first architectural project, a single-family dwelling, especially its beautiful facades and open planning à la Mies van der Rohe, fashionable in those days.

Sasha told me that in Paris he had attended preparatory classes at Ecole des Beaux-Arts for two years, but was not accepted, allegedly

The author sketching at the shore of Chud Lake. Pskov, Russia, 1959.

because he was Russian. These classes plus stints at Paris architectural studios put Sasha's designs ahead of my classmates like Lev Kozlòv, who had attended architecture school at Tehran University for two years, as well as Fèdor Gazhèvsky and me, who finished architectural/construction trade schools and had two years of practice at design offices. The rest of the group did not quite realize then what was expected of them.

Unfortunately, Sasha's edge at the starting line subsequently did him a disservice. He became used to getting A's with ease; then he became preoccupied with getting translation jobs, and gradually his edge vanished. A few years after graduation he left architecture altogether.

A Soviet architect could not survive on a salary. Everybody was moonlighting, though architectural moonlighting was not as well-paid as the translations Sasha was doing on the side. He had to support a family with two kids and could not be choosy. With different financial circumstances, he could have quietly put in a few years doing menial jobs at a state design office, and his architectural career would have turned out differently. Although it is hard to say how he would have fared at a Soviet office with his French mentality.

Sasha's greatest tragedy as an architect was his graduation project, "A Residential Complex in Far North." I liked it a lot. His main idea was simple and elegant: large residential blocks with schools and kindergartens locked inside the walls of multi-storied buildings. The apartments were an excellent version of the Soviet constructivist cells that came to Sasha from Le Corbusier's Marseilles project. The design was regarded highly, which led Sasha to believe that he had created a masterpiece that would put our whole school in the architecture history books. Through the rest of his life, his confidence never flagged.

I showed his project to my stepbrother, who had spent most of his life north of the Arctic Circle on the Novaya Zemlya Island. Mark tried very seriously to grasp Sasha's concept and then said, "Well, your friend doesn't know the North."

He explained that the low-hanging polar sun would be heating one side of the buildings only. Since their other side would be cold and the buildings were set on stilts (they had to be, with permafrost), incredibly strong winds would form in the inner yards — too strong for anyone to be there.

His designs were of course never used in real life — neither this, nor his subsequent ones. For the rest of his life he considered himself an unrecognized genius.

Sasha and I spent a lot of time outside school, too: studying for exams together and arguing about architecture and politics. I also grilled him on the subject of France and Paris. We kept going back to his parents' decision to return to the Soviet Union. Sasha invariably defended their actions and cited the incredible reception they got on their return.

According to him, in France his father had to provide for his family by working as a night watchman. His paintings did not sell. Shortly after his return he was admitted to the Artists' Union, got a free studio, and a year later got a solo show at the most prestigious gallery, Artists' Union Central Exhibition Hall on Kuznetsky Bridge. Several of his works were purchased by museums right away.

Sasha often said that life in the Soviet Union was better than in France. His family gained from the move; with their perfect command of two languages and no competition, they made a good living by translating for large publishing houses. When I pressed him about what exactly was better in the USSR for others, he was less than sincere, I believe. He fell back on the standard Party line about absence of unemployment and fear of the future and free medicine and education, etc.

I knew that under no circumstances could Sasha leave the country — even to travel to a socialist country like Bulgaria, to say nothing of France — and this depressed him a lot. He tried to go several times as an interpreter with a delegation, and he could not understand why he was being turned down. Moreover, he was denied chances to work with French tourists in Moscow, to say nothing of official delegations — French architects, for example.

In his youth Sasha had biked around Europe. I was especially stunned by his stories about Switzerland. I kept grilling him. How could he, just like that, hop on a bike and go to another country? What if he had chosen to stay?

"Why? I was fine at home. But if I wanted to stay, I would have to ask for a residence permit."

Accustomed to Soviet non-freedom, I at first would not believe these "fairy tales."

Yet Sasha's nostalgia-soaked stories suggested that he missed France and Paris. Back in France, his mother would talk to him about the buns called "French buns" in Russia and "Moscow buns" in Paris. "You will understand their true taste only back in Moscow!" Yet the Paris buns turned out so much tastier — beyond comparison.

It took the fall of the Soviet power and forty years for Sasha to be able to go back to Paris.

In 1960 we took a trip to Central Asia and the Caucasus.

As the president of student science society, I obtained an official paper from school saying we were on a special field trip to study architectural monuments. This helped us find shelter and sometimes simply open the doors of certain buildings, mosques, and madrasah, ordinarily closed to the public. We spent whole days hanging out in exotic places with our sketchbooks.

In Central Asia our schoolmate Andrey Yefimov traveled with us. Ours was a small school, about a thousand students altogether, so Andrey and I had known each other before. Andrey was a year older and frequented the dormitory room shared by my future wife Marina and two other girls, Lara Pevzner and Valentina Stepanova. He sketched their portraits. After this trip we became friends.

Thirty years later, in the early '80s, our daughter Lana brought a copy of *Soviet Life* magazine from the school library. She showed us the cover with Andrey's picture. "Do you know this architect Yefimov?" Marina and I were delighted to see his picture. He was the one who had introduced us twenty years earlier.

Andrey was a natural artist and constantly drew fantastic pictures of local life. Upon return he had an exhibit at school. I asked him if I could have one. "Pick any one," he said casually. Now Andrey's picture is framed at my office to remind me of the wonderful time we had in Central Asia almost fifty years ago.

In Tashkent we slept at the local polytech dormitory on the ground floor, with metal grates on the windows. At night we were awakened by strange sounds. Someone was trying to pick my shirt off the back of the chair with a long wire hook.

Once we bought some grapes on the street. Then we rinsed them in the irrigation ditch nearby and landed on the bench to consume the large fragrant fruit. And then we saw women doing laundry in the same ditch upstream, and further upstream a little boy peeing in the ditch.

In Bukhara we climbed the local madrasah to do some watercolors. We didn't notice that it grew dark fast. We tried to get down into the courtyard but discovered that the guard had forgotten about us and locked the door to the roof stair, and left. Nights in Central Asia were too cold to sleep on the roof. We shouted, but no one responded. We found a rope to climb down the outer wall, but it was too short. Still, we decided to give it a try. A local denizen saw us rappelling down the wall, took us for thieves, and ran off to get the guard. Fortunately, he took his time.

From the medieval town of Khiva we hitchhiked to Urgench, where we were met by a huge poster that said "Town of Urgench Greets Disciplined Drivers." It seemed that no other kind had ever made it to the town.

From Urgench the Town of Disciplined Drivers we took a plane to Baku — a small Ilyushin-14, popular in those days. It was a sunny day, and we had an excellent view of the Caspian Sea with ships and oil tankers. There were few other passengers, and out of curiosity we wandered into the cockpit.

If it sounds like the distant past from the safety-conscious twenty-first century, what we saw was even more exotic. Both pilots were seated with their backs to the front, facing the radio operator and the hostess. In the middle was an unfinished bottle of vodka and some candy. The four were busy playing cards.

The first pilot was genuinely happy to see us. He offered us a drink and proudly showed us a primitive wire construction under the ceiling that he claimed was "an autopilot of my own design."

We were too young to be scared.

In Baku we stayed with our classmate Nonna Selipanova, who showed us around and filled us in on the local news. Shortly before, Khrushchev had visited the city. The local authorities readied the city for two months. The central avenue that was part of his route was paved afresh — the locals called it "a million for a smile."

From Baku we took a night train to Yerevan. There were few passengers, and, after a full day of roaming the Baku streets, we were hoping to get a good night's sleep. But the moment we climbed into our second-tier cots, the border guards arrived. It turned out that the train was traveling near the border, and so they had to check our papers. My passport was fine, and I was about to go back to sleep, but Sasha's indicated "Paris" as his birthplace, and he was taken away. I dragged my backpack off the shelf and followed him.

The guards delivered us into a practically empty first-class car. They

During travels through Central Asia. An example of Soviet idolatry: next to the author is a half-life size "Great Leader" Stalin monument outside the local library. Bukhara, 1960.

locked us in a compartment with comfortable soft couches — a lap of luxury compared to the car we were moved from — and promised to release us the moment the train turned away from the border. We saw through the window that the railroad tracks were indeed running sometimes on the other bank of the Arax River, i.e. on Iran's, and then Turkey's territory.

Barely did we relax in our newfound luxury than the door lock clicked, and we had visitors: one was a uniformed KGB major, and the other one was in plain clothes. With his puffy face and pince-nez, the latter bore an odd resemblance to Lavrenty Beria, Stalin's KGB chief.

The interrogation took the form of a friendly talk: weather, Caucasus vistas, local customs, girls. A waiter delivered a bottle of Armenian brandy with snacks from the buffet car. The night was sultry; our hosts removed their coats. We were in our undershirts. Sasha instantly got suspicious and alerted me. "Watch out — they may try to rape us." He had an unmistakable nose for that sort of thing.

Indeed, after a few drinks, the Beria look-alike moved in closely and started tugging at my chest hair showing from the undershirt, while cooing "*pepe, pepe*" — whatever that meant — and cackling unpleasantly. With every glass, he moved in closer. Meanwhile the major tried to put his arms around Sasha, met with resistance, and focused on the bottle. Finally, after about three hours, we were left alone. Sasha had his passport back, and we could go back to sleep.

At the Yerevan train station, we came across a very nice young guy who was an architecture student at the local engineering school and who had arrived by the same train. We spent all our time in this wonderful city with him and his friends.

A few years earlier, the Armenians tossed the huge statue of much-hated Stalin off its pedestal and, shortly before our arrival, replaced it with an even larger female figure with a sword. The locals called her Alliluyeva, for Stalin's daughter.

Unlike me, Sasha was not impressed with Yerevan. I was happy to see the buildings designed by Tamanyan, my trade school days' idol.

We decided to hitchhike to Georgia. We rode standing up in flatbed trucks, just like local peasants, for whom this was the prevalent form of transportation. Somewhere around Sevan Lake we picked up a guy with a pig in a poke. Sasha, whose instinct was on the alert, told me to stay away from the pig man. Indeed, after a while, the guy offered me sex. This was not the first time I was thought to be gay, and I learned not to panic. But that time in the truck I didn't know how to get out of it. Sasha only laughed and jocularly suggested that I think about it. He would remember this for years.

In Tbilisi we stayed with Sasha's Paris hooker friends. They lived on the top floor of a typical Tbilisi residential building wrapped with terraces. They did not have much space and set out a folding cot for us next to the door. Sasha joked that, as two men sleeping together in a narrow cot, we would be taken for gays. Indeed, the neighbors chuckled unambiguously as they passed.

In Azerbaijan, we were told that all Armenians are gay. Armenians returned the favor. Georgians called both Azerbaijanis and Armenians gays.

One night our hostesses took us over to visit elderly friends of theirs who had also re-immigrated from France and, it turned out, fought in the Civil War on the Whites' side. After a few drinks one of them, formerly a Cossack officer, started reminiscing about "hacking at Jews and Communists." I called him names and got into a fight. It was not a good evening.

We made our way to Kutaisi and then planned to take a plane for a less than half-hour flight to Mestia, the capital of Svanetia (an ethnic enclave of Georgia). But Mestia was fogged in. A group of fellow passengers, all Svans, suggested we all pitch in, eight rubles each, to hire a helicopter standing nearby. But the pilot wanted more money. Then they took the same offer to the pilot of the plane, and after some hesitation he agreed. Sasha didn't like the idea of flying through the mountains in non-flying weather. Yet we joined the rest aboard a small biplane.

Kutaisi was drenched in sunshine, but, as we approached the mountains, the weather changed. We could not take our eyes off the landscape as the pilot skillfully climbed up the gorge, the wings barely clearing the steep, snow-clad ridges.

Like us, the Svans settled on narrow aluminum benches lining the cabin, eating sausages and cheese with homemade bread and loudly conversing in hoarse voices. Suddenly one of them glanced out the window and rushed forward, where he grabbed the pilot by the throat: "Where you fly, you bastard? Wrong way fly?"

The plane pitched, and we almost hit the mountain. Two other Svans grabbed their friend and pulled him back. One of them explained that we were indeed flying through another gorge — the original one was closed by the fog.

Suddenly we saw the taxiing strip under the plane chassis. The plane passed the hut that was the terminal and slowed down — but did not stop. The Svans started jumping out and throwing out their belongings. We, too, jumped onto fine gravel, and somehow managed not to get hurt.

People ran out of the terminal after the plane. Two of them managed to get hold of the wing and the tail. The pilot paid them no attention. He accelerated, dropping them, and took off.

In the local canteen we made the acquaintance of a Russian-speaking Svan who invited us to visit his friends. They treated us to a drink they called "beer," though it was actually rather crude hooch. It felt impolite to refuse. We passed out in no time. For a few days, we couldn't shake off the effects of this "Svan lightning" and felt drunk after every glass of water.

We told our new friend that we were planning to climb the Svan gorge to the pass to northwest Georgia, and he offered to help. He wrote notes of recommendation on pieces of paper to his friends in the villages on our route. Indeed, whenever we found these friends and handed them his notes, we were received as the best of friends and got a comfortable place for the night with plentiful food and drink.

I kept his last note and back in Moscow asked a Georgian classmate to translate. It turned out to be a series of unprintable words. Since the reception was of stellar quality, I can only wonder whether the combination of curses was the Svan equivalent of recommending a person — or, perhaps, that famed Georgian hospitality was inseparable from humiliating the guest?

Sasha subscribed to the original (as opposed to the censored Soviet version) *Architecture d'Aujourd'hui* magazine, as well as the Sunday edition of *L'Humanité*, the Communist newspaper that was the only French paper available in the USSR. During the long recess, he would settle in a secluded place to read. A Soviet Sunday paper was four pages long, but *L'Humanité* was about fifty pages, some of them with color pictures and chock full of ads. It was as foreign as a newspaper could be. Ever since Sasha and I had grown close, he would share news stories and translate occasional items. Although *L'Humanité* was a Communist paper, it was published in Paris, and, in order to survive, it had to present news differently from *Pravda* or *Izvestiya*.

In the spring of 1960, in the midst of our exam session, the Berlin crisis burst out. The Soviet press reports were scarce and safely removed from the truth. Sasha kept translating articles from L'Humanite, each one more troubling than the other. One day we went to the Sokolniki Park to study in a pleasant setting, and Sasha brought the latest issue. Comparing the articles to *Pravda*'s, we concluded that the world was on the eve of a nuclear war, bound to start any minute. Hence, there was no reason to read for the exam. We spent a whole day wandering about the park, talking about trifles and bidding farewell to the grass and the trees.

We did not pass the exam next morning, yet we still did not care.

The next summer, Sasha "the Frenchman," Yan Dautovsky from Macedonia, Nguyen Chick Luèn (future head of Architects' Union in Vietnam), and I — all from the same study group — were sent to Lvov in the western Ukraine for post-study practice. It so happened that Dautovsky's wife, a student from the Food Industry Institute, was sent to Lvov's winery-cum-distillery for post-study practice, too. Yan had an idea: we came to the distillery, introduced ourselves as students from the same institute as his wife, and asked to be shown around. She confirmed that we went to the same school, and for a couple of hours we were taught about wine production. Afterwards we were brought to the tasting room, which was our target area to begin with.

The drinks were brought in unlabelled lab retorts and served in turn. It

Lunch at high altitude during travels around Upper Svanetia (Georgia). From left are the author and Sasha Karvovsky, a schoolmate. Famous Mt. Ushba looms in the background. Caucasus, 1960.

was mostly cheap table wine and various sorts of port. We were supposed to guess the variety. Incredibly enough, we did most of the time, sending our hosts into rapture. "That's Moscow students for you!" (Possibly, they meant, "Boy, do the students drink in Moscow!")

As a result, we got completely drunk. I have no memory of how we managed to get back to the dorm. All I recall is Sasha dragging me and carrying Nguyen — who was rather diminutive — to the streetcar and muttering, "God, just don't let me lose him somewhere...."

Sasha's occasional stories about his life in France and the news from *L'Humanite* he shared with me were a serious factor in changing my worldview and leaving the mold of ossified Soviet conformism.

Sasha graduated and got a job as a junior architect in a huge Mosproekt design office, while I went off to Siberia and we lost contact for a long time.

In 1969 in Moscow, my wife and I rented a room on Festival Street near Rechnòy Vokzàl subway station. Sasha and his second wife lived nearby. We met a few times. He complained about his life and wished he had not left architecture.

The last time we talked was over the telephone in 2003. We exchanged our e-mail addresses. He sent me a story about our school years, as well as his verses, most of which I unfortunately didn't understand. I promised to send him my memoirs for his consideration. But then our son fell sick, and I withdrew for a few years. When I thought of Sasha again, he had died in a car accident.

Professors

I studied at the department of residential and public buildings design. We were divided into two groups. Our group was taught architectural design by professors Mikhail Sinyàvsky and Ismail Gaynutdìnov and instructor Avraam Urbach.

In his youth, Sinyàvsky was a promising Constructivist. When Constructivism became proscribed, he tried to adjust and switch to imitating the permitted fifteenth-century Italian Renaissance, which until then he didn't know too well. The façade architecture of Soviet neo–Renaissance that took the best years of his life consumed his entire creative potential and turned out to be a dead end.

He taught us at the fading period of his life, intimidated by endless troubles and quarrels in his studio, which consumed his attention and cut into his creative concentration.

The school had to invite a certain number of practicing architects for teaching jobs. Sinyàvsky was one of them, working "half-time," as it was called. Constantly busy at his studio and in endless haggling with architectural bosses, he didn't always show up for class. When he did come in, he was always worried. In a rare moment when he was dealing with someone's project, the whole group gathered around him. Some of his remarks just had to be put down on paper. Alas, we didn't realize it at the time.

These are some of his phrases, always concise and precise.

Urban planning: "An urban district is a big baby. A town of the same size is a tiny old man."

An urban planning project: "Your houses stand around like a bunch of scalded roaches."

About a student named Nonna Selipanova: "So petite and makes noise like a buffalo herd."

As he pointed out someone's lack of attention and observation: "Did you look at the projects in the hallway? Or did you look away on purpose?"

Vladimir Kozyùlya, the son of the deputy minister for construction, had very hard time with designing, and his sketches were absolutely atrocious. Once Sinyàvsky could not hold back any longer and spat out, "This is the kind that graduates and becomes our bosses."

Vladimir merely sighed — heaved, rather — with his whole huge body

Party time at the school. From left are Professor Ismail Gaynutdìnov, the author, Galina Karaseva, Zhenya Kumskova, and Nonna Selipanova. Moscow, 1961.

and said nothing. I don't think he reported Sinyàvsky to his father. He seemed like a decent person.

Unlike Sinyàvsky, Professor Gaynutdìnov was on the faculty and a dedicated workaholic, wrapped in his teaching. I still respect him. He gave intelligent critiques of our work. Once in a while he would cover them with tracing paper and draw something with a thick clutch pencil — something Sinyàvsky would never do, unless a sketch was truly terrible.

As an architect, Gaynutdìnov grew up in the era when decorative architecture zigzagged from Renaissance to Russian Empire styles to ethnic motifs and then back to Renaissance and so on. He stayed atop this wave in rough times due to his natural artistic talent and his natural Tatar wits. In his youth, as the only talented Tatar architect in Tatarstan, he was commissioned to build the Tatar pavilion at the National Agriculture Exhibition in Moscow. He stayed in Moscow. He went to graduate school and became a professor. He told us he was worshipped at home, with many titles and awards, and asked to come back — but for some reason he stayed in the unloved capital.

He honestly tried to give us knowledge — most of which no one was interested in any longer. Like Sinyàvsky, he regularly recommended that we get our inspiration from the foreign journals that now appeared in the school's library.

The other study group at the department was taught by the famous Barkhìns, father Grigory and son Boris.

Before the revolution, Grigory was member of St. Petersburg's Art Academy. Allegedly a *cantonist's* (Jewish soldier's) son, he walked from Siberia to St. Petersburg to study. By the time I saw him at the school he was very old and feeble — very short with a gray beard that came to below his knees, like a wizard in old illustrations to Pushkin's fairy tales.

His son Boris was one of the nicest people I have ever met — a kind, soft, cultured person. Unfortunately, I didn't get to know him very well. The last time I saw him was in 1989 when he brought a group of students and my ex-classmate (and his pet student) Andrei Nekràsov to Chicago.

(Andrei left me a business card that described him as a member of an international architects' skiing club. Perhaps it was risky for his career for the card to make reference to his teaching job in Moscow. The Soviet state had another couple of years to go.)

Boris walked around our house in Deerfield, a Chicago suburb, and grilled me on details. He called my wife "baby" and seemed to be genuinely happy that this structure had been designed by an alumnus of his school.

We had a huge apple tree growing in the back yard, and that fall it yielded a record crop. I brought two huge baskets of apples for his students. Boris was touched: "The kids save every penny, including on food. Thank you very much."

The Barkhins practiced an education system based on the hands-on approach. Fortunately, it was not based on their own projects. For them it was normal to put tracing paper on a sketch and draw their own versions, which sometimes led to a completely different design decision. But when it came to the final stage — presentation — they rolled up their sleeves and armed themselves with brushes.

While critiquing projects, Barkhin Sr. asked to spread the sketches on the floor. Helped by his son, he climbed a stool and assessed the sketches' quality from on high. Once, as he eyed Lena Melchakòva's sketch that followed his own sketches to a T and had been done with his help, he suddenly shed a tear. "So beautiful, so beautiful," he murmured, patting his eyes with a handkerchief.

Barkhin's group's designs were recognizable — they were done in the same hand. The plans were beautifully drawn and presented in the style of the latest foreign publications. The façades were washed in the best classical tradition of the turn of the century and were on impeccably composed boards — we thought of it as an inaccessible level of mastery.

At first we were envious of classmates placed in the Barkhins' group. But

Guests from Moscow in Deerfield. From left are Professor Boris Barkhin, instructor Andrey Nekrasov and the author's wife, Marina Berkovich. At right is the author's self-portrait from school days. Deerfield, Illinois, 1989.

by the fourth year many of us came to realize that while we could not present our works on the Barkhin level, our designs were more independent and original. And if, unlike those by our neighbors, ours pointed every which way, there was nothing wrong with it.

Now, many years later, as we compare teaching architecture according to the Barkhins' method with that being used in America, their contribution to teaching architectural design and the development of Soviet architecture actually does not look all that impressive.

In Moscow in 2005, a friend of mine, Russian architectural academic Alexander Ryabùshin, published a book called *Architects at the Turn of the Millennium*. Russians criticized him for not including any Russian/Soviet architects. "What could I do?" he complained. "None of them comes even close to western ones."

We could find fault with Soviet ideology, which killed every fresh growth, or with backward technology, or with the corrupted selection of human resources. But we should also keep in mind the teaching method that gave

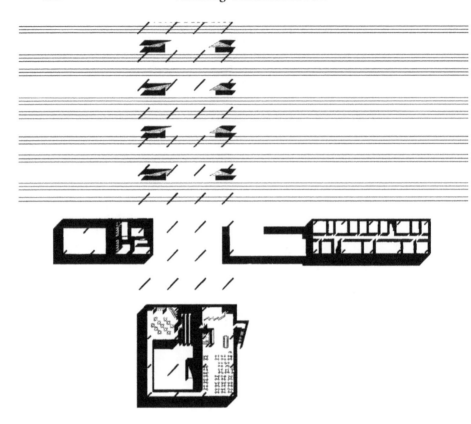

The author's student project for a railroad terminal. The complex was designed to serve as a major transportation hub for a city of 50,000. The main waiting hall is located above and across the tracks. Moscow, 1961.

priority to the graphic presentation of material and copying "the best" — according to today's fashion — samples. This is what our professors were taught to teach. The important thing was to prevent the student from standing out. How many times I heard: "Berkovich, stop trying to be original." It would be unfair to blame merely our school. This was the basis of the entire Soviet system. I didn't think even then that in their own way our teachers were trying to protect us, whether consciously or not.

Architects like Ginzburg, Leonidov, the Vesnin brothers, and Melnikov — those who made Soviet architecture famous in the 1920s — worked in much worse conditions. Yet they were made from other stuff and came from a different culture — the one I came across in the West.

In my last years of college I thought I would be designing, building, and teaching architecture. Life turned out differently. In the USSR, I managed to get into design only. In the U.S., almost by an accident, I got a chance to

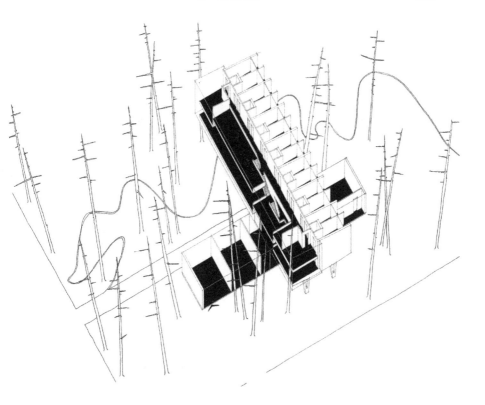

The author's project for a Creative Artist's Union Retreat, designed to host up to 30 artists, including private workshop areas with sleeping accommodations, a small restaurant and a community room for informal meetings. The construction was finished in 1968. Moscow, 1963.

teach, too. I was invited to University of Illinois School of Architecture to be on the jury — to critique and judge students' projects. I had a chance to see western methods of teaching architecture. Years later, I saw them closer when my daughter Lana attended the Yale School of Architecture. Helping a student develop his originality was the main difference from Soviet teaching methods.

But it was not just that in the USSR everybody had to toe the same line. There was no one to teach us, either. There were no real teachers left. Some of our professors like Parusnikov and Mèzentzev realized their professional impotence and drowned it in vodka. Others weren't even aware of it.

One such professor was Akìmov, famous for being Lenin's standing guard at the Bolshevik headquarters in 1917 and for being the brother of a well-known stage director. Our Akìmov was in charge of summer field trips to familiarize students with architectural monuments. His *mots* became part of students' lore. His famous phrase went, "Our side gets up and goes." When

The author's Moscow design office ID. Moscow, 1963.

asked where we were going, he would say, "Forward, always forward." He was also fond of oddly phrased — clearly self-taught — politesse: "My apologies, please," or "Thank you, please." These were his comments on the buildings shown: "Sculptural quality," "Painting quality," "Ruin quality," "Architectural quality." Allegedly, he also used "Fucking-A quality," though I never heard it.

One of the reasons for the backwardness of modern Russian architecture is the so-called Soviet mentality. Even after decades spent in the West we have a hard time squeezing it out of ourselves. My friend Vladimir Donchik, a Leningrad architect-turned-sculptor, thus described his creative torment: "You keep searching for something your own, something unique, inside of you, and then you stick your hand in your soul and you come up with the same goddamn hammer and sickle."

One should expect even less of those who did not go through the baptism of emigration, those who still believe that, as our former Rector Nikolayev put it, "Our school is number one in the world and the best one in Europe." Or those who live in the country where the villainous outfit called the KGB was never liquidated or condemned, but merely renamed — or where a person who once did the bidding of this monster is leading the country.

The Soviet power is long gone, but the Soviet mentality is still there. That is why, despite the wealth of talent left in Russia, Ryabùshin had no internationally recognized name to choose for his book.

One should give credit where credit is due. The Moscow School of Architecture was the best school of architecture in the USSR. One should also keep in mind that it was the only one.

The real value of the school was in its students. They were my real teachers, especially those in my year. It was from them that I learned presentation techniques, drawing, watercolors, a sense of composition, and the logic of approaching design. I developed my understanding of architecture by way of comparison.

After graduation, in the courtyard of the Moscow School of Architecture are (from left) Gary Faif, the author, Sasha Kisilev, the author's wife Marina Berkovich and a friend from Kharkov, Sasha Frishman. Moscow, 1964.

I learned from them, and they learned from me. Cross-pollination was our best professor.

Moscow Vice

In the fall of 1958, a month after I started my studies, I was approached by another student from my year called Sasha Batàlov. He told me he was a member of the Party Committee and I was being given a "social assignment." I was enrolled in the Special Public Order Protection Unit.

I already knew that all the students were enrolled in "public order protection." At least one night every two weeks, they were supposed to don a red armband and hang out in groups of three or four along Neglìnnaya Street and Trùbnaya Square, adjacent to the school. The main contribution to public order consisted of picking up the drunks off the ground and passing them to the cops.

The author's ID as a member of the Special Public Order Protection Unit. Moscow, 1958.

For me, Batàlov had something special. I was enrolled in a special unit that would be fighting prostitution, with Sergei Petròv, a senior, as a leader.

A Komsomòl Congress was coming up, and the center of Moscow was supposed to be cleared of prostitutes — perhaps so that the girls didn't distract the delegates from important business. Officially, prostitution did not exist in the USSR. Hence there could not be a law prohibiting it. The girls were picked up and taken to the precinct. Before being released, they promised in writing they would go straight home. The next day it was the same thing all over again. The authorities could not come up with anything smarter, but at least everyone was kept busy.

Our unit was assigned the south side of Marx Avenue, from Fedorov Monument past the Metropol Hotel via Theater Square along the Moscow Hotel to Manèzh Square. Among prostitutes, this route was known as the Bald Spot.

We were not supposed to turn onto Manèzh Square. The space in front of the hotel's main entrance on the square belonged to the so-called "good-time girls" — who were after adventures and did not charge for love. We were not supposed to detain them. We did look in, though, out of curiosity, and even spotted a girl from our school — a senior.

The shift was usually from seven to eleven or midnight. At first we were helped by local undercover cops who knew all the hookers on sight. Then we got to know all the local habitués and walked around by ourselves. We had to detain the girls at the moment when they made a deal with a client and got into a cab. This was not hard. They worked by themselves without pimps. The johns were detained, too, but they were seldom taken to the precinct.

We learned that Moscow's center was divided into turfs. The turf violators — generally suburban teenagers who had no idea of the rules — were handed over to us by the "competition." Once, however, the competitors led

The author at the Moscow School of Architecture. In the background is an exhibition of his summer works. Moscow, 1960.

us to a 62-year-old, grungy, drunken whore who generally worked the railroad station and thought turning a trick downtown would be easier.

Our prey varied in age from 14 to 60 and even higher. Some of them had factory jobs in Moscow and merely used the Bald Spot for moonlighting. Some lived in the suburbs. We even ran into a couple of girls from the textile mills at Orekhovo-Zuyevo, a few hours away by train. One girl was four (later five) months pregnant, and we let her go in a violation of rules until we saw that she was abusing our kindness. We ran into college students, too, which entailed fierce verbal battles. Police often sent letters to local Komsomòl organizations at the girls' places of work and study, which they didn't like. If they had neither school nor employment to show, they could be indicted for parasitism.

There were setbacks. En route to the precinct the girls started whining and promising they'd never do it again, even promising they'd never charge for their services again and offering to prove it — right now with us. With some patrols they got away with it.

Once this led to a scandal. Early in the shift, a unit led by Slava Glàzychev from my year (now a Ph.D. and an academician) was taking its detainees to the precinct — and disappeared en route together with them. The incident became the subject of a Komsomòl meeting. With Slava narrating the story in racy detail and begging forgiveness, the transcript would have read like a comedy show.

My service at the "vice unit" lasted for a few years. It turned out to be easier to get into than out of. I tried to quit several times, and always was warned by our leader Sergei Petròv of harsh consequences. I left "the force" later on when my good standing in the school was ruined already.

A few years later, one night my future wife Marina and I were walking to the Revolution Square subway station. As we crossed the Bald Spot, I was greeted by a few girls whose appearance left no doubt as to what they were doing there. This more than raised Marina's eyebrows. And I had to confess.

Top: The Revolution Day demonstration. From left are Lev Netsvetàyev, the author, Nonna Selipànova, Dima Radẏgin, and Lisa Liberman. Moscow, 1960.
Bottom: The author and his wife Marina Berkovich (Guz). Moscow, 1962.

Kòndos

In the fall of 1960, I was transferred to another dorm at Dorogomìlovo. Now I was sharing a room with Batàlov and Sòtos Kòndos, a student from Macedonia. We had a few Macedonian students, children of émigrés from the last Balkan war. We called them Greeks.

On the very first day Kòndos suggested taking turns using the room if one of us would bring a girl over. Sasha and I didn't have girls; we came from school late at night, and thus had no intention of taking advantage of the arrangement.

Kòndos picked up girls in the morning in the subway en route to school. Instead of proceeding to class he brought them back to the dorm. We got used to it and paid no attention.

One day one of the girls showed up out of turn and found Kòndos with the competitor. Enraged, she wrote a complaint letter to the administration, claiming she was pregnant by Kòndos.

Sasha and I were summoned to the administration. The investigation was conducted by Deputy Rector Shutìlov, who, rumors claimed, had been a Gulag camp commander in the past. He would not even listen to our explanations. Instead, he gave us a sheet of paper each and suggested that we put it in writing.

I wrote that nothing had happened in front of me. I had never seen the girls in the room (only once, in the evening, but they were dressed and were quietly drinking vodka). I did not deny that en route to classes in the morning Kòndos had repeatedly gone his own way. But what had happened later, I had no idea.

Sasha told me that he did not hide anything.

Shutìlov was not happy with my testimony. He said Rector's Deputy Lukàyev was counting on me. He thought I was someone they could rely on, someone who would be telling things honestly and in detail. Actually, since I was sharing a room with a foreigner (he got that right — despite Kòndos's Soviet citizenship, upon graduation he left for Greece), I was supposed to be reporting regularly on his behavior and conversations. Shutìlov would not let me go until I promised him I would. Later, he would often stop me in the hallway. Why was I not reporting anything? The reference to Lukàyev made me uneasy. But soon I forgot all about it.

A few days later the dorm called a student meeting, attended exclusively by girls. Almost all of them came from other schools. Each considered it her duty to speak and condemn poor Kòndos.

When Kòndos got the floor, he rose and said proudly: "If I'm such a bad person, let at least one of you get up and say I made her lose her innocence. Or that she was not satisfied with me."

No one rose. He turned ... and left.

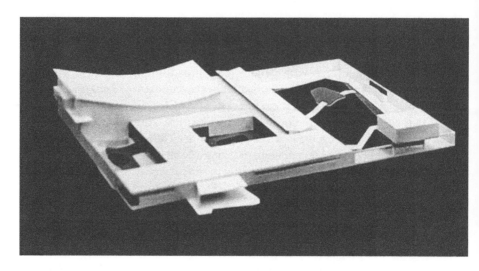

The author's student project for a community center in southern Russia. All elements of the complex (an auditorium for 700 people, library with reading room, youth and activity rooms) are grouped around a courtyard with a reflecting pool as one of the central compositional elements. Moscow, 1960.

Batàlov

Soon after the Kòndos story, Batàlov told me that he was being moved to the foreign student dorm in a high-rise on Lenin Hills. The accommodation was two persons to a room, and each two rooms had a separate bathroom (unlike in our dorm with a bathroom per floor). The only thing was that you had to write regular reports on your roommates — what they talked about and whom they met. But that was not such a big deal, right? Sasha offered me the same bargain.

Paying for comfort with informing was not my idea of the good life. I suspected that Sasha was merely a messenger and decided to give it a chance to go away. I told him I would think about it. Strangely enough, nobody from the administration approached me with that directly.

A few days later Sasha came back — had I made up my mind? "Nature abhors a vacuum." In fact, Deputy Rector Shutìlov, responsible for assigning dorm space, promised Deputy Rector Lukàyev to hold my spot for a couple of days — not more.

I didn't like it that Lukàyev's name came up. I realized this needed to be faced and told Batàlov rudely that I was not going to be an informer.

He took umbrage. "You shouldn't say things like that."

We never spoke about it again. He spent a few years living with foreign students, counting a year of studying abroad in East Germany. He came back to teach us the proper way of saying "Leipzig." He was very happy about his life choice.

As for me, I was soon moved to the ramshackle barrack of Alexèyevski Dorm in the All Union Exhibition area.

I once was an ideal conformist. I vehemently "exposed American imperialists" at Komsomòl meetings. I started having problems with the administration after giving up my chance at deluxe accommodations with foreigners. Yet it took me a while to put two and two together.

Sasha was a good-natured guy from Murom, deep in the Russian province. He entered school straight after the army. His freshman year he was sent to Kazakhstan right away to harvest the crops. There Sasha befriended the deputy head of the chair of Marxism, who became his "patron."

Sasha was a diligent student, but he had a hard time studying. His casual aperçus spread by word of mouth and became famous throughout school.

"Lisa Liberman has a wonderful grandma, especially her mom."

"More and more I can't do it."

"Garik Berkovich is a plain Russian peasant."

"Nothing gets in my head except for various thoughts."

"Compromise is when you come into a room and they are cursing inside and then they tell you that you are the one who brought about the curses."

In 1960, Sasha and I were in the same construction crew that volunteered to build housing for peasants. A few days after we arrived, he got drunk and fell from the hayloft, landing on a rake. He spent the rest of the time sick. At least he didn't become crippled.

Sasha was always fond of tippling, though I wouldn't call him a drunkard. Both Dima Radỳgin and he were sent to Kazakhstan to teach at a local engineering college. Not one evening was complete without booze. Dima's physique turned out to be weaker, and he became saddled with this problem for the rest of his life. Sasha was unaffected.

On his way back from Kazakhstan to graduate school in Moscow, Sasha got drunk and passed out in the plane's toilet. At the airport he had to be extracted by the squad team.

When we shared a room at the Dorogomilovo dorm, there was a string of thefts. Someone broke into our room while we were in class. Sasha figured out the culprit, a kid of about eighteen, and not a student. There were some families who had moved in during the war. He called Dima and Lev Kozlov and me into the room and gave the suspect the third degree.

I feel ashamed recalling this. Sasha put the guy on a chair and beat him to a pulp. The suspect didn't confess. Yet after a few days, he returned some of the stolen money. He said he had spent the rest.

Once, when we were already in graduate school, he helped Dima and me with our residential housing contest project. We overlooked that at the last moment he mistakenly added two bedrooms in the two-foot-high attic. (Neither did the jury. We got an honorable mention.)

After graduate school he became an instructor at our school. By now he must be a full-fledged professor.

Edith

According to Pushkin, Peter the Great cut for Russia "a window into Europe." In 1959, Khrushchev decided to follow his example and cut a door into the West (some would say the project never got past the peep-hole). For the "axe," Khrushchev decided to use an American exhibition in Moscow.

The ground for the exhibit was broken in Sokolniki Park.

As an architecture student in Moscow, I was curious about everything American, the architecture especially. I visited the construction site often, and sketched the erection of the main pavilion, a sphere designed by the great Buckminster Fuller.

In August, the exhibit finally opened. Although most of the tickets went to those with connections, as well as "best factory workers" in plainclothes, by a sheer miracle I managed to get one, too. Naturally, I headed straight for the architecture section, where a huge computer "answered" the visitors' questions. After standing in a long line, I got to pick a question from the list and, after pushing a button, received a printout of the answer. My query was about Frank Lloyd Wright, and I was upset about how primitive the procedure was. Such was my belief in the miracles of American technology that I had hoped that the machine would actually answer my question, rather than feed me something manufactured in advance.

As I stood there, re-reading the answer, I heard a fight starting behind my back. A drunken "prole," who must have received his ticket at his factory along with a bottle of vodka, grabbed a modestly dressed young man and yelled at him: "So you came to see the show, you kike? Why don't you shove off to your Jew-land!"

I came close, and being a devoted Soviet, tried to reason with him. "You shouldn't be doing this, shame on you, Americans are taking pictures." Nothing worked. Someone had already called the police.

A young American girl guide came up from behind to ask me in Russian, "What is this man saying?" Still a patriot, I told her he was a regular drunk and not worth the attention he was getting.

The drunken hoodlum kept exhorting that "all the Yids should be sent to Palestine!"

"Who should be sent to Palestine?" the guide persisted.

"The Yids!" he yelled before being hauled away.

The girl seemed about five years younger than I. She was a brunette with bright eyes and full red lips. I could not take my eyes off her. We fell into conversation. She turned out to be a sophomore from Cornell University.

Her Russian amazed me — though she had studied it for a mere year. I wondered if she came from an émigré family. Nothing of the kind — she just picked it as a second language.

As she offered me her hand, she eyed me attentively. "Shalom, my name is Edith."

She asked me a natural question: Why was I, a Jew, taking the anti–Semite's side? I hemmed and hawed as to how it was a rare occasion and that anti–Semitism in the Soviet Union was a thing of the past — the capitalist past. Inciden-

Edith Rogovin Frankel. 1959.

tally, the anti–Semites were not as active publicly then as now. Yet I, too, was a much greater fool than later.

She was called aside. While I waited for her, I lost interest in the rest of the exhibit. Finally, I got a chance to talk to her, and — in a gesture completely atypical of me — offered to meet her after the closing and show her the city at night. For example, I could show her the Moscow subway.

To my surprise, she quickly said yes, and we agreed to meet outside the park gate.

When Edith finally came, it was already dark, and she was not alone. She was accompanied by a guy named Joe. I was upset. And I recalled yesterday's newspaper article about CIA agents who had arrived using the cover of exhibit guides — including Joe, who was stationed near the voting machine exhibit. I asked him if this was about him, and he said it was — that he was the guide near the voting machine, that is.

Now I really felt sick. Joe, who spoke Russian better than Edith did, asked if I was afraid to talk to Americans just like that, in the open. He knew I could get in trouble for that.

Of course I was scared shitless. But I could not really show it. Anti-Soviet propaganda, I told Joe.

"Let me show you a trick," Joe said. "There are two men in identical hats following us — do NOT turn. Right now, they will pass us. Then one of them will turn towards us and look at his watch with its dial turned towards us. You will be part of the group picture. Aren't you afraid?"

Everything happened exactly according to this scenario. The clothing and the body language of the Men in Hats were painfully familiar.

I promised to show my new friends the most beautiful subway station. I brought them to the Palace of Soviets, now known as Kropotkin — the most spacious, bright and elegant station in the system. Both sighed relief and confessed they had expected something tacky, à la Komsomòlsky on the Ring Line.

Our "guardian angels" in hats must have been surprised, too. As Joe had predicted, they turned out to be subway lovers, too — and spoiled my evening. God forbid, it could have been my whole life. It took me a while to settle down and get to sleep on my dormitory cot.

Yet I wanted to see Edith again. Soon, I got lucky for the second time. I wrangled tickets for another hard-sought exhibit, one of Czech glassware. I traded one of them for the American exhibit in Sokolniki.

Edith asked me warily how I got the second ticket. She knew it was no simple matter and heard my explanation. Then she became worried that our meetings would land me in trouble and wondered whether I could get kicked out of college because of her. I kept toeing the Party line: This is a free country, and I have nothing to worry about. I told her what a great life we were living here, with free college education and scholarships and summer travels and hiking in the mountains.

We met without Joe. I wanted to come pick her up at the hotel, but she vetoed the idea. It turned out I was not the only Soviet she had met. A couple of young men from the Baltics came to visit her and were spotted. On the train back, they were assaulted and beaten up. One of them came back to Moscow and showed her the injuries. Now she was afraid something similar would befall me, too.

I did not risk inviting her over to the dorm. I did not want to scare her with our slum.

Her lovely accent and her cute mistakes in Russian charmed me completely. She seemed to be enjoying talking to me as well. Yet she was to leave a few days later. We exchanged addresses and agreed to write.

I gave her my best watercolor from the summer travels: sundown at the Pokrov church outside Novgorod. She gave me a catalog for the art section of the exhibit — a rarity, with all the copies gone on the first day. She signed it for me, too.

The most amazing thing is that no one summoned me afterwards. Our meetings had no visible consequences. I could only guess why. Maybe the picture was unclear, and they could not identify me, or accidentally I succeeded in losing the tails in the subway, or they were too busy with the guys from the Baltics already....

I sent her a few postcards, but never got an answer. I took umbrage and tried not to think about her anymore.

Over thirty years passed. One day our son Slava was looking for a book on the shelves and ran into Edith's catalog. He asked who Edith Rogovin was and why she signed it. I told him of our meetings. He was surprised: how come I had never tried to find her in America when we arrived twelve years ago?

I had no idea how to go about it. It's a huge country. She must have gotten married and changed her last name.

Slava persisted: it couldn't be that I didn't know anything else about her. Finally, I remembered. She had mentioned growing up in Buffalo, N.Y. Slava called the local directory. Buffalo had only two Rogovins. One of them was her aunt, and the other one was her mother. She told me that her daughter and husband lived in Jerusalem and would soon come to visit.

Two weeks later my phone rang. "Gary! You're in America! Mazel tov!"

It turned out that Edith's visit to Moscow — taken almost by accident — was crucial in her choice of career. At that point she still did not know what she would be doing. But meeting the boys from the Baltics and me and other visitors to the exhibition got her interested in Russia and the history of Russian — and subsequently East European — Jews. She married a British Jew and together they immigrated to Israel, where they got their Ph.D.s and were now teaching at Hebrew University in Jerusalem. They often hiked in the mountains. When I reminded her about my climbing hobby, she laughed. "I must have always had a soft spot for mountain climbers!"

She told me that my now-framed watercolor is hanging in a prominent spot in her house. She remembered me and wondered why I had never answered her letters. I wondered why she hadn't responded to mine.

We talked for over an hour.

That very night we had a visitor — Carol Avins, a Slavic professor at Northwestern, and one of our closest friends in the U.S. She listened to my story with undivided attention. Was my Rogovin friend the author of a famous book on Tvardòvsky? I didn't know, but probably. She was a Cornell graduate, an aliya to Israel, and a professor at Hebrew University. Everything fit.

Carol was stunned by our meeting and the reminder of what a small world we live in. When she was young, she was thinking of a career in music. It was exposure to Edith, or Dr. Rogovin Frankel, and her articles and books and speeches that led Carol to become a specialist in Russian language and literature.

The Honeymoon

The summer of 1962, my wife Marina and I traveled Russia. We were just married and remember that journey as our honeymoon.

One of our goals was to see what had happened to the "housing communes"— residential complexes where most services are delivered on the community level.

Most city residents then led a miserable existence in "communal" apartments, or large apartments in pre-revolutionary rental buildings that were now divided, one family per room. Housing communes would be an improvement over these: each family would get an apartment of its own, however small. The social design of these complexes was based on "liberating women" (i.e. from kitchen work and looking after children) and maximizing tenants' involvement in community affairs. Housing communes also promised economic benefits. Since everyday needs were met in a communal fashion, the living space could be cut to a minimum. In theory, that meant building more apartments for the same money.

The idea of the housing commune was supported by huge numbers of working people who were born in villages and had lived in the pre-revolutionary and Soviet-era barracks in the numerous fast-growing settlements outside the mammoth factories being built. These people were used to the traditional Russian communal way of living and wanted communal services because they would have a room the same size but their life would be more tolerable. They loved the idea that they would not have to use their space for cooking on the smelly kerosene stove, keep the perishables in a bag outside the window, do their laundry in a washtub, and use a bucket or a hole in the ground at the end of the hall for toilet. Instead, they would get a communal dining room, a laundry room with industrial washers, a separate toilet, and large public spaces for studies and recreation. They would also take their children to a kindergarten nearby.

At the same time the authorities — the client — supported housing communes for their beloved ideal of collectivization (full socialization and destruction of everything individual), which was in tune with the farm collectivization then being conducted in the country. By eradicating private life, the Party hoped to control family life as well.

One of housing commune projects we visited was in Saratov, on the Volga River. By chance we ran into an elderly woman who in the 1920s and 1930s had participated in the movement for the construction of housing communes and who was still living in the building.

She invited us into her place, got out a *samovar* (Russian tea-kettle), and told us her story.

In the late 1920s, together with other enthusiasts, she dreamed of the idea of "a man of the future." Although most of the population was driven to Socialism by force, she and her comrades naively hoped that in their lifetime the whole country would turn into one large commune. Being idealists, they believed in Communism and thought it was their duty to organize and build a cell of the future society.

Saratov then was a place with no money, no building materials, and no trained labor force. The future "communards" had saved for the housing for years. They toiled after work and on weekends. Finally in 1932, the complex was completed, and they moved in.

Because the food supply in the country was short, the kitchen factory, which was supposed to replace conventional apartment kitchens, was closed. Meals had to be cooked at home, but there were no kitchens, and so space had to be assigned on the landing at the end of each hallway — only three for the entire 120-unit building.

Thirty years later, the kitchen factory was still closed, and tenants were still using the makeshift kitchens.

The next problem: the kids were supposed to go to nursery school, but there wasn't room for everybody. And the facilities lacked proper sanitary conditions. The children were getting sick. Later they grew up and started families of their own. There was nowhere else to move because of the housing crisis. So they had to stay in the same place, in the small, already crowded apartments designed for two people. With all these hardships no one any longer had the strength or desire to participate in public life.

Self-management of the commune was soon dismissed by the authorities. The building passed into the hands of the government and the *communards* turned into tenants. The money they had spent on construction was "voluntarily" transferred to the "Fund for Socialist Construction."In the years of raging Stalinist repression, no one would think of protesting.

In the late 1940s, their grandchildren started families of their own. But the country was still in the same chronic housing crisis, so they brought their spouses (and later, children) into the same old overcrowded rooms, 15 to 20 square meters (approximately up to 200 square feet) each, which now accommodated more than three generations.

Many former enthusiasts died. Some were killed in the war, some passed away from old age, and many perished in the Gulag camps. The survivors had long forgotten their ideals in the constant struggle for survival. To their children and grandchildren, the ideas of the Communist lifestyle were alien. Few people in the country bought these "fairy tales" by now.

The hospitable woman in Saratov was moved by the fact that someone was finally interested in the honeymoon of her life.

Brought up by the Soviet system, we could not think that these experiments on humans — under the conditions and in the form that they had been conducted — could only have eradicated everything natural, personal, and inimitable from these people.

We were just entering our own post-honeymoon experience.

NSE

In the early '60s, I happened to witness a most interesting development at our school. A group of students at our department came up with an idea they called New Settlement Element, or NSE.

At first I thought it was just another folly of the administration's pets, especially since the NSE promoters included Andrei Babùrov, whom I disliked from the start. His father, a professor at our school, was one of the architects appointed by the Party to smash the architectural avant-garde of the '20s.

I had known him since 1959. Along with Fedor Gazhèvsky, I was helping our Professor Gaynutdìnov to develop a contest project for an experimental district in Moscow. Gaynutdìnov's residence units got the highest marks from the jury in this section of the contest.

The deadline was close, and we worked late, without raising our heads from the drafting boards. Suddenly a big guy, slightly drunk, burst in and noisily went on to look for something, throwing around drawings and boards. Gaynutdìnov asked him to be quiet. "You, Ismail, should shut up," the guy responded.

Fedor and I were in shock. Gaynutdìnov's lips and hands were trembling. The oaf left. We were without a clue. Just like that, quite casually, one could insult an elderly, well-respected professor?

Once Gaynutdìnov calmed down, he said sadly: "You have just seen the son of Babùrov. He can hurt anyone with total impunity."

But the NSE group also included Alexey Gutnòv, and that made me take it more seriously. I respected him. He was two years older and headed the students' Science Society. It was he who had helped me get film for my first summer trip. Then, when I replaced him in that position, he helped me learn the ropes. I really admired him. He was gifted, bright, and full of energy. A born organizer and great company. He was what the late constructivist Ginzburg must have been like.

The idea was to build new towns in "new settlement elements," or NSEs. Each was a complete entity that was not planned for growth. According to this idea, cities would grow by adding new elements, rather than by developing existing ones. This was yet another attempt to design an "ideal" city of the future, this time, out of NSE building blocks.

NSEs were living areas for 1,500 to 2,000 people, joined into larger areas of 25,000 each.

I don't know if NSE-ists knew, but in Central Asia this element of urban settlement, called *mahallàh*, has existed for centuries. Each *mahallàh* was about 2,000 people strong. This figure, arrived at empirically, is the maximally sufficient population of a primary cell of a medieval town. The size of a *mahallàh* allows its citizens to know one another and thus secures strong social connections. This is enough for economic expediency of the primary service network. A city grows by building additional *mahallàhs*.

Now our students used the same method for modern Soviet urban planning, basing it, naturally, on the Party's Marxist-Leninist program.

The sociological basis of NSE was developed by Georgii Dumentòn, a Marxism professor. (Later Dumentòn would move to an institute within Academy of Sciences. In 1964, he refused to sign a sycophantic letter from the institute to "our dear Nikita Sergèyevich Khrushchev." While he was being expelled from the Party, Khrushchev lost his job. Consequently, Dumentòn was treated with respect and fear.)

The social basis of NSE was a set of long-forgotten ideas of Constructivists' Housing Communes. At the same time, the architectural solutions were imitations of western projects of that day that found their way to the school's library.

When NSE postulates were first made public, I had not seen them before and did not understand much of what I saw. I admiringly peered at the recondite tables and charts. I was especially impressed by the project's strong suit — its presentation, including an incredibly well-made film narrating NSE's main ideas.

At the time I was deeply into constructivist legacy. I thought something very serious was taking place at the school. Stunning student ideas were in the air, aimed at the future of architecture. Analogies to projects by Ginzburg, Leonidov, and the Vesnin brothers came to mind.

My first sobering moment came when no one at the administration was overjoyed at my presentation on Constructivism. At first I thought it was due to the flaws in my work. Much later I figured out one of the main reasons. My work was initiated "from below," which was never welcome in Russia. It's too bad that our Rector Nikolayev never thought of entrusting me with research on Constructivism.

NSE was his baby. Nikolayev spotted a group of capable students with Alexey Gutnòv at the head, who had until then been brought together by amateur theatricals. Nikolayev did a good job of channeling the students' energy. If the idea of NSE had been born in their group, no one would ever have heard of it. But it was "dropped from the top" as a part of some complicated political game. Nikolayev created great PR for the project, involving the media. He even allowed those in the project to stay on at school for an additional semester — and some of them for a year — at state expense, which was utterly unprecedented.

Unfortunately, NSE came to nothing. Perhaps Nikolayev didn't have the guts to take it to the finishing line. Perhaps he got bored with it. Perhaps he was told upstairs not to stick his neck out, and he got scared.

I attended the NSE's final presentation. I remembered the speeches made by Nathan Osterman and Konstantin Ivanov. The latter declared he was ready to hire all participants and let them continue the project at his Architectural Theory and Practice R&D Institute.

Perhaps this was what killed NSE. Perhaps Nikolayev did not like this scenario. One thing is for sure: he failed at playing the NSE card to the end. The moment he realized it, he forgot all about NSE and got busy with something else. A vital, moderately original and interesting urban-planning idea came to naught. And yet as a phenomenon, NSE was a considerable Soviet achievement that went beyond our school. This was a breakthrough in the rigid Socialist official regulation of urban planning.

NSE had a great effect on me. NSE-ists inspired me to study the '20s Soviet avant-garde more substantially. They made me ponder the methods of scientific approach in this work and wonder if my worldview was wide enough.

The West did not notice NSE, though our rector created some PR there, too. The NSE book about their project came out in Milan in Italian and in New York in English. But NSE was an overly Soviet phenomenon. It could be taken seriously only within the framework of a socialist economy. Its authors tried to use the system's totalitarian advantages.

It looks like this flaw was shared by my Ph.D. thesis as well. Unlike the NSE developers, I was lucky to see it in person when, in early '80s, I had a chance to try out my ideas in the West. Bruce Graham, the principal of a huge U.S. firm called SOM was interested in my ideas in the area of housing and entrusted me with a manual on designing residential housing. I thought of a two-volume work. The first one, the analysis of experience, came out and is still being used. But I never finished the second one, which contained a prescription for action. One of the main reasons was that my old ideas belonged in the socialist economy framework. To raise them to a level unconstrained by a political system was to begin all over again. Thus they still gather dust, waiting for their time.

A few years after their triumphant presentation, the NSE developers were hired to teach at the architecture school — all but their main ideologist, theorist, organizer and leader, who formulated NSE's main postulates — the talented Alexey Gutnòv. Could it be that his mother's Jewish roots got in the way?

7

Siberia

From Moscow to Novosibirsk

The radio aboard the train announced that the head of state, Party General Secretary Nikita Khrushchev, had requested the Politburo to release him from his duties — for "health reasons," to be sure.

I lay on the upper cot and watched my fellow passengers discuss this epochal announcement with a great deal of agitation. I added my two cents in here and there, just to be polite. But my mind was elsewhere. I was depressed, and the rhythmic sound of the wheels brought no relaxation.

I had just obtained an architect's diploma. And yet I was traveling to Siberia to work in the land utilization business — for three years. Not of my own free will, but to work off my debt to the state for my supposedly free education.

Although the verdict appeared to be fair, it did not take much to realize that whatever the state had spent on my education it had earlier taken out of my pocket. It was but a fraction of what the state was taking away from us — the difference between the cost of what we produced and our tiny salaries. But even so, I was not worried about the "debt." I had already paid one in the form of three years of military service. At the time I had no doubt that it was natural and fair. How come I was depressed now? How come I found myself aboard this train against my will?

I spent the trip analyzing my conduct in the last six years, when I had attended architecture school. And I found more than one reason why I had ended up on this train. The main one was the absence of *propìska*, or Moscow registration.

Propìska is a simple word that stands for one of the most cherished chains that kept Soviet citizens in place. I doubt that a non–Soviet person would comprehend the awe we felt toward this magnificent chain, and the way we adjusted our necks to be comfortable with this chain.

Everybody knew that *propìska* could be "permanent," tied to the main residence and the place of birth; or it could be "temporary," for those who for some reason could not get hold of "permanent."

We did not have the right of moving freely about our own country; were we really justified in calling it our own?

Like everyone else, I was never outraged that the government should decide which cities and towns should be supplied with sausage and cheese and kitchen furniture. And that Moscow—the national capital exposed to foreigners' eyes—should be getting a lot more of these goods. Everybody was equal, but some were more so.

I treated this injustice calmly and for some reason never even grumbled.

I serenely watched the country denizens—in theory, food producers—besiege the food stores in the towns where authorities allowed minimal means of subsistence. I knew that these villagers were picked up and deported back to their villages to starve. I tried to believe the explanation that the state tried to satisfy the population's needs the best it could.

I saw that research, cultural, and educational facilities were concentrated in the same areas that got food. And I was not surprised that people tried to move there by hook or by crook from the areas with the artificially manufactured low quality of life.

I never argued the claim that *propìska* was the only means of holding people "in their place."

I closed my eyes to various ruses that the double-dealing authorities employed in order to support the system. Sending graduates to the areas for the less fortunate was just such a ruse, but I had never thought about it until it became personal. You don't learn from the experience of others.

I used to deal with more serious things like science and learning. Now that I had a chance to look around, the scales fell from my eyes. "Good chow" was not the only reason Soviet citizens strove to get *propìska* in big cities with higher quality of life. They wanted to belong to the elite, with a choice of jobs and schools and entertainment.

I knew the importance and the hard work it took to get in, ever since Yemelyàn Budyònny, the brother of a famous Soviet marshal and now an alcoholic VIP retiree had offered to arrange a Moscow *propìska* for me. At the time I turned it down: I didn't want to get involved in a dubious affair. I wanted to be without sin in the land where pulling a fast one amounted to a civic virtue. I was a romantic who had a very vague idea of the scale and the solidity of the web that held us.

Now I tossed and turned on the top cot. If I only had *propìska*, my whole life would have turned out differently. I would have found a job designing my favorite residential buildings. Plus I could be moonlighting enough to buy a coop and resolve my living problems.

Once you had *propìska*, finding a job was a snap. Skilled people who actually wanted to work, rather than do a nine-to-five, have always been in demand. If a person was politically kosher, he was impossible to fire. In a state without unemployment, everybody is tenured.

I could not bear thinking that I had had to leave behind my wife Marina, a college senior without a home, and our nine-month-old daughter Lana in an orphanage (though an elite one — for foreign students' kids).

At first I tried to find a job close to Moscow, which did not require a *propìska;* at least temporarily, until Marina graduated, and keep my family together. I even visited a place like that on the list for graduates. But hiring a Jew was out of the question. They belonged to the military.

Originally I had counted on staying at postgraduate school, with my top grades and a diploma thesis sophisticated enough to be a Ph.D. dissertation.

Many professors, all respected names in architecture, recommended me for postgraduate studies, including Graduation Commission Chairman Nikolay Kòlli and Architectural Theory Institute Director Konstantin Ivanov. They believed my thesis should be completed and enlarged into a Ph.D. dissertation. In 1964, it looked super-innovative in its introduction of computer technology in architecture.

Yet I did not get into postgraduate school. Then Ivanov tried to get me a position at his institute — but even he could do nothing in the absence of a *propìska.*

On the other hand, it was highly irresponsible and naïve and even juvenile to assume that even with a *propìska* a Jew was a shoo-in for postgraduate school.

A stunningly idiotic case of confusing dreams with reality, I concluded. Yet I was still young enough to be hopelessly caught in the web of "what-ifs." If I had a *propìska*, not only would I be working at a design office, but I could also get into postgraduate school part-time.

My future dissertation was as much of a sore spot — perhaps even worse — as my *propìska.*

Perhaps I was wrong to be obsessed with Moscow, I thought. But the alternative was settling down in Novosibirsk and becoming a land use expert, as the authorities mandated.

In the first place, I could not do it emotionally. Architecture was everything to me. And why should I? *A debt to the Motherland? Plizzz.* It was not quite clear who owed whom.

In Moscow I had friends and relatives and some connections. All I had in Siberia was the prospect of being the cock of the local walk. There was only one architecture school in the country — in Moscow — and who could doubt that its training was a cut above provincial architecture departments?

Fine. Let's say it's land use in Siberia for me. Could I go back to architecture by means of, say, changing jobs? Legally, not before three years' time.

Three years in the Navy and then three years in Siberia — isn't it a little too much? For the first time I questioned if I had done the right thing when I made no effort to dodge the draft, as I had tried to beat the post-graduate assignment to Siberia.

Then I thought, had it all turned out differently, I would have relocated to the provinces filled with enthusiasm. I would have sacrificed years of my life for the benefit of the state. Just to see what it's like. And if I liked it, I would stay.

And so I had been taken for a ride by the propaganda. Not me alone. Many graduates had. Had we left Moscow with the best of intentions, there was no legal way for us to come back. The rules of *propiska* were utterly draconian.

"Young specialists" who were "assigned" by their schools resorted to all sorts of tricks to get around the *propiska* rules. For example, they did not give up their registration and thus did not lose their "permanent *propiska*." When they arrived at their destination, they registered temporarily — for a bribe, of course, and without a mark in their internal passports, since you could not have "temporary" and "permanent" *propiskas* at the same time. Then, after their three years' exile, they would come home. The whole thing was illegal but was practiced widely. But it was only for those who studied in their hometowns and thus had a permanent *propiska*.

But there was no way back to my hometown of Kharkov. I had lost my registration there a long time ago. And even if I got it back, I did not have much of a professional future there — not with the traditional Ukrainian anti–Semitism.

When out-of-towners like me entered a school, they automatically lost their permanent *propiska* and got temporary one at school, which never entitled one to permanent registration. That's why a school would fulfill its forced-assignment quotas at the expense of "temps" like us.

I used to despise the "smart" out-of-towners, who did not bother with "small" stuff like learning and training and focused on what really mattered: getting a permanent *propiska*.

Marriage was the most widespread and absolutely legal means of gaining equality. Therefore the last months of school were the feast season of hasty marriages. Some of them were mutually profitable and even lasted. Yet more often they were blatant marriages of convenience.

If there was a baby in the family, or the other spouse needed to continue his or her studies, both graduates were entitled to "free assignment," i.e. picking an employer themselves. I was hoping that, with a baby and an undergraduate wife, I would be eligible. In any event, as a magna cum laude graduate, or a "red diploma" holder, I should have been entitled to the first pick of jobs.

Once I had used this privilege when I was assigned a job upon graduating from the trade school. As I entered college, I was confident, rather presumptuously, that I would earn the "red diploma." Otherwise what was the point of leaving my hometown, my job, my top position in the line for an apartment, and the third year of engineering college — and running off to Moscow? I was absolutely sure that, as a top student, I would have my pick of jobs.

The more I thought about it, the more my heartbeat was drowning out the knock-knock of the train wheels. The bastards did not give a damn about my "red diploma" and their own rules. And then I remembered the final episode of my "assignment."

When I realized I was barred from the postgraduate program and no laws, written or not, would let me stay in Moscow, I requested a still-vacant (clearly nobody's top choice) position teaching architecture in the shining metropolis of Ust-Kamenogorsk in Kazakhstan, in the heart of Siberia's coal country. This one surely would go through without a hitch.

Fat chance. This time a monkey wrench was thrown in the works by the school's KGB resident Lukàyev, who would not forgive me my virulent refusal to cooperate.

I was not regretting my decision — but did my reaction have to be so violent?

Reluctantly, I came to the most unpleasant part of my analysis. Certainly I had to shoulder some of the fault for my predicament. After all, Lukàyev was not the only one I had antagonized. That my own thesis advisor would vote against me — this was without precedent. That made me pause: never before had I experienced such a conflict with reality. Perhaps this was not only about *propìska*.

Perhaps my deepest youthful delusion was believing in the system. Of course six years of studies in Moscow had done a lot to erode this faith. Yet even now, riding a train to Siberia, I still deluded myself. I was still years away from real understanding — that would set me against the system.

After three days' travel, the train was about to arrive. It was already approaching the bridge over the Ob River.

I concluded I had to go back to Moscow. Although I had no idea how I would get out of this jam. No job was available without a *propìska*. I was facing a wall, and it was solid — unlike the rotten wall of Czarism faced by Siberian exiles fifty years earlier.

But first I had to come back — legally. Strictly by the book. That is, I had to get a release from my new job. Just like a serf. With a difference — a serf could buy himself freedom legally. The Communists closed that loophole.

And thus, Comrade Crazy Truth Teller, we have one option only left: I would have to demand "living quarters" on a legal basis. This would have to be my avenue of attack. Was I not entitled to at least that? I was a "young specialist" with a family. I should be entitled to an apartment or at least a room in the dorm. *And if you, gentlemen, cannot provide that, I demand a release.* Damn it, the law was on my side! It had to be observed, at least — sometimes!

I left my backpack and other belongings in a locker at the station. Then I boarded a streetcar and rode towards the seat of the new masters of my destiny: an office with the unwieldy name of *RosGìproZèm*. Or, rather, the Siberian branch of *RosGìproZèm*.

The Land Use Expert

RosGìproZèm is one of these ubiquitous Soviet abbreviations. This one stands for "Russian State Institute for Designing Land Use." I was sent to its Siberian branch, whose job was quite modest: developing the immense land of Siberia. This included measuring and developing it, as well as assessing fertility, cattle breeding, vegetable and orchard growing ... and nothing in this plethora of areas seemed to fit my architectural training.

I have to get a release from the Gypro, I intoned like a mantra as I headed to the office; then I'll say goodbye and head back to Moscow.

I was welcomed effusively by the director himself, Comrade Serpenìnov — short, graying, with a tanned complexion and attractive manners. He wore a blue striped suit with a tie and a white shirt. He seemed affable and genuinely happy to see me. Finally, he said. They had expected me three months earlier.

He rose from his desk, shook my hand firmly, put me in a comfortable chair — for VIPs, I assumed — and went on to inquire about my trip and my family and my health. He called in his chief engineer and union secretary; then the party secretary joined us, too. And then all together they set out to discuss my future and make plans for me. The setting seemed more than friendly. Another moment, it seemed, and we would be opening a bottle of vodka.

I was not overwhelmingly comfortable. I wanted to cut in and at least tell them that I was an architect, trained to design residential and public buildings. That I was an urban denizen who did not have a clue about country life and land development and their whole business. But while I was trying to find the right moment to cut in, my new bosom buddies, without breaking their friendly chitchat, called the personnel director and had my papers filled out.

I was sentenced to the position of land engineer with a salary of 83 rubles a month. I shuddered. How was I supposed to live on this money?

They noted my change of expression (I would never have made a good poker player) and instantly "lent me moral support" by promising "after some time" a promotion to senior land engineer at the salary of 105 rubles.

They went on to describe my prospects in the exciting area of land use. They segued into the joys of local hunting and fishing — so much so that they seemed to forget about my presence.

I took advantage of the pause and posed my most heartfelt question: What were the living arrangements like? I had a family, with a wife and a child.

The question did not catch my hosts unawares. No problem. Everything is taken care of. I could share a room with a very nice old lady.

They explained to me in the same patient and friendly manner that the old lady in question lived in a beautiful log house with a stove in the middle, where our hostess slept. I was to sleep on a cot behind a really nice curtain. The wash basin was by the door. The outhouse was no more than thirty meters away. The firewood was stacked next to it, and it was my chore to chop and carry it indoors, as well as to haul water from the well on the corner and clear the snow. All these chores would yield me a 10-ruble cut in rent — I would be paying a mere 35 rubles instead of 45.

I could not believe my ears. This was a fabulous turn of events — a legal chance to go back to Moscow. The niggardly pay was not good enough, but the absence of comfortable living arrangements for an "assigned young specialist" was foolproof.

I caught my breath and wrote a letter of resignation.

Then I bid goodbye and settled in the waiting room at the train terminal. "The worse, the better," I reasoned. "I could weather it for a week. They can't resist my resignation forever."

And once again I made a wrong move. I went to work. For the umpteenth time, I fell victim to my natural law-obedience. Perhaps even more importantly, many years of privation engendered a habit of constantly looking for ways to make ends meet. I never had a chance to pause and catch my breath. So once again, somewhere in the back of my mind, I had to be thinking, while this goes on, at least I'll be drawing a salary. Without it I could not survive longer than a week.

Novosibirsk, the capital of Western Siberia, looked like a relatively small place. It was a fifteen-minute trip by streetcar from the head office of Gypro in the outskirts to the section where I was assigned in the center of the city. The section's street address was on Communism Avenue, and to me its appearance fit the name: a tiny damp dark basement in a four-story apartment building. For the rest of my life I will remember the miserable, musty, toilet-tainted stink of this place.

The main staircase leading to the basement from the street entrance was,

The author (right) at a construction site. Novosibirsk, Siberia, 1965.

as usual in the Soviet Union, hammered shut. The one we used was in the backyard's area well and reeked of urine.

The basement ceiling was so low you could easily touch it with an outstretched hand. The rooms were criss-crossed with damp black sewer and heating pipes, all dripping. Some of them ran vertically in the middle of the rooms. The few tiny windows were "winterized" with newspaper strips glued along the perimeter. The unisex toilet was in the corridor and stank up the place. The bowl was tottering treacherously, unsurprisingly—people used it by climbing up with their feet.

My development section was at the other end of the basement from its "mother" topographical section. One day they decided that topographers should be put to work developing villages and made a separate section.

The section took up several rooms. One, about six by six feet, was taken by section chief Valentin Vasilkòv, an affable man, constantly worried, constantly sighing. Another room of the same size held archives. The next cell was for chief engineer Maklakòv. There were also two men and a few women with their drafting boards in other rooms. I was put in the corner near the door.

Two blocks away was another section that dealt with blueprinting, where I found myself on the first day. The locals hated it: the place generously stank of ammonia around the clock. That was not surprising, since reproducing the blueprints used an ammonia solution.

I was lucky to see this process in its prelapsarian form. The original transparencies were pressed against sensitive paper sheets and taken outside to be exposed to daylight, preferably to sunlight. Afterwards the sheets were brought back indoors and placed in special flat bins with ammonia solution, where they were held until they turned blue and white images came out. When I went to trade school fifteen years earlier, our teachers remembered this ancient reproduction method as something from their youth.

To compensate for exposure to harmful ammonia vapors, workers at this section were issued milk daily, which they could take home to their children. This was considered a major benefit, since milk was not always available in stores.

Besides, in foul-weather days, with not enough sunlight for exposure, the work came to a stop. Relieved workers grabbed their bags and ran shopping.

On my very first day, like the smart aleck from Moscow that I was, I came up with the idea of placing electric bulbs over the tables and using their light for exposure. This innocent idea brought derision and, I thought, hostility: "This is not Moscow, where they waste electricity." I was upset by this turn, but didn't know what to say in my defense. I am sure that eventually they had modern copiers with daylight lamps installed and I'm not comfortable thinking that they could be attributing this to my plotting.

Next door was a small binding shop. In the USSR, all blueprints were published as small book-like volumes. A blueprint was folded several times and then finely cut on the side to make a strip for glue. From experience I knew how to simplify the process, but, having learned a lesson, I kept my mouth shut.

My boss was Galina Bezborodova, a pleasant woman of about forty. She was a topographer by training (which was a highly respected trade in Siberia), and instantly admitted that she did not have a clue about her job and hoped to learn from me (!). In brief, she told me, the village development that she was doing included creating the so-called "production area," with a farm of six thousand sheep. My first assignment was to design it. She didn't have a clue as to how I was supposed to do it. Yet she explained to me that "ewes" were "girl sheep," as opposed to "rams," which were "guy sheep."

Although I was not planning to stay, I got down to some studies. My colleagues were happy to pile my desk with books on agriculture. The most useful one was *Land Use in State and Collective Farms*, edited by Professor Kuropàtenko.

The Kuropàtenko book enlightened me: the farms that grew grain were called grain farms — as opposed to cattle farms, though there was also a mixed kind. I also became enlightened on crop rotation and need to designate selection plots, on pedigreed cattle and progressive milking methods, and many other things from agricultural theory and practice.

Naturally, no one had ever taught me anything like it. Nor would I have ever gone off to the Moscow School of Architecture for this kind of knowledge. Yet for some reason fate decreed that I should learn it all.

I was aware that state farms belonged to the state. They hired workers and paid salaries. Collective farms were cooperative property, and their members' earnings depended on the income of the whole farm. I knew that collective farms could be in the red for years. But the media never told us that in that case the farmers were left without means of sustenance, which they had to derive from their private plots (actually, same went for state farm workers as well). At the same time, the authorities kept trying to limit the size of these plots. Professor Kuropàtenko agreed. He saw it as a way to motivate better work on collective land.

I had heard of this problem before, but never thought of it seriously. Now my boss Comrade Bezboròdova told me that cutting down the size of private plots was the main target of our "development." I had never thought I would be specializing in something like this, doing Expropriation Lite at my drafting table.

As I got into talking with my colleagues, the first thing I was told was that our office was "self-financed." I was familiar with that term. The state would not subsidize organizations, forcing them to pay their own way. In general, I liked the idea. Yet, as with any well-meant initiative in this miserable country, when an enterprise did pay its way, everything was fine. But if it generated profits that could be legally used to reward those responsible for it, the authorities eagerly took this money away — which deprived a rare enthusiast of any motivation to do something socially useful. But we knew little about it then and did not discuss it.

I was also told that in our case "self-financed" meant churning out projects. No one cared what they were about, since no one had any intention of implementing them.

My co-workers also let me know that Gypro Siberia had gone into development about a year earlier. It was obvious that they had gotten themselves into something relatively strange to them and they did not have a clue to what it was. It was all the doing of some Big Boss who heeded the Party's call to develop rural settlements and decided not to think about it too much and dump it into the land use specialists' lap. No one cared that land distribution and correct crop rotation had nothing in common with developing facilities for people. "They can learn. It ain't brain surgery."

It turned out that there were untold numbers of potential clients — all created artificially, like the whole agricultural reform. Since time immemorial, Siberians had done fine living in small villages. During the '30s "collectivization," the Soviets pushed them into state farms. This was of course an utterly political measure aimed at making peasants more like workers — a social class the Party was more comfortable with. The state farms were not producing well, and so in the '60s they were integrated into yet larger entities. Like all the economic problems of Communism, this one was not seen as inherent, but, rather, something that came from "not enough Communism." People were moved into larger settlements, which were built up without rhyme or reason, without concern for streets and roads and schools and stores. Now the authorities had decided to put the house in order.

In theory, large settlements looked like an idea whose time had come. They would save on communications, on land use, and on energy. I had grown up on "communist rationalist" utopias and found it all rather appealing. There was just one little thing that I didn't realize then: as you pulled people away from the land, you deprived them of a chance to feed themselves. Ultimately, this idea failed, like most Soviet ideas. But in my time, when complying with "Party instructions" was at its peak, not only did the authorities force integrated farms to move into these settlements, but also required them to order and pay for (they were "self-financed, too") the development plans.

Big money was involved. Work could — and had to — be done in a slapdash fashion. No one really knew what a project like this should look like. They must have made it all up themselves: plot of survey, general plan, plan of production area, civil engineering, the list of prototype structures — cowsheds, pigsties, residences, "people's club," and the like — and that's the whole project for you. Beside the plot of survey and the list of prototype structures, attached to add gravitas, it was all schematics. That was the official name: "Planning Schematics."

A few days later I was already assigned one of these schematics: development of a village. They figured I was sufficiently versed in this business. Or else they realized I knew at least as much — that is, as little — as they did.

"Development of Country Settlements" seemed to be far removed from my occupation. And yet this was the galley to which I was chained in the rotting basement of Siberian Gypro on Communism Avenue.

Comforting myself that it was just for a week or two, I rolled up my sleeves and reluctantly got down to earn my keep.

Looking back, I believe that the plot of survey was the only part of my project — and other projects, too — that had been done professionally by Gypro surveyors who took pride in their work. On the other hand, I found it hard to see what was in it for the farmers.

I had no idea of what was expected of me and how I should approach it. This sent me to my predecessors. The only new information in their "Planning Schematics" was that small plots adjoining farmers' houses would lose over three-quarters of their acreage to future construction. I started doing the same thing with even more diligence, leaving no plots at all. I think this is what any other ignorant extremist would have done in my place.

As I realized later, no villager would take these schematics seriously. They must have had a ball looking at my output.

I could assume that the "Schematics of Production Area Plan" that I was clumsily mapping out as part of my project was based on a completely fictitious perspective of economic development. I could not imagine that the basic data with which I had been provided were completely lacking in even faintly realistic economic forecasting. Therefore my "plan" could not have possibly interested the farmers and could not have been used.

The "Schematics of Civil Engineering" part of the project was to show the direction of precipitation downflow. This was generally made by surveyors, too, who had good topographic skills and quickly mastered that part of the civil engineering profession.

The villagers who had a chance to glance at this drawing must have wondered: did they really need it to see how rainwater would get into the river? Somehow it had managed to do so for thousands of years without a plan. I didn't understand that, either. Much later, when I had to tackle the subject more in-depth, I realized that the villagers would have a point. Since the Gypro prepared only schematics, they were pointless by definition. If the state came to build any of the streets we schemed, the builders would still have to turn to professionals for real blueprints.

Yet in those days I had a very vague notion of all that. I never bothered to wonder that the villagers were charged thousands of rubles they had earned in back-breaking labor for a few crudely drawn schemes. I did not have a clue why my bosses loved this work so much. Gradually, I realized why: they bore no responsibility for any of it, since everything was drawn so vaguely.

The way it might have happened was that a Gypro executive who had been engaged in surveying these farms simply stumbled on this get-quick-rich scheme. When Moscow announced that the farms were going to be integrated, the Gypro figured out that it had hit paydirt. One way or another, by the time I arrived, they had been churning out dozens of these plans.

Perhaps when they had just started out they were getting away with murder. Then a client tried to put one of their blueprints to at least some use — and couldn't. This led to the emergence of a vetting authority that demanded quality. Never mind they did not know what kind of quality they were looking for. In any event, our outfit had to start taking the schemes business more seriously. It was to bring in some pros. And in the Soviet Union that commodity had always been in short supply.

Unaware of any of this, long before my departure from Moscow, I was trying in vain to figure out what they wanted with an architecture school graduate. I was still hoping that the system was acting rationally.

The explanation was simple. It seems that at some top meeting someone must have once again complained about the ongoing problems of Soviet agriculture. Just to shut him up, the bosses promised to help with human resources. But the agricultural school graduates had all been assigned. Our school of architecture was next (perhaps alphabetically), and I was the only one left with questionable status. The fact that the job content had nothing in common with my training was irrelevant. The Party's decision to supply young specialists to Siberian agriculture was to be implemented.

Meanwhile, the Novosibirsk train terminal was becoming my home. Like all Stalin-era Soviet terminals, the one in Novosibirsk followed the blueprint of the well-known Cincinnati Union Terminal. But I wonder if architects Alfred T. Fellheimer and Steward Wagner would have recognized their creature on Siberian soil. The station's huge waiting area was always full. There were endless lines to ticket windows and information. The food-concession stand was mobbed. The passengers in transit were all over the place, barely seen under their huge bags. The place was filled with the stink of engine oil and ammonia and urine, with the deafening din of loudspeakers and the grating sound of train wheels.

At night most of the mobs were gone. Sometimes you could even find enough space on a wooden bench to take a nap. All my belongings were in a locker, so I was not afraid of being robbed. I kept my papers and money in the inside pocket of my jacket underneath my parka.

Soon I was being recognized by the station employees, policemen, and fellow residents. Some of the latter were homeless like me; others were in transit and failed to get tickets for a connecting train. I was even assigned the moniker of "Muscovite."

The nap was never longer than a couple of hours, since the police would wake us up several times a night and ask for an ID. Although the sergeant knew me, he had to "follow orders" that could not be breached: "Wake up, Muscovite, show your passport!" What if I was a bandit, or, God forbid, a spy?

The second floor of the station housed a so-called Repose Room — actually a few tiny rooms, and two of them included several cots, where you could stretch under a blanket and sleep in relative comfort — one room for men and one for women. The place even had a tiny shower with hot water.

I never learned the written and unwritten entry requirements to this small heaven. Or most likely — the combination of special permits and proper connections. I slept there a couple of times — the food stand saleswoman took a shine to me and put in a good word — but you could not spend more than one night at a time there.

Then "my" manager briefly put me up at her place, over her boyfriend's protests. Then she handed me over to her colleague from another food stand. This one did not have a boyfriend, so, like a biblical Joseph, I fled back to the terminal bench.

Worn out by sleepless nights at the terminal, I went to see my good friend Comrade Serpenìnov. I brought an ultimatum in the form of a request: either he provided me with living quarters, or he should give me an "honorable discharge." Otherwise I was going to the DA's office and filing a suit by the end of the week.

I was convinced that my walking papers were in the bag. The Gypro did not have an apartment for me or even a room. If they didn't let me go, they knew they had a lawsuit on their hands.

Concerned with my own vicissitudes, I had no desire to sort out their problems. In this conflict they were victims, too — no less than I. They needed a professional. Badly. And now they had one. Once they let me go, they would never get another one. What were they supposed to do?

The much-vaunted cot at the old lady's real nice hut had already been taken. But now Serpenìnov offered to put me up temporarily right at the office by freeing up one of the stinking cells. This ran counter to my departure plans. But exhausted by my train-terminal vigils, I agreed. I reasoned that it could not pass muster as "living quarters" and thus did not weaken my case. Although, come to think of it, it wasn't so bad — running water, hot water, and a warm toilet (though with a semi-broken dirty bowl), and it was centrally located, with two cafeterias nearby.

But it turned out right away that clearing even this tiny cell was a major problem. Its two occupants were somehow found spaces next door. The only person left was an elderly typist with a huge Underwood typewriter that might well have gone back to the Civil War. With the racket it made, no one wanted to give space to the old lady. Then I conceded that she could stay and work in the daytime. After all, she could type on my cot. But then it turned out that they could not find space for the first two workers. The scheme failed.

A few weeks passed. Serpenìnov was still affable. He claimed he liked me, as did the rest of the workers, and my living-conditions problem was to be resolved any day now.

I believed he was working on it. I started every morning by calling him, begging to be released. And then suddenly he told me he had pried a four-room apartment out of the city's hands — with one of the rooms going to me. The building was about to be finished in a month or two.

My only real chance to leave Novosibirsk legally was evaporating in front of my own eyes. I panicked and tried to make a scene — ineptly.

Then my bosses found an ingenious solution. In order to stall, they sent me on the road — to Altai. All I could was to admire their practical peasant skills.

Naturally, no one was concerned that no one could have become a specialist in the few weeks I had spent at Gypro — not to the extent that I could negotiate with clients.

This is how, little by little, without much drama, I started my Siberian Saga — like all sagas, sometimes sad and sometimes delicious. Absorbed in my struggle to return to Moscow, I did not quite perceive it as such, but I remembered the date: October 14, 1964. This was the day Khrushchev retired, and a former land expert, a lily-livered functionary named Brezhnev, got his spot atop Lenin's tomb. And in a manner of speaking, I got Brezhnev's place among the land experts.

The Bus

The jump-off point of my business trip to Altai was Pospèlikha, a district seat that I reached by first taking a night train from Novosibirsk and then changing to another one in Barnaul, the capital of Altai. In Pospèlikha, I was supposed to take a bus.

It was still dark and frosty, and I had to stumble through huge snowdrifts after a recent snowfall. Despite the early hour, the tiny, beat-up van was full. I was lucky to find a window seat in the back, next to the rear exit.

My fellow travelers, invisible in the predawn light, exchanged remarks in subdued voices. They talked over international affairs and discussed the weather. Some were asleep, while others smoked and cursed quietly. Soon the driver showed up, and we took off.

The moment we left town, the old, decrepit bus started shaking like an airplane in turbulence. Everything creaked and groaned as it struggled up through snowdrifts, never going over ten miles an hour.

I couldn't tell the dirt road from the rest of the landscape, and I was mystified as to how the driver found his way, especially when the road strayed from the line of telegraph poles. It felt like we were traveling on a frozen, choppy sea. Normally, driving along such surfaces makes me sick, but after a sleepless night in the trains and the cold outside, I relaxed in the warmth of the bus and fell asleep.

I was awakened by a sudden pang of anxiety. The bus stood still. The snow sparkled pleasantly in the bright sun. Outside, about a hundred feet downhill, I saw a small, purple-brownish wooden structure with a huge sign. "Diner." It was completely swept up in a snowdrift, and reached via a narrow, blue-shadowed footpath, at least five feet deep, made through the brilliant white snow. The bus was almost empty.

The unusual, seemingly-bewitched silence was disturbed by an odd hissing sound — as if a tire were going flat. Suddenly, a woman seated in front of me with a child in her lap uttered a heart-rending yell and froze as she pressed herself against the right wall of our poor carriage. As she yelled two children who had been napping in the seat behind me jumped into the rear door-well.

I saw that the hiss came from a huge metal rod, an inch-and-a-half in diameter, that had already pierced the seat right next to me and was now going through the seat of the woman in front. By sheer luck, it missed both of us. Three more rods, positioned at equal spaces from one another, were piercing the seats to our left. With seeming bloodthirst, one of these powerful "bayonets" had already penetrated the backs of the two rows of seats and now was pushing against the metal handle of the next one, bending it in the process.

The woman and I, having miraculously survived this attack, stared at these mysterious rods in silence for a moment until we felt the impact of a blow against the rear bumper. The rods started moving backward. It was then that I realized that the bus had been pierced by the pitchfork of a hay-stacker. The woman could not settle down the rest of the way and kept repeating, "Holy shit! Holy shit!"

The rest of the passengers popped out of the diner and stared at the scene before them. Then they rushed towards the bus like extras on a movie set following the director's command. The rush was led by our driver, wearing a huge fur hat and throwing on his beat-up coat. He was followed by a one-legged man carrying a crutch in one hand and an unfinished bottle in the other. Next came three women with bottles and packages of food, waving away the waitress that followed them. Two old ladies in black velveteen coats moved in cautious step, holding on to each other so they wouldn't fall. Bringing up the rear were a pack of youths who were already drunk, with fur hats and no coats.

It was a magnificent scene, worthy of a great director.

The hay-stacking tractor backed up to free the pitchfork. Then, as if nothing had happened, he drove off, its caterpillar tread making a jarring sound as it disappeared around a turn in the road.

By the time our driver brought the frozen engine back to life, the bus was full. And then we went on a chase.

If driving before was no picnic, now the bus and the passengers really were tested. We were tossed and turned, and at times rode at such an unbelievable angle to the horizon, with the sides of the bus cutting through snowdrifts, that a flop-down seemed inevitable. I was sure we wouldn't make it, and I reflected on the absurdity of dying in a tractor-chase wreck after having survived a pitchfork attack minutes earlier.

My fellow passengers did not seem bothered by this at all. They were busy consuming the booze they had bought at the diner and hotly discussing the accident, outshouting one another in excitement. Everybody but the kids and me was chain-smoking. The air, blue with smoke, was thick with curses.

Just as we finally saw the tractor, the bus was abruptly tossed to the right, and then into a U-turn. Somehow we came to rest on all four wheels, facing the traffic and stuck in a snowdrift.

The driver opened the doors and led the posse "to catch the jerk." I ran along, surrendering to the herd instinct and getting caught up in the excitement after a few gulps of vodka that had been offered by a fellow passenger.

We followed the caterpillar trail and soon caught up with the tractor. Its driver was impervious to our threats and curses and kept driving. Finally, one of the pursuers climbed into the cab and pulled out the ignition key. The tractor came to an abrupt stop. And it was a good thing, too — another twenty feet, and it would have gone down a steep cliff.

The momentum tossed the tractor driver out in the snow, and an empty vodka bottle rolled out of his pocket. It appeared that he had been drunk and asleep throughout the chase.

Now we had to tow the bus out of the drift. This turned out to be a simple matter: every other passenger knew how to drive a tractor. They found a cable, and there was plenty of enthusiasm. Half an hour later, we were back in the village to file a police report so our bus driver wouldn't have to pay for the repairs.

The tractor driver was known to the local police. "That's Stepan! From Kràsnoznàmenka! But where the heck did he find vodka at so early an hour?" Officially, no vodka was sold before 10 A.M.

"Maybe he stocked up the night before." I ventured a shy guess.

I was a laughingstock. "Could city folks hold back this long?" My city-slicker roots were too obvious.

Finally, the report was complete, and we were let go. The culprit was put to bed with tender loving care. "He has to start his shift soon."

The Lodging

By the time my bus arrived at the village of Kràsnoschèkovo it was getting dark. I called up the Lenin's Path State Farm, and in two hours a truck came to pick me up. Another hour later I arrived at my destination, a village called Nòvo-Shipunòvo.

I was billeted at the local medical attendant's office, not far from the village center — a small log hut with two entrances on opposite sides. In the back, about eighty feet away, I made out an outhouse.

The hut was divided in two: the attendant's living quarters and the office proper. The office half consisted of a tiny entry room with a wash basin, a hallway with a stove, and two small rooms: an office and a patients' ward that barely had space for two iron cots separated by a curtain. The attendant, a middle-aged, tall, lean man with old-fashioned round glasses over a lengthy predator's nose, assigned me one of them with a bedside locker. I used it to lay out my clothing over a briefcase with my belongings.

After a sleepless night aboard the train and a day in the bus, I fell asleep the moment my head touched the pillow.

Soon I was awakened by a loud conversation.

"So who are you?" the attendant asked.

"Well, see, Pàvel Shmelèv got knifed here the other day. And I'm his dad."

"He got knifed, all right — what do *you* want?"

"I'm, well, a job."

"What job?"

"You know, *job*. Any kind of job."

"You got nothing better to do at night?"

"Well, I'm kind of in pain."

"Go home. You stink like a distillery."

"Show respect for a cripple, Zakhàrych. Just a couple of drops."

"Some people ... how many times do I have to tell you? Alcohol is for medicinal purposes only. Me-di-ci-nal, you understand? There's not enough for everybody."

"C'mon, Zakhàrych."

"Go away, already. You know what time it is? Enough bothering people."

The attendant saw me awake. "They keep bugging me about alcohol. Or about anything. A granny showed up the other day. Ninety nine years old. Stomachache. Like she doesn't have something better to do. I had to take her to the hospital. Turned out she had appendicitis! We laughed ourselves silly...."

I sank back into sleep. Not for long. An hour later, I was awakened again, this time by voices and a woman's subdued groans behind the curtain.

From time to time a man whispered, "Quiet, Vàrya, there's a person asleep on the other cot." The groans and the squeaking of the bedsprings came to a pause. Then, after a short period, they started all over again, louder and louder. Something was going on.

I opened my eyes. The room was relatively light. Yet it was not the overhead bulb. Someone had been considerate enough to turn it off. The light came from a flashlight resting on the bedside locker on the other side of the curtain, which turned into a shadow theater. Peering closer, I realized something odd — on the other cot, an arm's length away, a woman was giving birth.

Later I could sleep only intermittently, between contractions. Finally, around five in the morning, a baby screamed, and his mother and I went to sleep, utterly exhausted.

Surveyor General

I got a lift to Kràsno, the district center, in a Russian-made GAZ, a clone of an American Jeep. Besides the silent driver Vassily, there were three of us. I sat next to Vladimir Zhelyàbin the fire inspector — youngish, tacit, and rapt in his own thoughts. Next to the driver was Fèdor Plòtnikov, deputy chairman of Ostròvsky's Memory collective farm — squat and plump, with a big head on a short neck, and excruciatingly talkative.

Once he found out that I was from the Rosgyprozèm Office in Novosibirsk, he grew animated and eager to share his thoughts. He thought I shared his interests, and I was in no mood to disappoint him. I was not about to explain that I was an architect shanghaied into land utilization only few weeks ago. Or that I was clueless about village life. I tried to keep up my side of the conversation. I asked questions, sort of. And he answered in great detail — greater than I expected.

"You ask me about materials. It's not good. One time we needed some wood to build cattle pens. We went to the forestry. They are charging nine rubles a cubic meter. That's up from four or five they used to. All right, what you are gonna do. So when can they deliver. Well ... some in the first quarter, some in the second and the rest in the fourth. But we need our stuff by May! So we had to send our own guys to get the wood. One way or another, the forestry charged us nine rubles per, plus travel expenses and meals for our workers — it came up to eighteen rubles per! And still it's better than having no wood at all."

I had a good mind to tell him it was a run-of-the-mill Socialist economy mess. But I was too sleepy to get deep into it.

My lack of response didn't make a dent as he went on: "So we had to build this brick apartment house. We signed up with the Farm Construction agency. They asked fourteen thousand. The hell with that, we said; we did it ourselves for six. Still, it's steep. Armenians built us a brick club building. And Gutsùls — from Western Ukraine — they build wooden and frame houses. They charge us ten rubles a day per worker, but they work hard from six in the morning to eleven at night. They don't malinger. Everyone gains."

I was aware of this semi-legal summer work. (In fact, forty years later all the construction work is still being done by seasonal workers, mostly Ukrainians, with Moldavians a close second.) Moreover, I knew that these workers were paid three times more than I, an architect. But I never gave it much thought.

Actually, I was enjoying Plòtnikov's speech. His melodious intonations and fresh lexicon, uncluttered by bureaucratese, fit in well with my impressions of Altai, exposing the everyday worries and concerns of the world I knew absolutely nothing about. Yet after two sleepless nights in trains and on the cot next to the woman giving birth the night before, my curiosity could not compete with fatigue and sleepiness.

Yet once again Fedor pulled me out of slumber. "That's a fine place to cut down a tree!" Now he was outraged at seeing a freshly felled birch tree at the roadside. "They cut down their own! No brains at all! Why can't they go to the state forest!"

What a strange turn of mentality we are living through, I thought. So it's no sin stealing from the state — by definition, a people's state, hence it was stealing from ourselves.

I still had not arrived at the understanding that theft is a sin by itself. The Russian saying went, no stealing, no living. Can't argue with folk wisdom, can you?

As we passed a snowbound ruin, Plòtnikov became animated again. "This used to be a rich peasant's house before the revolution, and then they had a commune here in the twenties. They lived by ring bells. In the morning, a bell rings to get them up. Second bell rings — time to wash up. Another bell ring, everybody goes to breakfast. Next bell ring, to go to work. Everyone goes to sleep. And this is how they lived until they finished off the cattle and whatever the previous owner had stored in his cellars. Then, since there was nothing left to it, the commune broke up and became Motherland Collective Farm, and their chairman became the farm chairman. When he retired, they put him on the Communist sustenance: To each according to his needs. But he didn't need much by then. He was a modest guy. He died recently. His wife is still alive, though."

I wanted to ask a question or make a comment, but instead nodded off again. It was physically painful staying awake.

I woke up when we arrived in Kràsno. The fire inspector, silent up to that point, became markedly animated, and suggested we stop by the local medical office. There we were met by his nurse girlfriend Valeria, young and plump, with a tanned complexion.

Valeria invited us over. Her house was well-heated. The smell was like something from a Chekhov story about middle-class denizens. She set a table, though I found the food odd, considering the season. First we had cold soup — kvass, a Russian malt drink, with sliced hard-boiled eggs and finely diced onions. This was followed by warm tea, served with neatly sliced ham and — again — hard-boiled eggs on the side. The tea also came with black currant preserve and a huge loaf of home-made white bread.

Everything turned out to be strikingly tasty. Accompanied with a bottle of vodka, consumed to "warm the soul," the feast did us good. Not everyone drank: the driver had had recent problems with the local road police, and our hostess only took a sip "out of respect."

The vodka put the fireman to sleep. He stretched out on the couch for "some shuteye" and was snoring within seconds. Valeria solicitously took off his shoes and threw on a cover.

Fedor and I went straight to the Party Committee. Why we did, I had no idea. As the only sober person, Vassily the driver was now in charge.

As if on purpose, farm directors from all over the district had been summoned to the committee for a meeting. My head, spinning from the consumed alcohol, suddenly stumbled on a quite sober thought: This is a real chance to cut my trip short. Who knows whether I'll be able to catch them at their respective farms? But today, they are all right here. What can be simpler than to ask for the floor and introduce the fellows to the joys of planned land improvement?

I didn't think even for a moment that I was originally supposed to travel to their respective farms and study the conditions first-hand. All it took was two days and sleepless nights in Altai and some vodka — and I was already thinking like a local.

Before facing the meeting, Plòtnikov insisted that we partake of a bottle of locally distilled port in the Party Committee's cafeteria. Thus reinforced, we barged into the auditorium to witness a voters' meeting with the candidate to the local Soviet.

After "reinforcement," my head was a complete blur. I watched a woman talk through the fog. I think she implored that a pre–K nursery be built at a closer distance. "There was this mother taking her baby to the nursery in a sled for over a mile, in the freezing cold, too. But the pipes burst, so the nursery was closed. The child's already frozen, and she has to take him back, too. So he landed in the hospital with bilateral pneumonia and has been there for a month and is still sick."

For some reason, she ended with a poem of her own, which I thought to be quite original — I can't think of another reason why it deposited itself in my memory. The translation is in blank verse, but conveys the emotion rather closely.

> A simple worker and a mother
> I grow rough bread for my Motherland
> I am proud I am able to give my vote
> Which is like governing my own power.

Plòtnikov sent a note to the presidium in my name: a representative of Novosibirsk Rosgyprozem office needed to make an important announcement. At that moment the local Soviet chairman was handing retirement certificates to local old-timers in a rather celebratory manner.

One of them said in response, delivered in an inimitable local accent: "You're wishing us to live to see bright Communist future. I just want to make it to spring when snow comes off the graves."

Oddly, I remembered many details of this meeting very well. Yet my mind firmly deleted right away whatever balderdash I delivered from the stage. At the end, the Party Secretary, the de facto czar of the district, came up and shook my hand. I suppose I really got into my part and delivered well impromptu.

The success of this speech prompted me to what I thought was a striking idea — to sign up the farms for land-improvement projects then and there. Strictly speaking, this was not a part of my mandate. But my section chief stuck a bunch of these blank agreements in my bag right before I left — just in case.

The Party district advisor, a slicker who steadily reeked of alcohol (actually, like most of those in attendance — now including me), volunteered to help. And so without further ado the two of us started twisting the attending directors' arms to sign the agreements I filled out on my knee.

Naturally, none of them was eager to sign. "Our hard-earned money for this 'project' no one needs?"

There was a lot of arguing and fighting — at first with the advisor, then among themselves. As they moved to straight cursing, no one could remember what the original source of discontent was.

Then one of them suddenly said, "Well, the last thing to talk about is spare parts" — which was always a sore subject. Everybody laughed and agreed to sign — after a little snack. It was getting late, and they had long ways to travel. The cafeteria was still open, though it had hardly any food to offer. Mostly booze. I don't remember what we were drinking then.

After the "snack," it turned out that out of nine directors one was still resisting. The advisor dragged the stubborn one to the "tsar's" chambers. Fifteen minutes later, the two were back with a signed contract.

By the time I began sobering up, it was all over. The farm directors were gone. I was sitting by myself in an empty auditorium with a bunch of signed documents in my hands.

I felt like shit. I didn't know why I was there, what I was doing, or who needed any of it.

Collective Farm Inn

By 9 P.M., I was getting sober. Along with the vodka vanished the sour aftertaste of dealing with the local leadership at the district Party Committee. It was time to think about shelter for the night. I had not slept for three days.

My new "friend," a functionary at the Committee, was determined to take care of me and brought me to a small, oblong wooden house. We fought our way to the entrance through tall snowdrifts. The tiny sign on the nondescript door was barely legible in the light of a snow-covered lamp: "Collective Farmer Guest House." Since I was brought by a local "boss," I had no problems getting accommodation.

The attendant, a big, fat, fiftyish woman, unhappy at being disturbed, collected my passport and pointed at the door at the end of the hallway.

The room was about ten by twenty feet and held eight metal cots. The sign on the wall said, "Consuming Alcohol Strictly Forbidden." The one posted on the opposite wall featured a vodka bottle in the form of a green boa constrictor wrapped around a miserable-looking drinker.

I barely had time to settle for the night as one of my roommates approached me with a proposal to pitch in for a bottle of vodka. Booze was hardly on my mind, but I dared not say no.

In view of the prohibition sign, the vodka was brought in a teapot. Chasers were potluck: a chunk of home-made kielbasa, a couple of hard-boiled eggs, a piece of chicken, half a bread loaf, and two giant pickles. There were only three glasses, and we had to take turns.

We did not even finish pouring when the attendant burst in—without knocking, of course.

"Tea, you said?" she grabbed the teapot. "Where did you get the hot water? Let me see. Who are you trying to fool here?"

She downed her glass without missing a beat and wiped her mouth in a textbook wino gesture. "You better keep it quiet. Or else I'll have you out in the cold in two seconds flat."

When the vodka was finished, someone found a three-liter bottle of moonshine in his suitcase. For some reason, it was poured into the teapot. The hooch stank terribly, and I tried to drop out after the second glass. But no. "What's the matter, city boy? We're too good for you?" They had my number, that's for sure.

Then it was showtime. The moonshine owner sang a classic Russian song about a lonely sailor dying far away from his mother, with everybody joining in with the saddest expressions imaginable. The next number was the song about the proud Russian Navy ship called Varyàg that would rather die than surrender. The emotions shot up, and so did the volume. Next-door neighbors banged on the wall. They obviously could not stand the idea of so much fun and dispatched their own "representative" to negotiate. We had to pour him some vodka, too. He went back and returned with his roommates and more vodka and a song about a lovelorn accordionist roaming the fields on a dark and cold night.

The attendant woman came back a few times, too. She could barely stay up and was hard to understand, slurring her words that by now were a string of curses. She brushed the glasses off to the floor and drank the hooch straight from the teapot's spout. Then one of the drinkers threw up, and his friends

pulled him outside to rub him with snow and bring him back to his senses.
Then my body went out of control, which I found really amusing. Someone
helped me take off my clothes and shoes and put me to bed.

By dawn, the party ran out of steam and the rooms filled with the sounds
of snoring and stink. I could not fall asleep. My head was spinning and my
body was taken over by a herd of huge, smelly bedbugs. I spent the rest of
the night fighting off these monsters. The drunkenness was gone, but sleep
was out of reach.

At six in the morning I stepped outside, washed my face with snow, got
dressed, picked up my briefcase, and headed for the bus station, where the
jeep from the 20th Party Congress Collective Farm was to pick me up. My
Altai trip went on.

My Circus

Back from Altai, I went to work straight from the train. I had lost a few
pounds and gained heavy stubble. My eyes were sunken from lack of sleep
and heavy alcohol intake. My co-workers were horrified. "Comrade Berkovich,
are you OK?"

"That's it," I grumbled. I was done here, I explained. I was packing up
and going back to Moscow. Whatever happens, happens.

I repeated this to Director Serpenìnov when he asked me for the report.
First he had to find me a place to live. Or else I was gone. You have to take
care of your serfs, too.

My skid-row look and determined voice had an effect. Despite himself,
Serpenìnov ordered a fake business-trip certificate for me that the Novosibirsk branch of RosGìproZèm was sending me to ... Novosibirsk.

This certificate provided a good legal loophole. More importantly, I had
a good contact at Hotel Novosibirsk via the cafeteria manager's friend. And
I ended up having a room all to myself. In the Soviet days, even with such
certificate, it would have been a coup to get a bed. And here I was with a
room, where I could take a shower and get a good night's sleep.

At the post office I was met with a pleasant surprise — a cable from my
wife. She was flying in the next day to join me for the holidays — the revolution's 47th anniversary. She had made money for the fare by donating blood.

The hotel room came in handy. We had not seen each other for over
three weeks, which was the longest we had been apart in our first two years
together — and it seemed like half a lifetime. We talked and talked and it still
wasn't enough. Yet the joy of the meeting was from the very first marred by
the coming sadness of parting.

A record player was playing nonstop in the lobby. The pop diva du jour, the impossibly glamorous Klàvdia Shulzhènko, kept crooning how she was "a simple working girl from a small town in Spain." I'd never be able to hear this song about Manzanàres River again without seeing Marina's eyes welling up with tears.

I saw Marina to the airport and came back to the hotel around midnight. Atypically, the place was fragrant like spring. There was a huge vase with fresh flowers on the clerk's desk. All my belongings — a backpack, a sketchbook, a frame for paper, and a briefcase — were stacked next to the counter in the lobby. Instead of the key to the room, I got an official letter. I had been kicked out of the hotel for "violating the residence rules." I had "a woman systematically sleeping in my room." The clerk on duty triumphantly announced that a copy of this testimony to my loose morals had already been dispatched to my place of work.

There was no one to argue my case with. The head manager, with whom I had an "understanding," was not back from vacation yet. I wondered if I still had any stuff upstairs. I was told I could go check if the new occupant wasn't asleep yet.

Upstairs, Schulzhenko was still crooning about amor. The new resident was deeply asleep. He appeared to be from Central Asia. In the middle of the room were two huge cardboard suitcases. One was half-opened and filled with flowers. That was the whole story. The likelihood of an Uzbek flower wholesaler getting a hotel room legally was nil. In the boss's absence, the clerk used Marina's visit as an excuse to line her — the clerk's — pocket with cash. And the flower trade was all cash and very, very profitable.

As I went down the stairs, the diva's voice followed me with assurances that love and song would eventually prevail over money. Preferably sooner than later, I thought.

I stuck the briefcase in the backpack, picked up the rest of my belongings, and left. The night was mild and uncommonly windless. Snow was falling in giant white flakes. Across the square loomed the huge opera theater. I was smack in the center of the city, with not another soul in sight.

Lost in thought, I proceeded south on Red Avenue; then I remembered someone saying there was another hotel nearby — but where? There was no one to ask. Just in case, I decided to comb through a few blocks to the north.

It was hard to say what I was banking on. The chance to find the hotel was close to zero. The chance they'd let me in was even lower, even with my fake business-trip certificate. Yet I loathed going back to the bench at the train terminal even more. As I trundled in the semi-darkness around snowdrifts, I kept humming a motto from a popular pre-war movie, "He who searches will always find."

(Needless to say, I was unaware that the sentiment had been lifted from the New Testament.)

The movie motto held true. After a half an hour of wandering around dark snowbound streets, I stumbled upon a two-story oblong brick structure, at the end of a street next to a sandlot, without any signs of life. Yet, by process of elimination, this was the only structure in the area that could pass for a hotel.

I circled it till I found a door, barely noticeable. There was no marquee or a sign — just a small step, invisible in the snow.

I knocked on the door. No reply. I knocked again and again, louder and more insistently and desperately. Finally, something — someone — stirred on the other side. The door opened a crack, and a sleepy woman peered at me. Perhaps concluding she had nothing to fear from me, she opened the door and asked my name.

"Aha," she said when I introduced myself. "Sorry, we were expecting you on the morning plane."

I was being taken for someone else, but this was not the time or the place to clear this up.

Without opening my passport, the good fairy stuck it in the desk drawer and handed me the key to Room 26. I realized that I just had witnessed a miracle, and it had actually happened to me.

Trying to be quiet, I got under the blanket on the second — vacant — cot and immediately fell asleep. It was already around two A.M.

When I woke up, I found myself locked in. The second guest was not there, and neither was the room key. And the toilet was somewhere in the corridor. It was nine in the morning on Sunday. I started banging on the door. Guests from next door came out into the hallway, loudly accusing each other of bad jokes. Finally they realized where the knocking was, and I was released. I was somewhat surprised to see my liberators wearing Gypsy clothes.

That was not the end of this unusual morning. Barely had I come back from the toilet and started putting on my clothes than the key in the door started turning. I grew tense.

The door opened, and a rather good-looking girl, wearing a rather revealing bathrobe and high heels, waltzed in. The room filled with perfume. I apologized that I was not dressed.

She said she had been told to come and unlock me at eight, but she slept late.

That's nice, I thought.

She spotted a can of Bulgarian beans in tomato sauce and a can of condensed milk that I had just got out of the backpack. Without waiting for an invitation, she flirtatiously "consented" to come in for breakfast. Then she said somewhat mysteriously, "Never known them to have a third partner." By then nothing could surprise me any more.

After she left, I went to take a shower. In the otherwise abandoned hallway, I ran into a Mongol, who, after he passed me, leaped in the air and then did several cartwheels.

Regardless of my inability to absorb any more surprises, they kept coming.

The shower room had several open stalls. I had barely soaped myself when someone knocked on the door and a woman's voice asked me to open up.

I told her this stall was taken, and by a man, too.

"I'm a man, too," she countered.

I told her I was not in the mood for jokes and I had soap all over me.

She said, rather politely, that no one was making any jokes. "Please open up."

I did — to face two dwarfs. Of male gender, yes.

As they were undressing, another knock came on the door. A female voice, again. This time I opened without an argument. Another dwarf— this time a woman. With a friend. Covering myself, I invited them to come in.

"That's okay," she tweeted. "We can wait."

The moment I left, the lissome twosome sneaked in. On my way back to the room I ran into a couple of more dwarfs walking with their arms around each other. I questioned my sanity.

Barely breathing, I came downstairs. At the reception was the dwarf woman I had seen earlier in the shower room. Now she was dressed up and had her makeup on. Sitting on the high counter, with her legs crossed, she was blowing smoke rings, the cigarette taking up half her tiny face. A regular Marlene Dietrich, no less.

The clerk was out for lunch, she informed me. If I wanted a cab, she would call one. Actually — did I like music? Especially early Shostakovich? And would I agree that he was influenced by late Rachmaninov? It was such a shame that the local philharmonic didn't have Wagner's *Valkyrie* in their repertory. "They have a very solid wind section, you know."

The Wonderland turned out to be a hotel reserved for circus performers.

The same night I met my roommate, who was a dancer at the local opera theater. It turned out that he shared a room with a friend who was registered elsewhere but was sleeping with him, and yes, in the same cot. They must be really close friends, I thought naively.

They were "terribly sorry" about the morning mishap. They were late for the morning rehearsal before the matinee. It was not a good idea to leave the room unlocked, and it was "terribly sensitive" to wake me up.

We struck a friendly relation from the start. When I was leaving for work, they were still asleep. And when they were coming back from the show, I was the one asleep.

Later I found out that the girl who had confused me that morning was a dancer, too (she called herself a bal-lerina). Naturally, she thought I was gay.

Soon I was friends with the manager and the clerks. They told me that originally I had been taken for a conductor from Minsk. Luckily for me, his tour had been cancelled. When the mess was eventually sorted out, they decided to leave me alone.

The adjoining sandlot had long been the presumed site for a circus building. For now, the city used this hotel for touring performers.

I liked it a lot there. It felt very home-like. In the middle of our floor was a communal kitchen — not a common feature at a hotel — with a sink for dishes and a small fridge and a few gas ranges along the walls. Several ranges had small, jury-rigged stepstools for dwarfs.

A week later I moved into a room of my own. I left early in the morning for work, I came home late from work, I got my room key, and no one ever asked me any questions. I decided to unpack and settle down. The room was great, with a wooden wardrobe for clothing, a hot-and-cold water sink and a mirror, and the bed mattress was remarkably even.

My next-door neighbors were a dwarf family, very pleasant and affable, though our communication was limited to a rare hallway greeting or sharing the kitchen.

I met other guests, too. A few rooms were taken by the touring Yaroslàvl Gypsy Song and Dance Troupe (two of them added to my confusion on my very first morning). The Gypsies constantly milled around in the kitchen, staying up till the wee hours. The reception clerk who kept their passports intimated to me that there were actually only two official "Gypsies" in the troupe, Yakov Migèlny and Nikolay Zhòlty; one "Gypsy" was Armenian, three were Russian, and six were Jews. Coquettish "Gypsy" girls often treated me to Ukrainian borscht and Jewish chicken croquettes — delicacies whose taste I had almost forgotten.

I started talking to Yakov, a nice Jewish guy, who told me that most of the troupe had come from Odessa, where anti–Semitism was very strong. They managed to "affiliate" the troupe with the Yaroslàvl Philharmonic, where Nikolay had connections. (Oh yes. The Soviet Ministry of Culture would not have any loose troupes running around; each one had to be under the aegis of a local philharmonic).

A month had passed. I was still haunted by thoughts of my slavish position in Novosibirsk and ways to get out, but now I was enjoying the roof over my head, something I had long yearned for. Truly, it was a lap of luxury. I was getting used to creature comforts, like my own bed, a shower whenever I felt like it, and a warm toilet.

The Architects' Club was nearby. I enrolled for drawing classes. I also signed up for courses in philosophy and English at the local engineering college — I needed to take exams in these to be eligible for a postgraduate degree. I started thinking about writing articles and getting moonlighting jobs.

Once in a while my neighbors would wake me up as they made noise, unable to settle down after the show. But I got used to it fast.

One night I had a hard time falling asleep because of the noise in the hallway. It was two dwarfs having fun. One was hiding at the landing and peeking out from time to time. The other one, next to my room, reacted by screaming and stomping his feet. I tried to reason with him. I told him the hour was late, that I needed to rest, that, as an actor and a man of culture, he should be respectful of communal living rules. Nothing helped. He would not listen; he merely lay down on the floor and kicked the wall. Our "dialogue" went on for some time. Finally, a young woman wearing an evening dress and high heels came out. She picked up the miscreant — "That's enough from you, son"— and carried him back to her room.

Yet there was a dark side to my paradise-like existence. The hotel cost a fortune: three rubles fifty a night, due weekly. The philharmonic paid for the artists, but I had to pay out of my own pocket—105 rubles a month on a salary of 83 (70 after taxes). Food alone was two to three rubles a day, so I already had to borrow from co-workers.

But then I found out that by law my office was supposed to be paying the hotel-living expenses of a "young" (i.e. just after college) professional. Or else they would have to "release" him — in other words, let me go back to Moscow! Suddenly my "inconvenience" turned into a real chance to change my situation.

I collected all the hotel bills and showed them to the director. He called his bookkeeper. The latter would not hear about it. There was nothing in the budget, period. He was not about to set himself up for trouble.

I went to the local D.A.'s office and filed a suit. They were in shock. "A young specialist," legally living in a hotel — suing a state organization. This made for a great story.

Two days later I got a call from the D.A. She had seen them all, she intimated, and she would get to the bottom of it. How did I manage to settle down in a hotel?

She offered me an alternative — to withdraw my suit. Then she started threatening me. There would be consequences, she hinted. Then she took a different tack, addressing my conscience: good specialists were needed in Siberia, and I had a great future here. My office had nothing but good things to say about me —

"Then they should let me go!" By now logic was no longer my strong suit.

Then the D.A.— officially, the defender of working people's interests —

went on the offensive again. "If you don't want to settle this nicely, I'll write a letter to your school, and you'll never get your graduation diploma." (In those days a diploma was held up for a year.) "You don't have Moscow registration. You'll never get a job there. And I'll make sure you'll get picked up for parasitism. Then you'll be back in our office—but in a different capacity."

Picking up on her tone, I responded with a demagogical tirade of my own, raising my voice to the screaming pitch: "The Party entrusted you with protecting Soviet citizens—is this how you live up to the Party's trust? I'm going to the Party Committee with a complaint against you!"

She grew quiet. Her temperature went up a few degrees. The makeup on her face was melting and dripping. With her pious mask gone, she dialed a number nervously. Shooting me hateful looks, she gave my director a good talking-to: "I'm sending Berkovich over. Deal with him yourself. But I don't want to see him again. Is that understood?"

The reference to the Party Committee worked. It is not as if they would take my side against her. But she would get a black eye for being unable to take care of me.

I rushed off to the office. I couldn't believe my good fortune. I knew they had no money to spend. They had to let me go! I had to call Marina. No—I would just surprise her. The first thing to do is to make up a list. First stop, the post office: the change-of-address form. Next, return books to the library. Pay the debts—which meant getting money some place. What about the ticket? I'll take a train—I'll make some kind of a deal with the conductor—what a great stroke of luck!

The entire "Politburo" of the office gathered in the director's office. They looked properly grim, from time to time casting fiery looks, enough to turn me to ashes. What did I care? In a week, I wouldn't remember their names.

The moment I came in, the union secretary rose, holding a package in his hands. Aha. This had to be my labor book, a passport-like document with employment record that follows Soviet citizens from job to job. So he was going to make a big deal out of it.

"Comrade Berkovich," he said in a funereal voice. "Please, sign here."

Wonderful. We are off—

"And count the money, please. The local union committee is granting you a non-returnable loan due to your extraordinary family circumstances."

Kuz'min

Looking for extra income, I got a local TV station in Novosibirsk to commission scripts for a TV series on architecture. Then I had to bring in an expert opinion of my writings. At the architecture department of a local school of engineering I was referred to "Comrade Kuz'min."

My heart jumped at the name. Could it be the same Nikolay Kuz'min, the Constructivist architect whose name was all over the media in the USSR thirty years earlier? It turned out that it was.

In the 1920s the Constructivists had been the avant-garde of modern international architecture. But in the early 1930s the powers-that-be concluded that this particular *garde* had gone so far *avant* that they were out of control; thus they had to be squashed. When the Stalinists got to destroy Constructivism, they looked for any reason to smear the movement in the eyes of society. Any roof leak, any imagined or actual flaw in design became an occasion for the gravest charges, including sabotage. This led to jails, camps, and executions. Kuzmin's Housing Commune project (*Dom-Kommuna* in Russian) was one such example.

At the time, city dwellers in Russia led a miserable existence in pre–1917 Revolution rental apartments where the rooms were split among families. To solve the problems of overcrowding and lack of privacy, the Housing Commune was proposed as a new type of social housing. Functions, such as cooking, dining, recreation, laundry were combined in common areas. So, for the same square footage and budget, the state could provide many more private, if very small, "social" apartments than traditional ones.

Kuz'min took those ideas to a utopian extreme. In his *Dom-Kommuna*, adults were to sleep in clusters of six (men and women separately) or in groups of two ("formerly known as 'husband' and 'wife'"). They were to take meals in the common dining room. There was to be no family in the customary sense. The children were to live independently, in effect, having convenient access to the parents only by means of "warm corridors." Meanwhile, those former "husbands" and "wives," though sleeping together, were in every other respect to dissolve in Kuz'min's highly structured collective.

This gave the authorities a reason to accuse all Constructivists of a satirical distortion of Communist ideas. I was certain that Kuz'min had been executed a long time ago. But he turned out to be alive and well, strong, lean, and athletic in his early sixties — and teaching architecture.

He spoke in short, abrupt, well-polished phrases. His movements were sharp and nervous. His opinions were unappealingly judgmental. And he continued to generate ideas.

When we met, he was enthusiastic about his project for a prefabricated building, whose components could be delivered by a dirigible and then assembled on the site. "There is nothing like a pure idea," he said. "Imagine a unit of dirigibles in the wilderness of taiga. They bring prefabricated concrete pieces along with a group of enthusiasts. They cut down trees and clear the space. Buildings are assembled horizontally on the ground. No heavy cranes, no expensive scaffolds. Work goes fast. Time is money. Everything goes on schedule. On an appointed date, the dirigibles come back. A quick order rings out, and the buildings are pulled off the ground and installed. Residents move in in an orderly fashion."

Like me, Kuz'min was sent to Siberia "voluntarily," though in his case the decision came from the highest place: Soviet leader Khrushchev personally. There was a time in the 1950s, when Khrushchev flirted with the "creative intelligentsia," and at one of these lovefests, Kuz'min got into a fistfight with the host.

The story was hard to believe. "Of course I could not get away with it," Kuz'min confessed to me sadly, and added in a completely childish way. "He started first."

I still wonder how he was able to hold on to his ideas, both naive and non-compromising, through so many years of so hard a life. I liked him a lot. Though not quite typical, Kuz'min helped me recreate a picture of those wonderful people who naively subscribed to the Communist ideal of social equality.

"Six Ninths"

One day I got a letter from Dmitry Linsky. He worked at a place whose full name was All-Union Research Institute of Physical Technical and Radio Measurements. Every hour the institute's famed beep of Exact Time was transmitted all over the Soviet Union from the town of Mendelèyevo near Moscow. Dmitry was doing lab experiments under Alexander Voronèl, a well-known physicist.

Dmitry told me that he needed a little gold in a hurry. The problem was that the gold had to be of high purity — practically without admixture, .999999 percent pure. That's what they called it, he said: "six ninths." The only place in the country where such gold was manufactured was a mysterious factory in Novosibirsk. Naturally, everything the shop produced went to defense and space research, which was essentially the same thing. It was impossible to obtain any of its gold through official channels. One needed several years to do it through Gosplan, the national planning agency. And even that was a hopeless venture.

Dmitry needed two grams of gold. "Can you get at least one gram," he begged. "You are our only hope. A historic scientific experiment depends on you."

He did not know either the factory's address or the name of a single official or its director. The address had a Kirovsky name in it, whether it was a street or the square, or something else, and no number.

I was not surprised. Due to the mania of total secrecy, an endless number of towns and villages or factories and research facilities were known only to a limited group of people — and then, under a name like "P.O. Box such-and-such." Those in on the secret had to swear silence in writing. When Dmitry wrote that this P.O. Box was producing gold known as "six ninths," he was disclosing a state secret. Fortunately, he knew he could count on me.

Naturally, these "boxes" were not listed in phone directories. You have to find them. And if I did, how would I get the gold? Nevertheless, "a historic experiment was depending" on me. In a country that worshipped its physicists — after all, didn't they put us in space before the Americans? — I did not need to be prodded. I decided to inspect Kirov Square, which was a fifteen-minute bus ride from my office.

I went there on a lunch break. In the freezing Siberian winter, the few passersby were covering their faces to escape the wind. It took me half an hour to inspect all the buildings. There was not a single sign that would at least hint at the presence of the mysterious "box." The lunch break was over, it was time to go back. Desperate, I grabbed a passerby to pop the question.

"Perhaps, you are talking about the six-ninths one?" He brought me to a nondescript entrance and rang the bell.

The door opened and instantly closed behind me. I was in a small dark room facing a small window. A man asked me sternly what the purpose of my visit was.

Hemming and hawing in confusion, I explained that I needed a little "six ninths." He told me to wait and left. Although at first I could barely see anything after the bright sunshine outside, soon my eyes got used to the dark. There was another door, and about fifteen minutes later another man came in and invited me to follow him.

As I followed him along a dark hallway, I could only think that I had gotten myself into another fine mess. I didn't have a Plan B. I could not give up Dmitry. I had to come up with something quick, and my head would not cooperate.

We entered another tiny room, also without windows, with a table and two chairs. It was hot inside, and I removed my winter jacket. Without waiting for questions that might put me further in the hole, I went on about the "historic experiment at the Measurement Institute," whose fate hinged on "six ninths." I embellished a little. I worked there, too, I said, in a lab next door, and was visiting Novosibirsk on business. And there was no way I could come back without the gold.

It was only then that I realized that I could be asked to show an ID. But that didn't happen. In general, the atmosphere was friendly. No one searched me, so an arrest was unlikely. The man held silent for a while and then asked how much I needed.

Barely containing myself, I said, "Five grams."

He fell silent again. "That's too much. Three maximum."

He gave me the number of their bank account and asked me for an address. I wasn't prepared for that, either. I wrote "Moscow Region, Village of Mendelèyevo, Measurement Institute, Voronèl Alexander Ivanovich."

I didn't know Voronèl's patronymic and added "Ivanovich" on the spur of the moment. A post office would not release a parcel if the patronymic did not fit. But since the institute was the recipient, we could get away with it.

I was a whole hour late from lunch — but the section head was away, and no one bothered me.

Five weeks later Dmitry reported that the gold had arrived, but they wouldn't use it. They hadn't believed I would succeed and had switched to another experiment — just as "historic."

Kisin

I had barely landed in Novosibirsk when I got a letter from my closest relative in Moscow: the always-helpful cousin Irena. She was writing to put me in touch with her husband's nephew Izzy Kisin, who lived in Novosibirsk and was "a good guy and a person of some importance. I already wrote him about you," she added. "I think you'll become friends."

"So how can I help you?" Kisin addressed me in the familiar "*ty*." An effusive Southerner (from Baku in Azerbaijan), lean and swarthy, with brown eyes and a mop of black hair, he was a mere seven years older. But I could hardly return the familiarity. The sign on the door of his office said, "Kisin Israil Moyseevich — Meteorology Institute, Siberian Branch — Director."

I told him how I was "distributed" to a local land utilization business that had nothing to do with architecture. My goal was to get out of it and go back as soon as I could. But the law was harsh — I had to spend a minimum of three years here.

"Why did you leave Moscow at all?" Kisin asked, surprised.

I had to, I admitted — in the absence of residential permit. If someone reported me living without it, and police came — I would end up having to dodge the law. Now I had to work here for 83 rubles a month.

Kisin gasped. "You can't live on this money!" He instantly called up their legal counsel.

"Yeah, you can't get rid of your 'masters' because of that," he uttered after hanging up. Upon reflection he said, "I wish I could get you a part-time job here, but there are no vacancies. However, I could fork over a few bucks from the Anonymous Fund."

The famous Anonymous Fund was part of a salary fund in a Soviet enterprise that was not earmarked to any particular person. It was sort of an emergency fund, unrelated to the office's main activity, and thus an area ripe for abuse. Millions of people prospered thanks to this loophole.

"You are an architect, right? I could commission from you, say, sketches for painting, let's see — our hallways! That's a few bucks for you. We'll give this place a bit of a fresh look, too. Of course, our housepainters don't need your sketches for shit. But that's not your problem."

"Now," Kisin went on — clearly, for him practical implementation never lagged far behind his ideas — "I got my head bookkeeper who is a real watchdog with money. Remember, this has to be done as cleanly as possible. I'm going to ask him over, and we'll make arrangements in front of him. Just don't ask too much, lest he get suspicious." He pushed the intercom button and asked his secretary to bring in "PPP."

The head bookkeeper was a gloomy hunchback with a red pimply nose and a suspicious look. His full name was Prokhòr Prokòpievich Propizèyev, hence "PPP." He modestly settled on the edge of a chair.

Kisin introduced me as a well-known Moscow architect. "Time to call in the housepainters, to give us a new fresh look, right? So, Comrade Berkovich agreed to do sketches for us."

PPP meekly tried to protest. "What the hell do we need with them?"

Kisin knew the drill. "We are a top-notch research facility. We are on the verge of being awarded a Red Banner to that effect. In two months we'll be getting a visit from the Moscow bosses. We have to keep up appearances." Then he addressed me. "Comrade Berkovich, how much will you charge for your sketches?"

I was unprepared. "I think — this might — cost" — I mumbled, staring upwards, desperately trying to come up with a figure. Then I took a deep breath. "Forty-five rubles." Inwardly, I decided I could not charge less — it was a big place, after all.

"Forty-five rubles?" Kisin echoed questioningly, and with air of slight distraction, as he gave the bookkeeper a pensive look. The latter stared at the floor in silence.

I got upset. Surely I had asked for too much. Now I'll never see that gig. And I needed it so badly. On the other hand, it was a huge building. And I had to measure the walls. No. I couldn't see anyone doing it for less.

Kisin looked at me again. "Comrade Berkovich, we are not doing just the lobby here. Please tell us how much you will charge for the whole job — both floors, the lobby, and my office."

I went back to calculations. The bookkeeper raised his eyes to look at me intently.

"The whole job?" I said.

"The whole job," Kisin said, looking at the bookkeeper.

"The whole job...." I drawled, stalling for time. He surely meant I asked too little. Suddenly, I felt daring. "I could do it for eighty-five rubles."

Kisin looked away.

"Er, Comrade Director —" the bookkeeper woke up — "are we going to paint the bookkeeping office?"

"Yes," said Kisin abruptly. "But we'll commission sketches for the bookkeeping office and your hallway from Comrade Berkovich later."

"How come?"

"We got no money," said Kisin tersely.

The bookkeeper left. Kisin rose from his chair and looked out of the window.

I broke the silence. "You told me not to ask too much."

Kisin cast me a look of sympathy and looked away again. Then, barely moving his head, he said, "I was afraid you'd ask over two or three thousand." Then he added, "Let's call it a day. We'll go to my place for dinner." And he called his secretary to get his car.

The Kisins lived in a small two-room apartment in a new building on the west bank of the Ob River. Kisin uncorked a bottle of brandy and we stayed up late talking. I visited them often. My cousin Irena proved right — we became friends.

In his previous life, Kisin was a glacier physicist. His Ph.D. thesis consisted of discovering and describing forty glaciers in the Caucasus. "We would rent a helicopter and go wild boar hunting afterwards. We would bring in a local boss, vodka, some girls. Have a barbecue in the mountains. Those were fun days."

Kisin despised the local population. "They are stuck up on their laws, like dogs in mangers. In Azerbaijan, life is different. If you need a letter from a doctor to get some sick days at work, everybody knew the rate: a ruble a day. No hard feelings. Everything's in the open."

Kisin was witty and charming, the soul of the party with a roving eye, and an all-round hedonist.

A few years later, Kisin got a job in Cuba, and I lost track of him. Many years later, my cousin told me that after Cuba he settled somewhere outside Moscow. I found him and invited him over.

The time was early '72, and we were talking emigration. Kisin thought that, without question, one had to take off, "before they closed the door." Yet the destination had to be America, not Israel.

Back in the Siberian days, Izzy once shared with me a story of his boss's business trip to the U.S. Upon return he told Izzy that in New York he had run into a store with a big sign that said Kisin & Sons. "I wondered if you are related."

Izzy commented: "I wasn't about to admit that this was my uncle!"

Now I reminded him about his uncle. Yet Izzy was not planning to leave. Too old, he said. When I told him I was feeling the same way at 36, he laughed at me — and stunned me with his detailed knowledge of the minutiae of filing emigration papers. My wife and I were still babes in the woods about this dangerous-for-the-Soviets business.

We had a pleasant evening. We did not suspect it was going to be our last one. A few months later Izzy was dead of cancer.

Following our first meeting in Novosibirsk, Izzy went to Moscow on business. He visited relatives and told them about our meeting and "sketches negotiations." He was a marvelous storyteller, and the whole incident, first re-enacted by him and then embellished with extra details, both real and invented, became a part of the family lore and a favorite at the family table to tease me with until our departure for the states.

In Novosibirsk, Kisin set out to help in all seriousness. At first he started describing all the good things about local life, of which the best one was "an acute shortage of professionals." Once he heard out my problems, he grew quiet. Then he said, "Of course you could have a brilliant career here in a few years. What is wrong with the land use business? I don't completely understand your obsession with architecture. But since all you want is to be reunited with your family in Moscow, let's put our minds together." And he started plotting out various courses of action for me.

"It will be hard to get you out by proving that you are being used improperly as a specialist. They'll always come up with an excuse. So you put pressure on them about living conditions? That's a good move. That's your only legal loophole. But that is not foolproof either.

"The best thing would be to get them to fire you," he reasoned. "What do you think?

"Surely you have had a chance to see the errors and stupidities that take place in their business? You must have — you have a fresh eye. Wrong decisions are being made every minute. On all levels, from your immediate boss to the director. Am I right?

"What you have to do is launch a criticism campaign on all levels. Don't pull any punches. Raise your hand at every meeting. Use every opportunity, no matter how specious the reason. You have nothing to lose. These are ideal conditions. You will get a reputation as an egregious nitpicker. No one likes that. Especially if you ignore the rank and rip into the highest-placed targets. After a while, you won't even have to ask them — they'll fire you of their own accord."

I loved his advice. And started working on it promptly.

My Brilliant Failure

To be released by the Gipro office as a "vicious critic" required a considerable moral effort. Simply criticizing was not a problem. To do it "viciously," I had to play a role — I had to undergo certain internal changes. And in order to deliver professional criticism I had to master the complexities of the area I had just started learning.

I had never studied the basics of agriculture and their relation to village development. I had not even the faintest thought where to obtain this information. I had been taught how to design buildings. I had to reinvent the wheel, in other words.

First, I developed an abstract scheme. I separated the traffic of cattle and machinery from that of people. Then I grouped housing into cul-de-sacs with backyards opening on back — dirty — roads. That brought me to a diagram of a bunch of fingers sticking out and into one another, with the public center on the cusp of residential and production areas along the through road that divided them. Then I placed the cattle compound downwind, between grazing areas and the transit road. Next, I tried to tie this conceptual idea to the real situation in several villages at once. Things began taking shape.

We toiled under the section's Chief Engineer Ivan Maklakòv — a native Siberian, tall and big-bodied, with light eyes and blond hair, a round face and an upturned nose. He always wore a well-starched white shirt and a yellow-orange necktie with broad blue stripes, a burgundy red coat and a vest of the same color. He spoke in a loud, convincing voice, especially when talking nonsense.

Maklakòv was considered a major expert on village affairs. Our directors lured him away from "competitors" about six months before my arrival. He knew how to wield the project lingo. He was not popular in the section, mildly speaking, and was disrespectfully called "Van'ka" behind his back, after a folk-tale character who was a dumbbell and whose first name just happened to be the same as Maklakòv's.

Maklakòv loathed me at first sight. He instantly concluded I was after his job. Yet I had a hard time taking his fear seriously.

From the start he found fault with everything I did. He could not stress enough my ignorance of agriculture and the country way of life. (Which, of course, was absolutely true.) He made a show of correcting me and announced my errors out loud, whether real or imaginary ones. But I had to give him his due. Of course he was basically ignorant in planning. But he knew village life very well. All his "village layout" ideas were based on a peasant's common sense.

"Don't get upset, Gary." He assumed an expression of paternal condescension. "Everybody makes mistakes at the beginning. We'll teach you. Sure, your professors taught you that bread grows on loaf trees, ha ha."

He corrected my designs with a thick crayon on the tracing paper. I neatly traced his scribbles and turned them into sketches. On his next visit he critiqued his own instructions, just as condescendingly. I kept tracing. And so it went.

Soon our work came up for examination at the regular production meeting — a perfect stage for me to play the part of the "vicious critic." I pinned our materials to the wall and started off slowly. I tried to be undiplomatic and pull no punches. As a result, I got a huge kick of enjoying free speech.

The meeting was chaired by the office's Chief Engineer Lukyànov. I used his presence to cast a few stones at the administration, too. There was no organization here, I said. Everybody just went his own way without getting any direction, and no technical information, either. We were on a deserted island. Our bosses were asleep at the wheel. And so on.

The results could not have been more unexpected. The administration did not take umbrage. Two days later I was called in to be informed I had been promoted, and skipping a position, too. I was made "group leader" and given a salary of 120 rubles (a time and a half increase). The group was made of my recent supervisor Galina Bezborodova and her friend Valentina Gusèlnikova — a topographer, too.

More than ever, Maklakòv became reinforced in his worse suspicions about me.

I had been in Novosibirsk for nine weeks, and my chances of going back to Moscow had not gone up a notch. Yet I was not discouraged. I decided I was on the right course and had to raise the level of my "vicious criticism" — make it more vicious and insistent. I kept orating at weekly meetings at my section, at union meetings and the technical council meetings. And I voiced criticism every time I ran into bosses of any level.

Soon I was sent on another business trip to Altai. This time I was traveling with Maklakòv as his deputy. I had long wanted to find myself tête-à-tête with him in order to talk things over. In essence, our goals dovetailed. Both of us wanted to rid the office of my presence. Why could we not join our efforts?

We had a heart-to-heart through an entire evening, but we did not come to an agreement. I tried to tell Maklakòv that I saw no prospect for me at the Gipro, that I was there against my own will, that I wanted to go back to Moscow to be with my family.

He didn't believe a thing. He called me a wolf in sheep's clothing. Not for nothing did I show off at every meeting. Going after his position was merely the first step; ultimately I was after the director's chair, too.

The conversation was not completely useless. I realized I had to aim my criticism high. If Maklakòv really thought I was going after our bosses, then the best thing he could do for me was to convince them he was right. I had to go on alienating the administration.

I had an occasion to do that in February, seventeen weeks after my arrival in Novosibirsk.

Actually, it started just before the New Year when it turned out that there was no money to pay the salaries. I was in shock. This couldn't happen in the USSR. It looked like either the accounting department had overlooked something, or something unexpected had happened — but a few collective farms and even two state farms had not paid on their accounts.

There were three forms of property in the USSR: state, co-operative, and private. The third one had nothing to do with us. Individuals did not commission projects. And getting paid by state farms was relatively simple. In the worst-case scenario, someone at the Party committee called the bank, and the required sum was transferred to our account even without the farm's say-so. Of course it was against the law. But the Party authority always trumped the state. A *kolkhoz* (a collective farm) was a different story. Of course you could put the pressure on the chairman and threaten him with the expulsion from the Party (and it was done, too). But the bank could not do anything without his signature.

I didn't know then that running out of payroll funds was not so rare in small state outfits that were supposed to pay their own way. I had an architect friend who was sent to work in Turkmenistan. He told me it was a usual thing at his office. The director would go borrow a sack full of cash from their night watchman named Muratàn. (Everybody was paid in cash in the USSR). The old Turkoman sat on the porch of the office in a pensive mood, selling opium and hashish — "not on the job," of course. He did not charge his boss interest. But he tsk-tsked disapprovingly: Not good business, boss.

We didn't have a Muratàn of our own. Hence Section Chief Vasilkòv could not think of anything better than to send Maklakòv and me around the villages to collect debts for the payroll. Fortunately, the country proletarians paid up, though reluctantly.

Once we plugged that hole, the Altai regional Soviet nixed three of our projects. They came back to us with devastating critiques. The clients immediately put a hold on payments. The projects had been signed by Maklakòv under Chief Engineer Lukyànov's direct supervision. I was told to redo them. I refused, under the pretext that I was doing urgent work that would guarantee timely pay. Then my group was made larger by adding a few more people. Now I had half the section under my supervision.

What I did next was real chutzpa (though of course I didn't know the word then). I made a condition: no one, even Chief Engineer Lukyànov, was to interfere with what I was doing. Also, as I re-worked the designs completed under his supervision, I regularly dropped remarks about his incompetence.

Opposite: The contest project for an experimental settlement in Siberia. A bird's-eye view of the central area. Novosibirsk, Siberia, 1966.

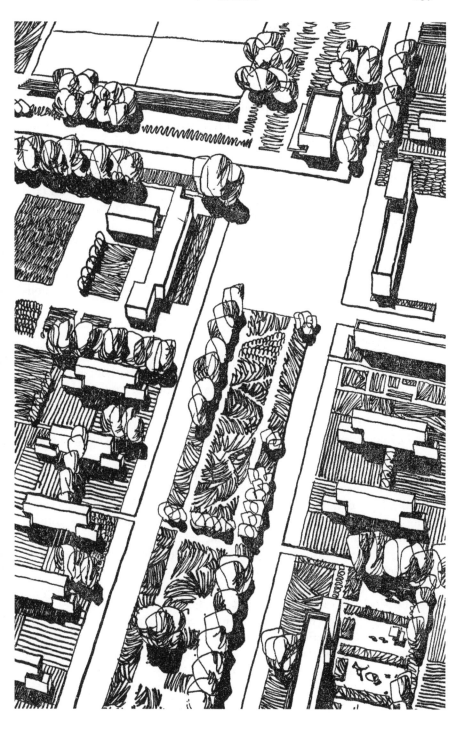

With Lukyànov's wife in my group now, those remarks just had to be passed along to him. From the point of view of my plans, things could not be working any better.

A week later, before the redone work was shipped, Director Serpenìnov, accompanied by Lukyànov, showed up at our section to take a look at the blueprints and sign off on them. Suddenly this turned into a public airing of the work done. Maklakòv came out with three pages of notes that led one to conclude that the blueprints could not be shipped in their present form. I had to go on defense.

It took me no time to switch to offense, though, and personal attacks, too. I reminded everybody how Serpenìnov couldn't meet the payroll (and accounting was his direct responsibility). I charged the director with negligence "verging on criminal."

Then came Lukyànov's turn. The deadline was the next day, and he trusted their analysis to the ignorant Maklakòv — is this what you do before the deadline? Where was he when this shabby work was being done under his supervision last summer? Didn't he realize that serious work cannot be done by amateurs?

By then I had really gotten the hang of Soviet bureaucratic demagoguery, and I was cherishing my impunity.

The workers at the meeting did not know which way to look. Lukyànov, barely containing himself, signed the stack of blueprints without looking and left. Serpenìnov followed suit. I folded the blueprints in a roll, took it to the post office, and went home.

I thought I had done a fine job scandalizing everybody. There was no way I could get away with it. Triumphant, I went to visit friends and shared with them a bottle of Armenian brandy.

The next day I came to work in an uplifted mood that seemed to be shared by no one else with the exception of Maklakòv. The latter grinned contentedly. For a day, that is; and then for another. But on the third day something changed. Maklakòv arrived at work and passed to his office without greeting anyone. Then Vasilkòv and he locked themselves in for a long powwow. Before lunch Vasilkòv vanished, while Maklakòv went next door to the topography section.

The next day Serpenìnov himself showed up at our section, accompanied by Mochalòv from the technical section.

The meeting was brief. We were informed that Maklakòv was leaving us "voluntarily." Our section chief Vasilkòv was promoted to chief specialist at technical section, while his predecessor in the job, Mochalòv, was being appointed to Vasilkòv's former position.

Then everyone was dismissed, and I was asked to come by Vasilkòv's office. My heart beat fast — did it work, after all?

Co-workers at RosGìproZèm included (front row, from left) Nadezhda Lukyanova, Nadezhda Tyunina, Galina Bezborodova, unidentified, Valeria Gusel'nikova, Julia Kaufman, (back row) three unidentified people, Vladimir Bukreyev, unidentified, Lyudmila Belozerova, Eugenia Soboleva, and Yekaterina Suvòrova. Novosibirsk, Siberia, 1966.

In the presence of our former and coming supervisors, Serpenìnov announced that the administration was appointing me to Maklakòv's position — the section's chief engineer, with a salary of 165 rubles. It was twice the original salary at the office that I was receiving a mere two months before.

I was shocked. And I was upset. My first hundred and twenty-four days in Novosibirsk (I counted them religiously) had ended in a total fiasco. As a "vicious critic," I was a complete failure. I failed to get fired.

8

~

Exodus

The Graduate

Early 1967 finds me at a tiny desk in a diminutive room in Moscow, working on my Ph.D. dissertation.

My desk is crammed. It is the same with the hard-as-nails sleeping couch that takes up the rest of the dark closet, two steps long and three steps wide, converted into a rental space. And I am the one who rents it.

My closet is accessed from the landlady's room. Whence from the shadows come odd-sounding sobs, uttered by Ksènia Mitrofànovna, 73, my landlady herself. Only a half hour earlier, belligerently drunk, she was sprawled on the floor, stretching along my desk. Which of course kept me from concentrating on my work, and I had to drag her back to her room.

She has not had a sober moment in two days, babbling nonstop. Just as she is now:

"My kids ... my babies ... all that I want for you ... all the best ... can't do nothing about the head, can I...." The weeping resumes loudly.

"Got to get a refrigerator. It's just sitting there. Lots of refrigerators. Just sitting there, that's all." I surmise she had signed up in a waitlist for a refrigerator. Now years later, her number has come up and she should be buying it.

"The old woman, she neeeed help, and there's no one to help 'er," she goes on wailing. And then suddenly she begins to snore.

There is nobody but me to feel sorry for Ksènia. Her granddaughter Natasha has gone out. Her daughter Tanya — Tatiàna Pàvlovna — is in the hospital. There is nobody else. But my empathy does not count. I am a tenant — a stranger.

I have been staying at her place for only a few weeks. My arrival was preceded by a series of attempts to move in with my wife in Moscow. This is a tale full of adventures, all miserable and some even funny.

The author's ID as a postgraduate student. Moscow, 1967.

The story started six months earlier when I returned to Moscow from Siberia. For a few weeks while I was taking my entrance exams for architectural graduate school, I stayed with Aunt Shura, my mother's sister, sleeping on the floor in her granddaughter's room. Then I got a bed in the graduate dorm, though it turned out to be a fiction. The tiny room meant for two was taken up by another student, Tòlik Hamzà, and his wife, living there illegally.

My wife Marina worked in the small town of Mendelèyevo outside Moscow, where she had a cot in a dorm. We had counted on a room in the graduate dorm. We would live there as a family, with our baby daughter, for the three years of school. In the meantime I would find a way to get a regular apartment. I still believe that if I had figured out a way to deal with the dorm's director Alyòna, this would have worked out. My graduate life would have turned out differently. But I never developed a talent for giving bribes.

While Hamzà's wife was away, I slept on the other bed. When she returned, they moved their beds back together, and I went back to the mattress on the floor. Soon Alyòna the director suspected "a violation" and took the mattress away. "No more than two people per room!" Of course I had a right to chase Hamzà's wife out, but it never occurred to me — perhaps out of a sense of solidarity. To return the favor, Tòlik courteously agreed to make room for cartons with my books.

I went to Aunt Shura, but two weeks later she voiced displeasure. I took the hint and refrained from further visits.

Unaware of my breakup with Aunt Shura, Marina came to visit me on the weekend. We had to spend the night in the transit lounge at Kazàn Railroad Terminal. The wooden benches were not the most comfortable place. And each hour or so the police chased everybody outside. Then we moved to Yaroslàvl Terminal next door. Here the cops were more laissez-faire.

Back at the dorm, Hamzà's wife left again, and I had another two weeks on the bed at my legitimate residence.

None of this benefited my academic progress. Between one thing and another I could not work on my thesis. Moreover, my friend Dmitry and I decided to enter an architectural contest. We toiled around the clock, hoping for a big fat award.

Concurrently I was attempting to rent a place. Late evenings I went to an informal "apartment exchange" in Banny Lane, where potential renters and landlords congregated on walkways when police were not around.

On a rainy autumn evening, Marina and I ran into a rather good-, and more importantly, cultured-looking old lady (actually, she was about fifty-five) called Larìssa Lalètina. She was thin and short-ish, with a small sharp nose and generously applied lipstick. She was dressed in an old, worn-out coat and a sharp-topped fur hat, and carried a small backpack.

Lalètina introduced herself as an "inventor in the area of cartoons." She had to go to Tbilisi for a year — or even longer — on a matter pertaining to a patent. She could not leave her apartment to strangers. "Too many items and books that I value as memories of my late husband." She liked us, "a young couple that inspired trust." If we paid two months in advance, she would charge us a mere fifty rubles a month. That was steep, but still looked like a stroke of luck. We went to take a look.

Lalètina's room was conveniently located almost in Moscow's downtown, on the fourth floor of a huge 1930s apartment building. While she was opening the door to her room, her neighbors in the communal apartment eyed us with curiosity through their doors kept ajar. Naturally, they were not enthusiastic to see us, but I was hoping we would get along.

The room was spacious, with large windows and bookcases lining the walls. There was not much furniture: a couch, a table, three chairs, a huge wardrobe that faced the door (a few steps from it) which, together with some hanging hooks on the wall, formed a mini-foyer of sorts, and, finally, a divan in the corner between the wardrobe's back and the wall. The place was strewn with personal items, cartons, leftover food, empty milk bottles, books and newspapers — it looked like a dorm room more than anything else.

Lalètina took off her coat and went to the communal kitchen to make tea. When she came back, she all of a sudden offered to let us stay for the night. "I can tell you don't have a place to stay. So feel at home. We'll have some tea with cookies, we'll chat. If you want to rent it, you'll bring your things tomorrow, along with the money. I'll be leaving two days from now. And tonight you can sleep behind the wardrobe. I'll hang a curtain for you to keep private."

We were ecstatic. We got our things together and we borrowed money wherever we could "for a few days." I moved to Lalètina's place, and Marina went back to Mendelèyevo to wrap up her affairs.

Two days later Larisa showed up wearing a brand-new raincoat and a pair of pretty shoes and told me that her departure was delayed for mysterious reasons. Something very strange had happened to Manàna, a Tbilisi relative of hers. I found especially suspicious the part that dealt with the mysterious Manàna's father. His last name was Zhukòvsky, and he lived on Zhukòvsky Street in the town of Zhukòvsky, "with two daughters in a two-room dacha, but with a piano and a refrigerator." The latter I found quite touching.

"Well, that's not too bad," Lalètina reassured me, looking away in a stealthy fashion. "We can get along; you are a cultured man, and you don't get in the way."

I had just enough culture to get the picture. I told her that this turn of the events did not suit us at all, and I was moving out tomorrow. Therefore I asked her to return the money, minus two nights. She said I could do whatever I liked, but she could not return the money, because she had already spent it.

While we were sorting things out, Marina called from a pay phone, happy to report that she had just gotten paid and was on her way. "We'll pay our debts!"

I briefed her on the latest developments, which upset her to the extent that she left the phone booth without her wallet with her salary. It's all true. It never rains, but it pours.

We rendezvoused that night in the graduate room of the Moscow School of Architecture. The deadline of our design entry was nearing, and we worked through the night. Then she went back to Mendelèyevo, and I went back to Lalètina's.

Here another surprise awaited me. The door to Lalètina's room was blocked by a new lock with combination code. The gloating neighbors crowded the hallway. They had been instructed to call the police the moment I showed up — and one of them was already busy doing just that. I tried to tell these law-abiding citizens that it was all a misunderstanding and I was here to retrieve my things.

All the while I was mechanically toying with the code on the lock — and suddenly I felt a miracle taking place: the lock opened. I told the instantly forlorn neighbors I had received the code from Lalètina and they scattered, disappointed.

Naturally, we were not going to share a room with Lalètina, and I was back on the street. For the next two or three weeks I slept in various dorms. Sometimes on a row of chairs in my "legit" one, but more often I crashed at fellow graduate students.' I was too busy finishing the contest entry to worry about shelter.

And it worked: we won, and got paid handsomely.

At the post office where I was getting my mail, I found a letter from my academic advisor Professor Meyerson. He was nervous. The deadline for the outline and detailed description of my thesis to be submitted to the Academic Council was two weeks away. It had to be approved by him beforehand. And I had not even shown him a single page yet! This could have ended in being kicked out.

"The graduate affairs director has been trying to locate you," Meyerson wrote, trying to be as polite as possible. "He is concerned that you show up only on the days your monthly stipend is paid."

I had to attend to my academic affairs. But I could not give up on the shelter business either.

Barely had I moved my belongings into a locker at the railroad terminal when I ran into Boris Moskalèv, a retired lieutenant colonel. Moskalèv stood six and a half feet, and looked way older than his middle age. We went to see his two-bedroom apartment in a deluxe building near Riga Terminal, on Mir Avenue, which had been built to house Soviet secret police KGB cadres. I liked it very much.

Moskalèv claimed two military degrees — an Armor Troop Academy and a General Staff Academy — and a command of foreign languages. He taught at the Armor Troop Academy and his bookshelf held a number of books on the strategy and tactics of tank warfare, authored or co-authored by him. Some of them were in foreign languages — Polish, Romanian, Chinese, Albanian, and others. He told me that he was temporarily not working for medical reasons and offered me one of the bedrooms that was accessed directly from the hall — thirty-five rubles a month. I agreed right away. Unlike Lalètina, he did not ask for rent in advance — just a loan of six rubles, which I provided.

Marina went to Zaporozhye, Ukraine, to bring in our daughter, who was staying there with my wife's parents, and I moved in with Moskalèv. I planned to put the room in order in time for my wife and daughter's arrival.

At first I came with my briefcase only, my suitcases still in the locker at the terminal. On the second day the colonel asked for another loan, this time fourteen rubles. I was apprehensive, but I complied. We agreed that I would bring my suitcases in a couple of hours. It took us a while. I insisted on having a key to the apartment, and he used various excuses to keep it away from me. Finally we agreed that he would be waiting for me.

When I came back laden with suitcases, the door was locked. I kept ringing the bell and knocking on the door for quite some time. I could see the light in the hall through the keyhole and distinctly heard someone's steps, but no one would open the door. It was ten P.M., then eleven. At half past midnight I took the suitcases back to the terminal. As I left it, I glanced at Moskalèv's apartment. The lights were on in every room.

I ran up to the seventh floor (the elevator was in use). I kept banging on the door and slamming the doorbell. Then the elevator arrived. Its door opened behind my back, and the professor of the Armor Academy and his wife stumbled out — colossally drunk. I had to help them insert the key — and then immediately slid it in my pocket.

Inside, we were met by a decent-looking girl named Zòya who turned out to be renting the other bedroom, accessible from the living room. (She had not opened the door out of fear). The landlord and his wife slept in the living room with no furniture but an armchair.

Although his wife was introduced as Elèna Dmìtrievna, her real name turned out to be Lìda, and of course she was not his real wife, who, along with their fifteen-year-old daughter, had moved out long ago.

My first night was far from quiet. It was filled with noise and cursing. This exchange reached me as I was barely awake:

PROFESSOR: Where am I gonna sleep? Get out!
LIDA: Go fuck yourself.
PROFESSOR: Move your butt!
LIDA: Go fuck yourself.
PROFESSOR: You can't say a word without fuck. (Beat.) Am I ever going to teach you cunt to stop cursing?
LIDA: Go fuck yourself.
PROFESSOR: Get out of here, you fucking whore!

A thud of a body against the wall — Lida hollering — heavy footsteps in the hall — doors slammed — strange voices.

I finally woke up and realized that I was in the next act of my graduate comedy-drama.

While talking to Marina on the phone the same day, I slightly hinted to her that perhaps it would be premature to bring our three-year-old daughter to Moscow.

When I came back I discovered that someone had used my bed — the door to my room was not locked.

The next night someone attempted to break in. At the last moment, Moskalèv threw them out. In the morning, following Zòya's advice — she had been renting from Moskalèv for a while — I cut in a lock.

Lida reacted to this development calmly. "Boris won't like it." Then she added flirtatiously, "You know he has moral scruples."

So I noticed, I said.

Lida herself was a sight to behold, with a huge shiner, a split lip, and a torn blouse. The professor-colonel's soulmate worked as a saleswoman at a vegetable stand. Today was her day off.

"I wish I had not rented my place" — she had a two-room apartment of her own — "to the Georgians," she murmured, filling the small hallway with vodka fumes. "You'd make a so much better tenant. It will be so hard for you here," she added sympathetically. "You have to write your thesis."

If it were not for her outside-the-barroom appearance, she did not sound like the person from the night before.

"You wouldn't have, by any chance, three rubles till tomorrow," she purred sweetly. "I'll pay you back tomorrow when I get home from work."

I had to turn her down.

By my wife's arrival, I felt quite settled at Moskalèv's. Of course the drinking and the cursing and the fighting went on night after night, but there were creature comforts, too: a subway station next door, a market, a railroad terminal, a bus stop, and a grocery store at the ground floor.

Actually, it was the latter that caused all the problems. The moment Moskalèv stopped by the store, he was set upon by all sorts of characters who offered to split a bottle with him. (Resisting the temptation was beyond him, not with his "system severely injured by serving the Motherland in armored troops.")

After the first bottle, the characters remembered that Moskalèv lived right upstairs and felt like paying a visit. But there was no food in the house. And so, instead of leaving, they felt like giving their host a solid thrashing. While the phone was still working, I would call the police, whom the guests feared enough to take off. Then the phone got turned off, but I still would pick up the receiver and pretend I was calling the police. At first it worked, but then they figured me out: after all, most of them were regulars. For some reason, they spared me. At least they never beat me up.

My wife could not stand the apartment from the start. When Marina first came, she carelessly left her fur coat outside the room in the hall. In the morning, the coat was still there, but someone had picked its pockets. Oddly, there had been no party the night before — which meant, no strangers. I raised the issue the next night, and Lida and Moskalèv feigned ignorance. I offered a "compromise," after a fashion. I would take the money out of the rent. "Just four-fifty less and that's it."

The colonel seemed to agree, but Lida, who had already had a few on her way home, was indignant. "Boris, what's wrong with you? This is an outrage! There was three rubles at the most!"

Marina did not like it that the bathroom door did not have a lock, either. Moskalèv's "wife," a cigarette dangling in the corner of her mouth, would march in unceremoniously while my wife was taking a bath. Then she would settle on the corner of the bathtub and, provided she was sober, engage in lengthy conversations on the meaning of life.

Eventually, we got along. I made good use of this time: I straightened out my affairs at school, I prepared the plan for my thesis, and I had Meyerson approve it.

In the meantime, I made friends with my neighbor Zòya, who was a fellow student from out of town taking courses by correspondence. She told me that Moskalèv's real wife was suing him for divorce and the apartment. His days here were numbered, and so were mine.

At the apartment exchange, I ran into a meek and quiet old lady called Ksènia Mitrofànovna. She lived in the easternmost Cherkizovo neighborhood, which was not easily accessed. It was 15 to 20 minutes by streetcar from Sokolniki subway station. It was a small place: a room and a closet, which I was renting. The apartment was barely enough for Ksènia, her daughter and her granddaughter — but a tenant? What do you need with a lousy thirty rubles, with such inconveniences?

It turned out later they were saving for her granddaughter Natasha's eighteenth birthday party. Natasha's father, a geologist in Tyumèn, Siberia, had sent the money for the purpose — and it had already been spent. Hence, they got a tenant.

I brought my things and settled down. I was told that previously the closet had been occupied by Grandma Ksènia herself, who now moved to the kitchen. Ksènia worked as a night watchperson and rested in the daytime on the couch or Natasha's cot, while her daughter Tatiana was at work and her granddaughter was at school.

Of course the tiny dark closet could not compare with Moskalèv's room. And moving in my wife was out of the question, to say nothing of our daughter. But it was quiet, without drunken fights, and I could hope that this was an intermediate solution, until something better turned up.

We got along. As a rule I spent weekdays in the library and came to my closet late. I felt peaceful and comfortable. And I was not worried about having to pay the thirty-ruble rent in advance.

According to Ksènia, her son-in-law had an important job in Tyumen. "Three years he's been there. They gave him a huuuge apartment — three rooms. Tanya went to visit."

"Why don't you move there," I asked, "instead of crowding here in one room?"
"Who'd wanna do that?"
"How's that?" I knew what this was about, but I wanted to hear it from her.
"You lose Moscow registration that way."
"So?" I egged her on.
"Can't it get back. Me, I don't really need it. This is for Natasha."
"What does she need it for?"
"She'll meet a cultured person. An educated one. In the country, it's nothing but drunks."

A week after I moved in they started preparations for the birthday celebration. The main thing was to get enough food and drink. First came the booze in the form of a few cases of vodka. Then the chasers: pickles, pickled tomatoes, sauerkraut, and marinated mushrooms. Everything was purchased in untold amounts, which took its toll on storage space. I had to shrink my living arrangements. Then came the hors d'oeuvres, stored on the balcony, which was also used for the cakes and pies and pierogis baked by Grandma Ksènia. Interestingly, all of this cost a lot more than my rent could bring in.

On the birthday, the room was turned into a banquet hall, which meant pushing aside most of the furniture and moving the rest to the neighbors.' The tiny kitchen table combined with sawhorses and a few boards served as a table the size of the room. Other boards were placed on the chairs, making quite comfortable benches.

The gala was attended by twenty-five guests, including Marina (who had visited me a few times and won the landlady's approval) and a few of my schoolmates (invited to bring up the men's contingent). Among the others, five were Natasha's schoolfriends, and six came from her mother Tatiana's office, headed by her supervisor and his wife. The rest were invited from next door.

As usual, we started by toasting and imbibing — lightly. That is, we were mostly drinking vodka out of eight-ounce glasses. Then came the dancing, which meant taking apart the bench and moving the table closer to the couch. We danced the tango, foxtrot, and waltz to the record player.

One of my friends picked up a guitar and sang a few popular songs, with others singing along. Then came more toasting and drinking. And then, "heated up," the guests really moved to cut a rug, which was something fast and rowdy, combining Ukrainian and Georgian dancing. This was accompanied by more toasting, without rhyme or reason, heeded by few. That segued into more drinking as the guests started falling into groups. Some settled on the couch and sang; others danced more.

In the chaos everyone forgot about hot food, to say nothing of dessert, since Grandma Ksènia, who was in charge of the above, became smashed after a few glasses, just as the "ethnic" dancing started.

I don't know exactly how the fight started. I stepped out on the landing to take some fresh air. I went back in when I heard the sound of the shattered mirror in the hall.

What happened was what I had least expected. Even by Russian standards we had more than enough booze. Twenty bottles of vodka alone, plus brandy and port. It took its toll. What seemed in the beginning like a well-behaved crowd transformed into a raging mob. A fellow worker of Tatiana's attacked a neighbor with a chair. Others tried to break them apart, but another guest banged him on the back of the head with the guitar. The victim's wife grabbed the offender by his hair.

The rest was hard to see through a wall of cigarette smoke or hear against the background of the record playing at full volume and everybody yelling at the same time. The schoolgirls tried to sneak out of the room. An old neighbor grabbed a chair to hit someone and missed, with the chair landing on the record player. En route the chair caught the chandelier, and the food on the table became covered with fine dust of broken glass. This damage made the room quieter and darker. My friends managed to drag Natasha's frightened girlfriends outside.

At the same time Tatiana sat in the corner, watching the scene with horror, her face increasingly pale. Eventually she had to be laid out on the couch, and someone called the ambulance. It turned out she was having a heart attack....

A week passed. The apartment was still a disaster site. Grandma Ksènia turned out to be a chronic alcoholic. Left without her daughter's supervision, she was constantly "sampling" little stashes of vodka hidden all over the house, and gradually got out of control. Natasha and I found some of the stashes and took them to the neighbors.

Right now she has awakened and has been cursing nonstop. I'm trying to focus on my work. It is Sunday, and I need to get ready for tomorrow meeting with an expert from the Invention Committee.

Yet Ksènia is getting worse. Now she is addressing me in an almost sober voice. "You educated ones ... you can't give a break to an old woman.... Why don't you say something, eh?" She breaks into weeping. "Tanya, my baby, my darling baby doll —"

Now she changes tack. "I'm an utter drunk, this is what I am," she declares in a steady voice. "But if we had any kinda order in the house —"

Suddenly, a crash and a horrifying holler. She had gotten up from the couch and, aiming to stay upright, grabbed the curtain, which collapsed on the floor with the curtain rod.

As I try to get Grandma from under the curtain, I realize her head is bleeding. Afraid for her, I head for the kitchen. There is no refrigerator and no ice, but I find a rag and put it in cold water. Just as I am about to wring it, Grandma Ksènia emerges behind me, her head bleeding profusely.

"You got what you wanted, you bastard!" With these mysterious words — what kind of nightmare is she having? — Ksènia collapses again, this time through the open door on the concrete landing floor.

The neighbors rush out because of the noise. I push them aside to behold a gruesome tableau. En route to the floor, Ksènia must have hit the metal banister, too, and her face is smashed. Her grey tousled hair is splattered with blood, which forms a puddle next to her head.

The momentary silence is broken by Grandma opening her dulled eyes, which circle the landing, as if looking for someone. Then, in a barely audible, yet clear voice, she declares: "The Jew killed me," and goes unconscious.

The Inventor

It all started with a ballpoint pen I received as a gift. In 1966 Moscow, Russia, a western-made pen like this with refillable rods of four different colors was an awfully valuable present.

It gave me sheer pleasure while writing out the description of my invention. "I should take out a patent," I told my wife. "They will issue me a license, three percent from the gross sales — a coop is guaranteed by the end of my graduate school."

"I see," she said. "You want us to have a schiz of our own."

The pen worked like a dream. Soon I learned to switch the colors with my thumb, without the ballpoint leaving the paper. The descriptions and the schematics appeared soon enough. I was working on a design for a cellular-type, multi-story residential building, erected with the use of prefabricated modules. I typed up the text on my long-suffering, East-German-made Erika portable, which was always at hand, or at least under my trestle-bed, and I ran to call Comrade Schtèrenberg.

Actually, I had been meaning to patent something for quite some time. It sort of started when I attended a lecture given by Vassily Pantelèyev at the Moscow Architects' Club. Pantelèyev, mustached and pink-cheeked, was some kind of pooh-bah at GOSSTROY (the State Committee for Construction). Despite his rank, he spoke in an intelligent and friendly fashion. On the one hand, it was clear from his speech that architectural inventions were not patented in the USSR. On the other, he called on everybody "not to be thwarted by obstacles" and patent their inventions. "Invent things," he urged us, "and come on over, and we'll help you break through the mire and together we'll prove that it is possible and necessary." It sounded great, especially the "break through the mire" part.

I called Pantelèyev the next morning, and we agreed to meet at 2 at his office the same day. As I was checking my coat at the GOSSTROY cloakroom, I saw his familiar, self-satisfied face at a distance, heading for the exit. He must have completely forgotten about our meeting. I managed to intercept him, and we spoke outside. He liked one of my long-cherished ideas and briefly explained how to put together an application. He ended on this encouraging note: "It shouldn't take longer than 3 to 5 years."

Something about my reaction to this rubbed him the wrong way. He threatened me. If I quit halfway, he would call my school and make sure I didn't get my Ph.D. Otherwise, he promised me all sorts of assistance. "Call me if you have problems," he said as he gave me the phone number of a "useful and responsible person" called Faìna Gurfinkel. He concluded by advising me to get myself a co-author, preferably from among those "particularly in the way."

Thus a few days later I got to see Comrade Gurfinkel, who turned out to be a young woman, rather zaftig, and very pleasant and attentive. She spent the first hour telling me about the vicissitudes of patenting life. Then she complained that her department had to share a tiny room with another department. Then I learned that she was also planning to enter graduate school, that she was still single and just happened to have an evening free. In the final analysis, she was of little use. I had to call Comrade Vladimir Shterenberg from the Central Research Institute of Experimental Design of Retail Buildings. Most importantly, "it would be a good idea to get a co-author from among the leadership." And she instantly called Shterenberg on my behalf.

We met the next day. He was short and thickset, a retired officer — a colonel, I think. Short gray hair and small eyes behind thick glasses. Despite his age, he was still full of energy and desire to work. We talked briefly about my application and then just chatted for another couple of hours.

Then I ran off to the library to work. That's when my pen really came in handy!

Finally, the application was ready, and I was back at Shterenberg's office.

"I haven't seen what you wrote," he said, "but I'll bet it's pretty bad. Don't argue. No one writes a good application on the first try. This is what I do myself: I write one and then I sit on it for a week or two. Then I take another look ... what did you think? Besides, you don't know how the expert thing works. You think an expert has the time to make heads or tails of it? Of course not. I was an expert once. You get five minutes per application at the most. That's impossible for doing quality work. And don't pay any attention to my coughing and sniffing. It is not an infection, it is asthma. My point is we'll have to work hard on your application."

Then we went over every phrase of mine again and again as we edited my writing, line by line. I could barely move my tongue after endless arguments.

"I'm sorry, but you have to write for the lowest common denominator," Shterenberg repeated. "By no means should you make the expert think."

At the end he encouraged me. Unless someone else had exactly the same proposal, I should get a patent.

He had more advice. "Are you planning to apply personally or as an associate at your Institute? I recommend the latter. And you should also find out if there's someone working on something similar. You should consider using him as a co-author. One way or another, your work will land on his desk for the review." (He was really prophetic about this. Why didn't I listen?) "Is your academic advisor a decent person? No, no — don't get me wrong.... But if it goes through him, perhaps it's worth your while to offer him co-authorship?"

The next day I retyped the application, put the finishing touches on the blueprints, and took off for the Institute's BRIZ (Inventors' Bureau). There

I had to deal with Comrade Lev Balk, a relatively young man of strikingly Semitic appearance, complete with swarthy complexion and the beginnings of a protruding belly.

Balk spoke concisely: "I am a lawyer. Your business is inventing, and my business is presenting it. Trust me. I'll write you an application and we'll get it reviewed. If it comes from me, the right people will sign. That's right. Today I'll get him to sign off for you, and tomorrow I'll get you to sign off for him. That's how it's done."

He told me that he had attended Moscow's Special Air Force High School Number Four, where his classmate was the son of the famous pre-war hero pilot Chkàlov. I learned also that lately Balk had been frequently traveling on business to the Siberian Academy of Sciences ("five times, a month apiece"). And if that alone were not enough to arouse my envy, he had spent his last visit basking on the beach, where he had an affair with a 20-year-old beauty ("they got a lot of that stuff there, if you know how to go about it").

Finally, we talked shop. At first Balk was not particularly pleasant. But after reading the application, he tried to persuade me not to quit. I never considered it.

He explained to me that my application contained an "interesting idea." It just had to be "cleared" of architecture. "You can't patent architecture." He asked me if I had shown it to any of "our experts." I hadn't? I should. And don't show off your scruples if you have to "get a co-author. Your name will still come first."

"Alphabetically, you mean?"

Oblivious to my sarcasm, Balk assured me that the real author's name always comes first.

Seven years later I heard a story about Lev Balk from my newly found Jewish refusenik friends. Eventually, Balk made up his mind to leave for Israel. According to the rules, he needed to bring in a release letter from his parents. His mother was dead set against his departure. Lev was not discouraged; he forged her death certificate and brought it to the visa section, along with a letter from the cemetery. He got his exit visa. But a few days before his departure his mother smelled a rat and went to the visa section. One can imagine the panic and confusion. The head of the section in charge of Israel exit visas called up and summoned Balk to her office. (In a shabby irony, a typically Soviet one, her last name was Isràileva.)

Balk agreed to come in the next morning. Meanwhile, he changed his airplane ticket for Vienna for the same morning. Before he left for the airport, he asked a friend to stay at his apartment to answer the phone. Comrade Fatimà Isràileva kept calling, her temperature rising, and the friend, who introduced himself as Balk, kept politely telling her that he was on his way to her office. Balk had well-founded suspicions that he would be taken off the plane in Moscow or not let off the plane in Vienna. Things like this happened. Finally, the friend got a call from Balk from Vienna and left the apartment.

Balk directed me to the section that dealt with problems similar to the one I was working on. Gently but insistently, they tried to talk me into abandoning the idea. "Your idea is interesting and original — perfect for a brilliant article. But in our business, patenting is just not done. Everything we do here qualifies as invention."

Naturally, they themselves patented everything in sight. I didn't pick any of them as co-authors and paid for this in spades with a few years of correspondence and red tape at the Inventions Committee.

Meanwhile, I got a letter from my mother-in-law Rosa from Ukraine, who happened to be a patent expert. She complimented me and assured me that from a formal standpoint I had no problems. She had no doubt I would get a patent. This was a business she knew like the back of her hand. She was also insistent that I should get one of my bosses for a co-author. Unfortunately, I did not heed her advice.

I fought my way through a variety of invention authorities, and three years later obtained a patent.

Coincidentally, it was my dear mother-in-law Rosa who gave me the wonderful four-color ballpoint that started the whole ball rolling.

Moscow's Map

In the late '60s my Soviet friend Mark Guràry found a job at the Moscow Planning Institute, located smack in the center of Moscow on Mayakovski Square. On a sunny day Mark would spend his lunch break on the steps to Mayakovski's monument, where he fed the pigeons and gawked at the huge tour buses that kept unloading an endless flow of foreigners.

Once a foreign tourist unfolded a huge city map a few steps away. Mark could not resist the temptation to take a look. This was not a city plan that was sold in kiosks under the guise of a "map," but a real geographical map on the scale 1:2000, with every street and lane listed. Noting Mark's interest, the foreigner offered it to him as a souvenir. "I have map in hotel," he explained in broken Russian. Mark gave him a pin to reciprocate and rushed back to the office to brag about his new possession.

Though his office was engaged in city planning and constantly needed a large-scale city map — as did the planning offices of other Soviet municipalities — these maps were a state secret and kept under lock and key, off limits even to the planners. The top secret artifact — or, rather, its fragments — was kept in a special room under a KGB man's watchful stare, and you needed to

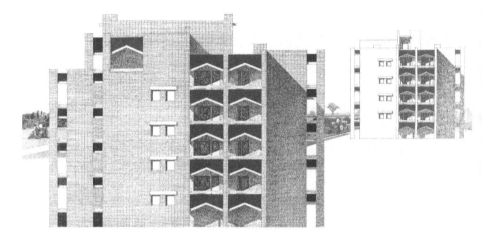

The prototype apartment building project for the River Volga area in Tataria. The building was repeatedly constructed at numerous locations around the town of Naberezhnie Chelny. Among the advantages of the project were efficient apartment layout, the presence of small public areas in basements and on roof terraces, and split floors which utilized the hilly terrain of the region. Use of local vernacular architecture motifs also contributed to the project's success. Moscow, 1971.

file a request in writing, have it approved by successive bosses, and finally get a clearance. Now Mark serendipitously had made all these obstacles vanish.

For the first time in their lives, professional city planners saw their city in its totality, rather than in fragments spoon-fed to them by the KGB. Even their section chief did not have clearance to see a map on scale this large. The entire institute gathered to see this miracle. And, of course, the KGB representative was not long in coming.

"Let me take a look," he said. "How interesting indeed. An excellent map. Where did you get it? ... Aha, from a foreign tourist. May I?" He folded it neatly and carried it away to the KGB's "first section."

By the end of the day Mark got worried. It seemed that the KGB man was taking his sweet time "looking at" the map. This did not bode well. He plodded off to inquire.

"Ah, come in, Guràry. Sorry, I cannot give it back. We consulted with proper authorities and they say we should place your map in the special storage and mark it 'state secret.'

"I can't show it to you either. You just don't have the proper clearance. Yours is too low-level.

"Dismissed."

The Map of Israel

It started with Sasha Frishman, a friend from trade school days. He called me from Kharkov. He was going on a business trip. He would change trains in Moscow and stop by to see me. He showed me a Soviet-printed map of the Middle East he had just bought in a kiosk. Besides Greece, Cyprus, Turkey, Syria, Lebanon, Jordan, and a chunk of Egypt and Saudi Arabia, it accommodated a tiny Israel as well.

The Yom Kippur war had just broken out, and the Soviet papers were awash in stories of "Egypt's valiant victories," with pictures of Israeli war prisoners and names of captured towns. I was worried. Where are these, near Tel Aviv? But Sasha's map put my fears to rest: the towns were next to the Suez Canal.

I asked Sasha to get me a map like that too, while they were still available. It turned out it was too late — he had bought the last one. Two days later he was supposed to be coming back from his trip, and I talked him into lending me the map.

From time to time chief architects at our office were supposed to deliver lectures on the current international matters to their fellow workers. I decided to take advantage of this situation to make a Xerox copy of the map — in the guise of a visual aid for my forthcoming lecture.

The copying room fell under the jurisdiction of Section One (or, put simply, the KGB). Thus one had to make a request in writing for a paper to be copied, and the request was to be approved by the section manager and the office director. But on that particular day none of them was in the office — and my request was approved by the deputy director in charge of housekeeping.

The woman who made the actual copies liked the map and made another couple of copies, for a friend and for herself. Her friend showed the map to a friend from another section, who in turn reported it back to the same deputy director — who turned out to be a retired Gulag camp commander. Maps of Israel are circulating among personnel, the vigilant friend reported.

The former camp commander got scared. Finally, the brave Arab fellows were finishing off the Israeli aggressor, while right here in his bailiwick, Zionist propaganda was going on! Which he had approved of personally! Trouble was on the way.

A quick investigation pointed at me as the resident troublemaker. Now it turned out that I had obtained his signature by misleading him. The request never mentioned "the map of Israel" — only a visual aid for a lecture on the Middle East. Only one copy was allowed. And I "condoned" unlimited production. And the only explanation was that I must have hooked up with Zionists, and all together we were Israel-bound (on foot, apparently). That's what I needed the maps for!

Top: The author's ID as a chief architect. Moscow, 1971. *Bottom:* The author's architects' union ID; the right page shows the union's payments. Moscow, 1975.

The suspicions were bolstered by something that had happened a year earlier, when Yuli Dubovòy, our department's chief engineer, applied for an Israeli exit visa. A general meeting was called where the "masses" were to denounce the traitor. I told the meeting that we shouldn't dish out dirt and create an enemy. He was an old guy, past forty. He wouldn't be able to master the language or find a job. How would he benefit from emigration? On the other hand, he was going to reunite with his son.

The reaction of Party Secretary Galina Zhdànova was: "Berkovich, quit your Jewish tricks."

Now, a year later she had no doubts: I was leaving, too.

The office opened a file on me, and it grew fast. Interrogations at the director's office, explanations in writing, and finally a full-court self-criticism session at the trade union and general meetings. The apparatchiks demanded that I make a full confession and name the names of leading Zionists. At the same time, Israeli Zionists were on the offensive, making minced meat of Arab armies. Zionist tanks were outside Cairo!

I asked Director Makhankò to help. Until recently he had treated me very well. We knew each other from the architecture school, where he was a

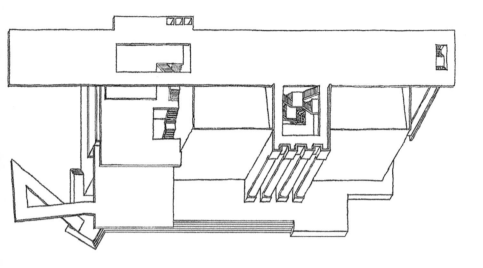

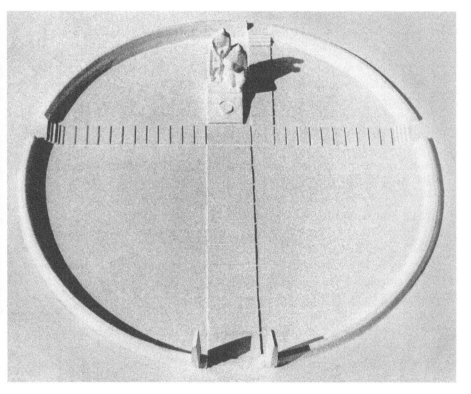

Top: The project for addition and reconstruction of an exhibition pavilion on the grounds of "The All Union Exhibition of Achievements" in Moscow. The new exposition hall floats above the existing Stalin-era building. Moscow, 1970. *Bottom:* Scale model of the project for the Fallen War Heroes Monument. The sculptor was Mikhail Intizarian. The architect was Gary Berkovich. Moscow, 1962.

few years ahead of me. But we were almost the same age, since I had served in the navy. He was a nice enough guy from a military family, a capable artist and a good architect, and with his politically impeccable extraction he could not help being spotted by someone upstairs. His career went into high gear. First he became chief architect of an office similar to ours, and a few years later director of our office. He was a talented architect, but he had to spend more and more time in meetings at various Party committees and ministries, and this takes its toll.

Six months before the Map Scandal, our relations hit a snag. The office was getting together a group of architects for a trip to Yugoslavia. My name, along with those of other Jews, were deleted from the applicants' list. The explanation was brief: "Don't you understand what the situation is like?"

Actually, I didn't, and started protesting. "Boris, couldn't you leave at least a couple of names for appearances' sake?" Meaning my own, of course. I was aiming to get in on the strength of my personal relation with him.

Boris gave me a cold stare, pretending he had no idea what I was talking about. After all, it was not he personally who crossed out the names, it was the so-called troika that formally ruled every Soviet office: the Director's Office, Party Committee and Trade Union Committee. The list itself was confirmed on the basis of the union committee's recommendation.

I went to see the union chairman. He referred me to the instruction from the Union's Central Committee and, after a little pressure from me, even named a specific person. I ran to the Central Committee, which was a mere ten minutes' walk away. Over there — complete denial: no one had ever issued any instructions like that.

A good friend of mine listened to my story and wrote an anonymous letter to the Central Party Committee on anti–Semitism at our office.

This was good timing. Brezhnev played the game of détente with the West and wanted no extra trouble. His advisers could get big black eyes if a copy of the letter found its way to the Voice of America or the like. A week later, seven Jews were included in a group of thirty, and we took a trip to Yugoslavia. The local union secretary was made a scapegoat and retired. And I became the chief suspect as the letter's author.

My mother-in-law seemed to have the gift of prophecy when she opined that I wouldn't get away with the Yugoslavia trip. "They'll never forgive you," she said. "Why are you sticking your neck out? What the hell do you want with this Yugoslavia? You're ruining a beautiful career. Especially since you're not planning to leave."

It was true that I did not plan to emigrate. I was already thirty-eight, and my adventure days were gone. I had a family, children, a co-op apartment, and an interesting, well-paid job, with plenty of opportunities to moonlight. I knew everybody and everybody knew me and everybody helped one

Left: The author's six-year-old son Slava. Moscow, 1976. *Right:* The author's ten-year-old daughter, Lana Berkovich. Moscow, 1974.

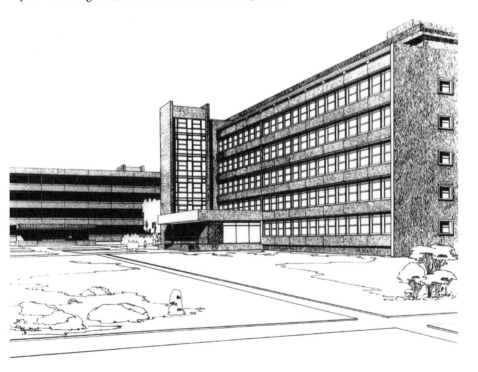

The project for the R&D Institute Laboratory building. It utilizes precast catalogue elements. Moscow, 1969.

The project for a civic center in the small town of Tereze in a mountainous region of southern Russia. The design integrated a group of small open courtyards surrounding a central plaza, connected by shaded walkways. The complex included a commercial block (supermarket, restaurant and hotel), a cultural center (a 700-seat theatre, sports hall, an outdoor movie theatre), an administrative block (village council offices and hall, and post office), and a traditional Eastern open market (bazaar). Moscow, 1971.

another. "Out there" was completely dark uncertainty, even if I got lucky and was granted a visa. And if it was denied? Did I have a right to take a risk? Of course I didn't.

I went back to Makhankò with my tail between my legs and asked him to stop the persecution. "You know very well I am not going anywhere. Look, I spent years saving for a co-op, slaving to get a degree. Do you want me to quit? I could do it right now!"

It turned out that I had exaggerated both my value and the extent of our friendship. I disregarded the old saying about no one being indispensable. And I found myself without a job.

At first I wasn't concerned. "Where there's a neck, there's a yoke," the saying goes. Well, not quite. No one was willing to give me a job. I applied for jobs at one design office after another, armed with recommendations from friends who worked there. After initial approval, my applications hit the wall of the personnel department. They had their own sources, and the sources said that I was being suspected of the intention to emigrate to Israel.

After a couple of months I realized the consequences of my rash act and went back to Director Makhankò. This time he wouldn't even see me.

I became an unemployed Soviet, devoid of all rights, benefits, or means of sustenance. This was the last thing in the world I wanted. I had put my family at risk.

Konstantinov

I spent almost six months in vain attempts to get a job. But an unfounded rumor that I was planning to leave for Israel followed me like a shadow. I applied to every architectural office I could find in Moscow and finally lost hope.

Then someone came up with an idea to try the synagogue. Never mind that I was an architect. *The* synagogue, for there was only one synagogue for a quarter of a million Jews in Moscow in 1974.

I spent an entire Saturday milling in a huge crowd in front of the temple on Arkhìpova Street, clueless as to what I was supposed to do. I grew desperate. Late in the evening, a short old man with a long beard in a yarmulke came up. "What are you doing here — a young man without a hat?"

I told him my story. He looked at me fixedly and drawled with a Yiddish intonation: "So you are an architect, hm.... And you are looking for a job.... And you need help...."

Yes to all questions. He pondered for a while and then said, "I think I can help you. I know a place where they will offer you a decent architect position."

After all my fruitless efforts I was stunned. Why didn't I come here earlier? Go ahead — tell me at once!

The old man gave me a long look and concluded with a slight smile: "The position I am talking about is in Israel, my dear. Do not waste your time here."

After I overcame the initial shock, it dawned on me that he could be right. Of course I hated the regime — who didn't? Of course I had given emigration some thought. But at thirty-nine I deemed myself too old — and then I was married, with two kids. To cast my family and myself into an abyss of uncertainty? Yet it seemed like my choices were limited.

Little by little, both my wife and I were growing used to the idea. We felt we were cornered. We saw no other way out. And before long I made up my mind.

Now, as a first step, I had to figure out how to get an invitation from a fake relative in Israel. We did not know any real ones there.

To obtain that paper was no easy task.

When, finally, we applied for an exit visa, a question on the application form demanded the relationship with the person in Israel we were joining and the reason for it. The invitation was signed by an Ezra Berkovich. Ignorantly, I deemed it to be a woman's name. Hence I wrote, "This is my loved aunt who left for Israel before I was born. Now she is aged and needs my help."

Soon I was called in for a chat. I didn't sleep all night. They had found out something! And really, they discovered that in my version of history, the date of "Ms. Ezra Berkovich's" departure from Russia preceded her birthday. We were caught in a lie! What would they do with us now? But the official politely suggested that I just change the order of the dates. The Wonderland of Soviet games!

In the meantime, suddenly, in late April of 1974, I got yet another phone number of an architectural office in Moscow where I had tried my luck already. Like elsewhere, no one would talk to me seriously. A Jew who is rumored to be ready to take off to Israel? And there were enough Jews in their office already.

A former co-worker who gave me the number insisted that I give it another shot. This time I should come see Comrade Konstantìnov. After some hesitation — was it really worth another bit of frustration? — I called and asked for an appointment. I badly needed an income.

At first blush, Konstantìnov's name was a blank. Then I remembered: he was the architect who got a Lenin Award, together with Isakòvich and Mèzentzev, for designing a memorial complex in Ulyànovsk (Lenin's hometown) for Lenin's centennial.

Konstantinov's studio was a part of the Central Entertainment Buildings Design Institute and was located in an abandoned basement in the center of Moscow on infamous Lubyànka Street — that is, next door to the KGB headquarters.

The basement location did not bother me. I had worked in worse circumstances in Novosibirsk. Besides, with my mind made up about departure, it didn't matter where I would be spending the remaining time in Moscow.

The tiny cell taken by Konstantinov was permeated with a smell of alcohol as potent as in a pub. It was furnished sparsely: a desk, a drawing board, and some kind of improvised workbench with a building model barely visible under some papers. Two empty glasses and a plate of homemade *pirozhkì* (meat patties) rested on a blueprint turned upside down and serving as a tablecloth on a desk. A lunch break.

The host, a sloppily dressed middle-aged man with light eyes and long, uncut blond hair touched by gray, introduced himself. "Konstantinov, Mikhail. You look familiar."

The woman on a stool next to him was good-looking and shapely, about forty-five, with the engaging appearance of a Russian beauty from a classical painting. "Natalya Minàicheva. 'Natasha' is fine."

I was invited to the table, and the *pirozhki* plate was pushed my way — have a taste. I was about to show my work, but Konstantinov interrupted rudely: "Who cares about your shit. Tell me straight. Are you taking off for Israel?"

This touched a nerve. Who the hell was he, to knock my designs without even looking? What about his own? The reference to Israel took me aback, too, and I denied everything.

"You're right. No point in going there. Same shit as here."

I was not about to argue or lecture him on anti–Semitism and Zionism. I just needed a job. Something to live on. My wife's salary was next to nothing. Working architects had no savings. There were no unemployment benefits in the Soviet Union in the absence of official unemployment. And we had already sold all the possessions we could.

"You should go to America instead. That's a different level! They really have high standards there."

That was a nice turn. I looked around. Konstantinov reeked of vodka; Natasha, less so. They poured me a glass.

I accepted and dug into the *pirozhki.*

"See," Konstantinov said, "the word is that you are planning to take off—"

There you go again, I thought. If you don't want to hire me, why bother inviting me? Patiently, I waited.

"—and I don't give a shit." He gave me a full load of his vodka breath.

Now, that's a different story. Not bad for a lead-in.

"This is what's going on here." Konstantinov reflexively fingered his besmeared, loosened necktie. His shirt could do with a spin in the washer, too. "*They* are really in a deep shit with the project. They haven't done dick. And the money's all spent. The deadline is six weeks away. No way can they meet it. This will be a major black eye and a reprimand in their Party cards."

For some reason he chortled happily.

"So they dropped the project at my door. They'll think my Lenin Award will get them out of trouble. Ha! I don't give a fuck!"

Instinctively, I shot a glance at silent Natasha.

"Not a damn thing can they do to me," he concluded. "I'm not a member of their Party."

That was quite something to say to a stranger in a first meeting. And within a stone's throw of the KGB headquarters. How fiercely he had to hate the regime!

He reached for the bottle, but Natasha stayed his hand.

"Not a chance of meeting the deadline," he said. "And there's no one to do it anyway. I heard you are a hard worker. And you've got nothing to lose. Israel Shmisrael. What are they gonna do? Our guard dog at personnel had to bite the bullet on this. I already spoke to him."

What? He hadn't seen me, he didn't know me, but he had already spoken to personnel! He didn't want me to waste a trip? But even if he was only concerned about not wasting his time, that wasn't too bad. I was beginning to like Konstantinov.

"While all this is going on, at least you'll make some money. You've been jerking off for six months, I've heard. You ever worked as a design architect in charge? What are you shooting for?"

I asked for two hundred twenty, which was my salary at the last job.

"That's good. Don't take anything less. Use your timing. They'll pay you anything. Natalia — how about a drop? There must be one apiece left, am I right?"

I got a corner in his office, next to an old model. The following day I was working on the "prototype palace of culture with an auditorium seating 700."

Before long and unexpectedly, we became friends. He told me that in his youth he dreamed of a soccer career. But then the war broke out, and he was drafted. In a few weeks he was shipped to the front line. While they were getting out of the train car, German planes came in an air raid — and he lost a leg and another one was deformed. After the hospital, he went to an architecture school. He got around with crutches on an artificial limb.

I shared with him the World War II story of my stepfather, who volunteered and had both his legs shot out. Thinking he wouldn't make it, the medics at first gave up on him. Then, miraculously, under heavy bombardment, he was delivered to the hospital. And both his legs were saved from amputation.

Konstantinov listened earnestly and asked for details.

As I got deeper into the designing job, I began to see the reason for Konstantinov's gloating laughter. The deadline was six weeks away, while there was enough work for six months. But indeed I had nothing to lose. I just wished that I had the invitation from Israel in my hands sooner.

After a six-month hiatus, I was itching to do something special, which was impossible by definition. The project was dubbed "prototype." Beginning at the studio level and the Institute's Technical Council, and on through endless committees and ministry experts, anything even marginally out of the ordinary would be gradually chiseled out of the design. It was a story as old as bureaucracy itself.

The program read, "The building's image must be comprehensible and close in spirit to the masses of all the regions where it will be constructed."

No "artsy excesses," like "unjustified" walls, canopies, or finishes. The construction spans had to correspond with the standard prefabricated concrete elements from a wretched all-nation catalogue. Windows, doors and fixtures should come from there too. Every bit of indoor square footage had to be saved, with no more than 5 percent deviation (preferably on the economy side). That was the essence of prototype design — save money. Every saving in the design of my palace of culture and every flaw caused by that would be repeated each time it was erected. No wonder that everything built in the Soviet Union — or any other places where these principles are being followed — looks so shabby.

The more I looked, the harder time I had understanding how I would solve this problem. On the other hand, I had the splendid advantage of irresponsibility. The departure was growing more real.

Of course I tasted this advantage fully only when I applied for the exit visa. But even as I took the decision, I already felt the delicious lightness unknown to anyone who never stepped outside Soviet society.

This helped provide an ideal mood for work. I was no longer susceptible to any dogmas. I was free to show or not show my sketches to whomever I wanted. Free to heed or not to heed advice and choose whatever I deemed fit. Free to follow or not follow the decisions of the Technical Council. I was not afraid to risk my career, for I did not expect to have one anymore. I could meet the deadline or not. And I was immeasurably happy that I had found the job.

Yet, as I had long discovered, I had an unhealthy penchant for difficulties. And old habits die hard.

First things first: I'd meet the deadline. For my own sake, not for theirs.

Second — obviously — I'd do the best job I could. Once again, I'd show them for the shit that they are with their Soviet anti–Semitism, chasing me out of the country. (Thank goodness they did it.)

The deadline was six weeks away. Minus a week for the Technical Council. The "submission" proper — execution and graphics — would take a week to ten days. Well, here the requirements were more serious than those at my last job. That meant having to add another week. Two and a half weeks left. Then I had to run it by the engineers — that's another week. This meant that for sketching proper — to come up with the design solution — I had altogether a week and a half left, two weeks maximum. It wasn't much, but it wasn't hopeless, if one worked twelve hours a day.

At any rate I had to arrive at the final design as soon as possible. I instantly thought of an *idée fixe* I had had for a long time and was dying to use. The question was whether it would work with this particular project. Then again, checking it out would take all the time I had. On the other hand, I would spend no less time developing a different one. So I was resolved. I had an

idea. And I couldn't afford to doubt it. Nor would I show it to Konstantinov
before time. What if he didn't like it? In fact, the notion that neither he nor
I gave a damn about the project was a façade, after all. But how could I hide
my work from him if we were sharing the same room?

Fate weighed in on my side. Konstantinov's studio was ordered to relo-
cate to a new high-rise on Vernàdskii Avenue. The entire Entertainment
Buildings Design Institute was being moved into the new quarters from myr-
iad basements around the city. Due to my extraordinary circumstances, I
talked Konstantinov into releasing me from the hassle of packing and moving, and he let me work at home for almost a week.

The happiest person about this turn of events was my three-year-old son
Slava. He had long adored my study. He moved his little chair in next to mine
and demanded paper and pencils and crayons and paints and brushes. We
encouraged him, admired his work, and saved it religiously. Now he had joy
galore. Dad was working at home, and he could stay on his little chair all day.

Many years later I would realize that in terms of typology, the closest
analog of the Soviet "Palace of Culture" is a synagogue. Regardless of the
content, both have a main auditorium with a foyer, adjacent lobbies and toilets. At the temple, there are weekend classes. A Palace of Culture has rooms
for various hobby groups, with auxiliary rooms. Instead of an extra praying
chapel, there is a special meeting auditorium. In a synagogue, the main prayer
auditorium and a Sunday school have to be able to be used autonomously,
and the same goes for a Palace of Culture auditorium and its auxiliary spaces.
Of course certain things do not match. A Palace of Culture auditorium, especially one seating seven hundred, has to have a real theater stage, properly
equipped, which synagogues don't need. God comes with His own gear.

I have always thought — this was my *idée fixe* — that unless it is specifically
stipulated otherwise, it would be nice to put the auxiliary areas of a Palace of
Culture around an open space — a courtyard — with greenery and a fountain.
Then, regardless of limitations, there should be a formally attractive, sharp,
volumetric composition, to say nothing of my favorite two-story high rooms
with balconies, stairs, and interflowing spaces. Not for nothing had I been
worshipping at the altar of Constructivism.

After a week of reclusion I brought the sketches to the new location of
the studio, where I had been assigned a space next to Konstantinov's office.
He stopped by just before the lunch break, stared at the sheets long and hard,
mumbling something — whether approvingly or not — and, without saying a
word, hobbled off to his office. Natasha was already ready with vodka and
pirozhki. I knew that after lunch he would be too drunk for a serious conversation.

Next day I came early. Konstantinov looked gloomy: he was not enthused
with my design. Yet he thought it was worth a shot. All he could say was that

nothing like that had ever been shown at their Technical Council. "Ain't our kind of stuff, as they'd say."

Then, all of a sudden — as he was wont to — he became mirthful. "Ròsanov's sure to have a stroke!" Ròsanov was the institute director. "Serves him right! And we'll pretend we didn't bring in anything unusual. What the hell!"

When Natasha came in, he asked for her opinion. "What do you think — are they going to flip at the council?" And then: "What? You actually like it? Are you serious?"

Konstantinov shook his head and sighed deeply. "You're really something," he said to me. And once again I could not understand whether this was reproach or approval.

Then, after a long silence, he squeezed out of himself. "What is there to fear? We should follow the assignment closely — what else is there?"

He need not voice a warning. I had had experience dealing with technical councils and ministry experts.

The next day I stayed late working, as usual. He sat next to me and started taking my sketches apart, detail by detail. Never before had I received such intelligent advice. I was struck by his professional objectivity.

It was my "luck," so to speak, that, while working at other offices, I had gotten used to being the top dog. That night, however, I heard a lot of interesting stuff about my project in particular and about Architect Berkovich in general. For some reason, I did not take umbrage. Of course he interwove his comments with "I don't give a damn," that "my idea ain't worth shit," and in general "there'll never be any good architecture here." Yet he was as carried away as I was.

He did not manage to change the design radically. Once he saw that, he started look into it detail by detail. I defended my decisions wherever I could. Yet it never came to fighting. We ended up having a friendly conversation. In fact, this is when our friendship started.

Before he left, he turned to face me. "So you are bailing them out? What for? They won't thank you."

In the morning, Natasha told me in confidence that Konstantinov had spoken well of my sketches, and, most importantly, told her to help me with putting together the mock-up orders. By then I knew that Natasha and Konstantinov had worked jointly for decades. They finished each other's sentences, and she treated him with motherly tenderness. And now he lent me her hand.

Of course the final design of the Palace of Culture was nothing special. As expected, the Technical Council made mincemeat of my work. And, without missing a beat, unanimously approved it for release with high praise.

After much torment, the ministry approved it, too. We got a cash bonus,

The author (left) and architect Mikhail Konstantìnov. Moscow, 1987.

both for quality and for finishing two days before the deadline. Director Ròsanov had not expected me to be so fast and begged a two weeks' postponement. Instead of a Party reprimand he got a bonus, too — naturally, much larger than ours.

After such success, I was immediately demoted (my original position "did not fit the corrected personnel structure"). Konstantìnov was right: I got no thank you. Then they cut my salary (I don't remember the excuse). But at least they didn't fire me.

For I got lucky again. Konstantìnov received a new project that was both urgent and delicate — two beachfront villas for Brezhnev in Foros, Crimea — and this is how I was given an extension on my employment.

Meanwhile, further work on the Palace of Culture project — construction documents — was shelved until the next deadline. It was finished a few years later by Michael Shapiro, whom I barely knew at the time. We met much later in Chicago after he emigrated, and he reassured me that he had made no changes.

Incidentally, I remembered that Konstantìnov and I had met once, in passing, about five or six years earlier. No wonder he had thought my face to be familiar when I first showed up in his office.

It was at the Architect House, a clubhouse of the Architects' Union. I used to stop by there every free evening. An excellent and always well-brewed coffee was served in their cafeteria. And in the library I could leaf through recent foreign publications.

The prototype project for the Palace of Culture with the auditorium for 700 people. The main objective of this project was adaptiveness to diverse local conditions. Among its features were the multi-use of spaces and the separation of paid admission activities (movies or plays) from free ones (lectures, seminars, and private meetings). Moscow, 1974.

On a night like this I found myself with a cup of coffee in one hand and a glass of brandy in the other and my briefcase under my hand stuck in the middle of the chock-full room, desperately looking for a place to sit. Through the thick cigarette smoke I saw a table for four with three people at it, also with coffee and a bottle of brandy. In Russia, with its acute shortage of public spaces, it was common to share a table with strangers. They were not quite forthcoming, but I didn't take offense (in fact, they could have told me it was taken).

Nonetheless, I tried to down the burning hot coffee as fast as I could, especially since I recognized one of my fellow drinkers — a certain Boris Mèzentzev, whom I could not stand ever since I learned about him from the history of Soviet architecture.

Mèzentzev was one of the designers of Kharkov's train station and a high-rise at Red Gate in Moscow. He was a Stalin Prize winner and belonged to the generation of Soviet architectural mandarins I hated so much. Back in the mid–'30s, these architecture barons, filled with unbridled ambition, were quick to grab the positions left vacant after the purge of Constructivists — my honest, uncompromising heroes.

The mandarins' main creative drive was endless lack of principle. In reality, they occupied a wide spectrum, from eclectic décor to a version of western modernism that became approved at the time.

My arrival made them fall silent as they examined me. I was tempted to paraphrase a well-known joke — You've never seen a Jew? — but then I noticed that one of them had clearly Semitic features, too.

Mèzentzev broke the silence as he reclined on the banquette, freeing a good chunk of the table from his considerable belly. "Are you an architect?"

"Yes."

"What school did you go to? Our school? ... What year? ... So you must know who I am."

Something about his tone made me take umbrage. Or perhaps it was the brandy taken on an empty stomach. I felt an irrepressible urge to strike back. I wondered in response how exactly I was supposed to know him.

"What do you mean, *How*? I am a professor. Everybody knows me there." And he named his name.

I could not stand the sight of him. "I don't recall that we had such a professor." And then I wondered if he remembered me.

"I can't know every student!"

There are plenty of professors, too, I parried.

"But I've been teaching there since '35!"

"What faculty?" And then I delved into his work — what exactly had he built, etc.

Our conversation was quickly going beyond civil discourse. The member of the threesome with a Semitic face lifted his glass and offered a toast. "To friendship."

But I was still full of vinegar, and so I just had to convert one cliché toast into another, even more of a cliché. "To friendship among nations," I said — a favorite of Soviet officials when delivered at official receptions, but sounding more than ambiguous in this setting.

In an unwarranted show of familiarity, Mèzentzev changed from *Vy*, standard among strangers, to a familiar *ty*. "What do you mean by that?"

Happy to see I got his goat, I said I was offering a toast to the friendship among nations of our great country — Russians, Ukrainians, Uzbeks, Armenians, Jews....

"What are you driving at?" Mèzentzev finally exploded. His generous consumption of brandy also showed. "My wife is Jewish — her name is Bella! I have children with her! My friends are Jewish! Garik, tell him!"

My pale-faced Jewish namesake at the table nodded in confirmation.

That was the favorite line of all anti–Semites, "My best friends are Jews." Oh sure, and he is an exception to the rule, I thought with sarcasm. Perhaps we should find out. But then I realized I had gone too far. I really had a scandal in the making on my hands. And I had promised my wife so many times to behave! What was this sudden eruption all about? Perhaps I was taking something else out on this fat apparatchik who went by the hallowed — to me — designation of architect. (Why on earth did I raise the Jewish question? Later I would discover he was not as bad as the rest.)

Later on I figured out that the other two drinkers were Isakòvich and Konstantinov, both on the verge of winning Lenin Prizes. Yet Konstantinov had taken no part in the fracas. I think he just became smashed after the eight ounce glass of brandy. Anyhow, Konstantinov might have a hard time understanding my feelings toward Mèzentzev then. To him, Mèzentzev was a charismatic professor, a former mentor, the soul of a party, and an effective leader. Like most of the Mèzentzev students, Konstantinov fondly called him "Boss."

In fact, Mèzentzev was a relatively minor figure, compared to the big villains who had inflicted horrible damage on Soviet architecture. But even then, when he, a provincial lad who had started as a pawn in a big political game, was rising to prominence, he did not care what kind of game he was involved in.

Konstantinov did not recall the incident. I did not know how he would react if I reminded him. Yet I noticed that his attitude towards Mèzentzev had changed lately.

He told me that Mèzentzev had once called him to brag that he had just "snapped up" a commission to design a Lenin Memorial and tried to talk Konstantinov into joining him. "This is foolproof, Misha! Don't you get it? A Lenin Prize is as good as in your pocket!" With his political diversions, how could he find time to think about architecture?

The country was stirred up by dissent. And Konstantinov's gradual transformation was part of this process.

To my colleagues, I was a mystery. I stayed in my little nook outside Konstantinov's office without showing my face from behind the drafting board. For lunch, I brought a sandwich from home. I came in before everybody else, and left only when the guards chased me out. But the main thing was that I was friends with Konstantinov, and — which was envied by many — was made a part of his inner circle, which previously consisted only of Natasha.

At first they thought that Konstantinov simply had gotten himself a fellow boozer to drink with. But how could a Jew be a boozer and a friend of Konstantinov's?

I had no idea that my new friend had a reputation for being an anti-Semite. One of our structural engineers, Gennady Zelikman, told me about it. We went back to this contradiction more that once and could never figure it out. All we could come up with was an old theory that every anti–Semite is supposed to have a Jewish friend.

In our talks with Konstantinov we had long ago gone beyond talking shop. His favorite subject was ranting against the regime. At first I was apprehensive, afraid of being set up. But soon we were trading banned Samizdat books and discussing it all, from Solzhenitsyn's *Letter to Leaders* to Leon Uris's *Exodus* to Max Dimont's *God, Jews, and History*, which the same Zelikman, now a part of the circle, read in English and translated to us on the fly.

Zelikman was rather short and slender, with brown eyes and a typical Semitic appearance. He drove a beat-up Russian Fiat and moonlighted by selling secondhand western items brought by his wife from Helsinki, where she originally came from. He was a good engineer and fun to be around. He was the first to note that Konstantinov was changing. He had become softer and more social, and, most importantly, his anti–Semitism had lost its aggressive edge. He even seemed to drink less. Gennady jocularly suggested my influence.

Through Gennady I met the rest of the office Jewry, who used to avoid and scorn me for befriending Konstantinov. They included a pretty young woman named Yulia Ferdman, whom I gave a *chai* pendant once. She didn't know what *chai* stood for, but in fifteen years she did end up in Jerusalem after all, along with another mutual friend, Gennady Rottenstein. Another friend, Rena Rogachèvskaya, now has her checkups at the office of a doctor whose house I designed in Glencoe, a neighboring Chicago suburb. And she is also a member of the synagogue in Glenview, another Chicago suburb, where twenty-three years later my son was married. The world is a small place indeed.

This was the time when my Jewish self-conscience reached its peak. I divided the world into "anti–Semites" and "non-anti–Semites." I behaved in a manner so pugnacious and defiant that Konstantinov more than once reproached me for dwelling on my Jewishness.

I wished my mother had lived long enough to see this. I remembered how I had naively parroted others who denounced Zionism and "Jewish nationalism," the scourge of all things. How I had preached "internationalism" and "assimilation." How I made a point of dating non–Jewish girls. How I tried to change my name. Not for nothing did my poor mother — along with the rest of the family — in despair call her son an "anti–Semite."

Soon, Natasha's husband, Yevgeny Fedorov, joined our circle, in absentia. He worked for the Science Council at the R&D Institute where I had done my Ph.D. thesis. And we were not the best of friends. I thought him an anti–Semite. Now, because of his wife, he was technically part of our group. In fact, according to Natasha, he devoured all the banned publications I loaned to her, sometimes staying up all night, and they would heatedly discuss them later.

That made me think that perhaps not all anti–Semites were alike. Some of them might be beset with doubts. "Of course the Jews are evil Yids. But they are persecuted by the evil regime. Does that put us on the regime's side?"

By the time the Palace of Culture project was due to be released, we finally obtained the fake invitation from Israel. But Marina refused to travel with a toddler and in general was not prepared to take this huge leap. There was nothing left for me to do but wait until she was ready. I was hoping that our new friends — refuseniks who had been refused exit visas and who helped me get my precious invitation — would help change her mind too.

I did not rule out that we might find ourselves in a situation similar to them. Once you applied for a visa, you were guaranteed to lose your job, and if you were refused, what would you live on? I practiced my wood-carving skills. Who knows ... I could sell my works to foreign tourists. I registered myself as a "Russian folk artist" (if the famous Soviet Jewish singer could be a "great national artist" in a Muslim republic in the Caucasus, what would stop me?) and even managed to sell a few works.

Art was one of our subjects of discussion with Konstantinov. He especially admired the Renaissance. During his education as an architect, the "Zholtovsky School," which worshipped Cinquecento, was dominant. Konstantinov used to bring his own watercolors, reminiscent of that style. Yet he was open to others too. I was bringing my woodcarvings to the office, and showing them to our circle, especially to Konstantinov. Most valuable comments followed.

Now, nearly all of my energy was taken by the new project. Barely had the Palace of Culture blueprints gone out for the ministry's approval as the new race-for-deadline broke out.

The Party's Central Committee had to build two villas in the Crimea — fast! At first the project was assigned personally to Director Rosanov — it was for Brezhnev, after all, and the job of court architect was quite a prize — why not give it a shot? Yet, according to the rumors, when the master saw the sketches, he uttered a sound interpreted by the majority as a hum of disapproval (the minority held it was a plain burp), and Soviet architects had another problem on their hands. Ultimately, the project landed in Konstantinov's lap. He had already won a Lenin Prize, which, the bureaucrats hoped, would serve as sure-fire protection.

The profound mystery was this: why were Brezhnev's villas to be designed at the Entertainment Buildings' Design Institute? What kind of shows were planned there? Could they have anticipated that seventeen years later the villas would serve as a set for the not-so-funny drama of Gorbachev's arrest during the August 1991 coup?

The mansions were to meet the standard modestly termed "enhanced quality." The square footage was unlimited. Structural solutions — as we wished. All the finishing materials, appliances, water taps, lamps — everything was purchased in Austria and Finland. Experts were dispatched on special shopping trips abroad to do the selection properly. Money was no object.

Each villa had a huge cellar cut into the rock, which contained auxiliary spaces: bedroom suites for the residents and servants with communications centers and autonomous life-support systems in case of a nuclear attack.

The villas were situated on a lightly wooded, slanted plateau, its southern boundary a thirty-meter, rocky, vertical bluff, where a special elevator and a tunnel would lead to the beach. On the west, it bordered on the already existing Party Central Committee vacation palace. This is where our architects and engineers would stay on their field trips: free spacious suites and ample meals, pools, saunas, wet bars — and the ready-to-serve, ideologically cleared young females.

Driveways, footpaths, and general landscaping, including pools and fountains, were done by another design institute. We had to present just general sketches.

It turned out that Fidel Castro's visit had been scheduled for the next summer, and Brezhnev was determined to receive him in a new palace. This is why two buildings were being built — and in an unimaginable hurry. We had barely started working on the sketches, while in the Crimea they were already detonating the rock for the pits.

Since we had met, Konstantinov had never touched the subject of my presumed departure. Now he invited me to his office, closed the door, told me about the forthcoming project in Foros, and asked me whether I had any fears about working on it. We both knew what he meant: whether my participation would endanger my chances of getting an exit visa. Clearly, they would not let me out of the country with information like that.

I had yet to formulate my opinion. Later on, I would realize that there was nothing systematic about the Soviet system. But I already knew that it was a lot easier to get a visa late in the year than early. People who applied in the fourth quarter had a much better chance of leaving, even those who held "secrets." Ultimately, issuing visas in the Soviet Union was no different from manufacturing light switches or designing Palaces of Culture — everything was a matter of meeting target figures, and only in the last moment.

It was frivolous of me to work on Brezhnev's villas, but it was the only job I had. If I lost it, I would not have enough money to make it to departure.

At least I decided to forgo the lap-of-luxury field trips. Yet the moment I turned down the first of them, my wily Jewish colleagues drew instant conclusions about my emigration intentions. Although I did not say a word to anyone, the dangerous rumor started anew. But this time it had foundation.

Encountering the KGB

I have been detained by the KGB three times in my life.

The first time was in the fall of '52. I was seventeen. I was examining the interiors of the brand-new Kharkov train terminal with a camera in my hand. I had almost finished the roll of film, when I was suddenly grabbed by two silent, muscular guys who seized my camera and dragged me to a room on the second floor. Cursing loudly, they handed me over to a lean, middle-aged KGB lieutenant with a huge blue nose. He asked me, using the same curses and barracks language, why I was "photographing an object" he "was in charge of."

He was not satisfied with my explanations that I was a student of architecture and I wanted to have pictures of such a unique building. He demanded that I open the camera (he didn't know how) and expose the film. I took off the cover. He saw the film, cursed again, and had me kicked out.

I didn't even have time to get scared properly. In the evening I developed the roll and found that only a couple of shots were ruined.

My second time was almost a year later in Kiev and also stemmed from photography.

This was my first time in Kiev and I felt lousy. What happened was that after I graduated from trade school with all A's, the administration refused — in violation of the rules — to refer me to the Moscow School of Architecture. Thus I thought I would try for the Department of Architecture at Kiev's engineering school, or at the art school. Kharkov didn't have even those.

In 1953, however, any sane person realized that Kiev was off limits for a Jew. And it was true. Neither at the Ministry of Higher Education nor at either school would anyone speak to me. Nonetheless, I decided to stay for a few days to sightsee.

I roamed the boulevards and parks on the hills over Dnieper River, seeking distraction from nasty thoughts. I knew the local architectural monuments from books. I stood in awe in front of St. Andrew's Church, designed by Francesco Rastrelli. I passed by the funicular to the monument to Prince Vladimir. I took a few pictures at Soviet Square outside the Party Committee building designed by Landbard, a well-known architect. Then I crossed Vladimir Descent towards Podol and climbed to Pervomàysky Park. I passed the library and a small stadium that I did not photograph to the Ukrainian Supreme Soviet building designed by Zabolotny, a local favorite. This one I had to photograph: it won a Stalin Award, after all! Finally, I could see all these buildings in person. Then I went down to Kirov Street to see the Ukrainian Council of Ministers building designed by the famous Fomin.

I enjoyed the luscious greenery, the quietness of deserted alleys, and the fragrance of countless flowerbeds.

Until I was awakened by a rude holler: "Citizen!"

The policeman materialized out of nowhere. "Documents, please," he said in Ukrainian.

He stuck my passport in his pocket, confiscated the camera, and told me to follow him. I tried to find out the reason. Suddenly a nondescript, tiny old woman popped out from behind him and muttered in quick Ukrainian that I was the man taking pictures — she saw it with her own eyes.

I was almost happy. An adventure, at last — I hadn't come here for nothing.

The policeman and the old woman brought me directly to the Fomin-designed building. Great! I wouldn't have dreamed I could get inside this guarded "administrative building."

We entered the gigantic lobby, with employees looking like gnomes from the Grimm fairy tales. The marble, the granite — the grand aesthetics of well-considered details. Wow! Fomin — the founder of Soviet architectural style — really knew his stuff. It was truly a stroke of luck to be brought here.

But I wasn't given a chance to sightsee. There was a door — huge, double-height — on the right, with a KGB sergeant standing guard. The policeman whispered something to him, and a minute later he gestured for us to come in. The grandma stayed out.

I was led into a grand room, comparable to the lobby. The walls ran upward to the unlit coffer ceiling. A desk with an armchair and two chairs in front of it seemed like toys on the shiny parquet floor next to an incredibly tall window. This was the "heroic" Stalin style. Later I learned that Speer, Hitler's court architect, was so delighted to see this building in 1942 when the Germans occupied Kiev that he wanted — after the war — to offer its architect, Ivan Fomin, a job.

In the room we were met by a KGB officer and a man in plainclothes who was hard to see in the dark corner.

The policeman saluted. "I've caught a spy, comrade major." He handed the major my passport and added that I had a Soviet document and that I spoke Russian well.

The major toyed with my passport as he read my name aloud. Then he told me to take out the film.

I objected. It would be exposed and the pictures would be lost.

"Quiet!" He cut me off and asked the policeman if there were witnesses. The cop popped out from behind my back. "With your permission —" He re-emerged with the old woman. "She saw it."

"That's him!" she hollered, pointing at me. Then she donned her glasses with one lens broken. Then she told the major she had followed me ever since she saw me at Soviet Square in the morning.

I felt goosebumps. Some adventure. I might stay here for quite some time. But the old lady — she had followed me for over two hours!

"He looked cultured," she narrated, fixing her glasses and picking at her gray woolen jacket. "At first he looked like he was looking for something. Maybe he got lost, I thought. But then I saw he had a camera! I wondered what he was doing next to the Party Committee with a camera — so I followed

him. And then he took it out! A decent man wouldn't behave like that—
right?" She fell silent, fatigued by her long story.

"That's right," the major said, eyeing me steadily.

For some reason the cop stood at attention.

"Then I knew he had evil things on his mind. So I hid behind a tree.
When he saw there was no one around, he started clicking his thing."

I opened my mouth to protest—I never hid when taking pictures! What
was going on here? Taking me—a Komsomòl member—for a spy? But before
I spoke—

"This guy—" the cop butted in—"has been planted by the English to
spy on us."

"Such a nice-looking boy...." The old woman sighed as she looked at me.
"And a spy—imagine that." She took out her handkerchief and blew her nose
loudly.

"You should have called a policeman," the major said.

"If I stepped away, he would have run off," she countered. For some reason she started studying her well-worn canvas shoes. "Then I got bored behind
the tree. You couldn't watch in silence. Who knows what he would do next.
A half-hour later, I could see he was up to something. I got scared and ran
away. He looked worried."

My God, was she ever observant! True, I was thinking then of finding a
toilet.

"This is when we picked him up," the policeman reported.

"I see." For some reason the major addressed the policeman in Ukrainian. "And then what?"

"With your permission, comrade major.... When she told me, I started
thinking. Assessing the situation in development. He wouldn't be hanging
out here for nothing. So I reasoned: what's his next step in this game he is
playing? Surely his intention was to weaken the struggle of all the people of
our country—then I knew I had to arrest this good-for-nothing. But it was
all in the timing...."

"Why didn't you do that right away?" the major said critically.

"I wanted to get some advice. What if he opened fire? A bullet or
more—"

Poor guy. So it was true that policemen working near government buildings were not issued live ammo—just in case. Truly, this was a unique government that was more afraid of its own police than of criminals.

So far the whole thing appeared funny. Not from every angle, of course.

After a pause the policeman went on: "Everybody knows what the enemies of the Motherland intend to do—"

"Thank you." The major cut him short. As he paraded past me, he
dropped: "I have no doubts about your spying."

Now the fun was gone. What did I need these silly pictures for? How would I get out of this mess? How could I prove I was not a spy? My poor mother. I could be sent to Siberia, and she wouldn't even know.

I started rambling, explaining that I had just graduated from a construction trade school as an architectural draftsman, and I was interested in famous Soviet buildings, which was my specialty. (They looked at each other importantly.) I had no idea I could not take pictures. And I was not interested in government structures.

"Nobody cares about that," the major commented philosophically. He pulled my film out of the camera and inspected it against the light. "Aha!" he cried out. "Here's the evidence — I can see the Supreme Council and the Party Committee —"

I knew that you couldn't see anything on undeveloped film. But he spoke with such confidence! What if there was something I didn't know and you could indeed see something, at least in the first moment when you pull it out?

"Do you still refuse to confess?" the major said.

Then I recovered my senses. He was lying through his teeth. What could he see there? I answered calmly — or so I thought — though inside I was still trembling with fear. "I didn't photograph anything like that."

"These deeds should be punished severely," the plainclothesman suddenly said from his dark corner.

The policeman, still behind my back, said, "He took pictures, comrade major. We have a witness."

"Did you both see him taking pictures of proscribed objects?" the major asked.

"No, only she did."

I kept insisting that the old lady was confused. Let's look at the film together. Where do you see the Party Committee?

"Enough playing innocent!" the major cried out. "I'm asking you for the last time!"

"He wouldn't tell me either," the policeman said plaintively.

"That's okay," the major said menacingly. "Our boys know how to get it out of him." But there was something new in his tone, I thought. A touch of uncertainty?

Now I had to do something, before they opened a case and passed it along. Then it would be too late.

"You exposed a roll of my film," I murmured, surprised at my chutzpa, and demanded further. "I'm asking for compensation."

"He's just showing off," the policeman commented. "He knows what's in store for him."

Silence fell. The major kept pacing the room. The plainclothesman remained in the dark.

"All right," the major said. "Are you continuing to deny everything?"

As if I had another way out. What was I going to do now — confess? The idiot exposed the film and can't prove anything anyway. Suddenly I felt a cold sweat again. I had another roll of film in my pocket. They had not searched me. What kind of security operation was that? But they still could —

At that moment the plainclothesman remarked sarcastically, "Some spy, with a Jew name. What are they, stupid? It's a crock of shit."

"Comrade major, asking permission to leave," the cop said shyly. "Duty calls."

The major let them go and moved on to the next charge. My resident registration was in Kharkov, so what was I doing walking around Kiev without a stamp in my passport? I realized that the worst was over, so now I felt free to lie and tell them I had arrived in the morning and did not have time to stop by the police station. What about the train ticket? I threw it away.

At least I thought of telling them I used a train instead of the bus, which arrived in Kiev in the evening, which would make it easy to establish I had already been in Kiev for three days (and one was supposed to register within 24 hours).

But I could tell that the major was getting sick of this story. After another hour of bickering he gave me back the passport and the camera and told me to go away. Now I went on the offensive and demanded compensation for the ruined film. That was risky. But I had already settled down, the trembling was gone, and I could treat myself to a little fun.

Besides, I noted that the major's tone was different from the one used towards me a year earlier at the Kharkov train terminal. The Committee must have received some new instructions, perhaps in the wake of Beria's arrest. Or perhaps I was just dealing with a different person. Finally, the major had enough of my lip and cried out: "I'll see you once again, you won't forget it!" And he called the sergeant to take me outside.

Twenty-two years passed. Stalin's body was carried into Lenin's tomb and then taken back out. Beria was executed. Khrushchev retired, not exactly of his own will. Andropov came to rule the KGB.

It was early summer, 1974. One evening after work I went to visit our new friends the Korenfelds. I was dressed lightly, no coat, and had a bottle of wine in my hand.

The streetcar stopped outside their apartment building. As I crossed a small garden in front, I spotted two young men on the bench, reading newspapers. Something about their reading seemed deliberate, I thought, and wondered whether they were holding them upside down, as they do in comic thrillers. I also recalled that at the streetcar stop I had run into an odd-looking, nondescript man who was pacing with a mien that combined concentration and diffidence. And then I became ashamed of my paranoia.

A few years earlier, Ilya and Lily Korenfelds applied for an exit visa to Israel. They were turned down and became "refuseniks." They were well-known among Moscow Jewish activists. Deprived of work and savings, they survived on foreign Jewish help. Both Ilya, a former army officer and until recently an engineer, and their elder daughter Lucy were idling away. His wife Lily, until recently an Intourist interpreter, taught English privately, and their younger daughter Natasha went to school.

The first time I met them was when I asked them to arrange for my invitation from Israel, as a first step in the process of emigration. They passed our personal data abroad. Once we found out that Lily was teaching English, Marina and I started attending her group. The classes were not classes as such — we had tea with candy and cookies and wine and vodka with goodies bought with foreign currency. We soon became friends.

At the previous "class" it turned out that the Korenfelds were taking off for a few days' vacation in the South and that today's class would be the farewell party. Marina stayed at home with the three-year-old Slava, who was under the weather. I promised to come home early.

The building was dark. The bulbs are out, I thought. Faint light came from the only second-floor window, never washed. I had the uneasy feeling that someone was hiding in the dark. I mocked my fears again, but less confidently.

In this building the elevator stopped on landings between the floors. As I left the elevator, I heard some kind of stirring in the dark. Now I no longer had doubts: it was not paranoia, and the Korenfelds had visitors — the KGB. They had already told me before, with a laugh, that their apartment had been blocked a few times in this manner. The telephone had been turned off the day before.

To avoid the risk of detainment, I went to the floor below theirs and rang the bell on the first door in sight. Fortunately, no one answered. Then, maintaining legitimacy, I returned to the elevator and pressed the first-floor button.

Before the elevator moved, I started frantically trying to come up with a story, all the while trying to get rid of the trembling inside. Sure, the two on the bench could detain me. Of course I was guilty of no crime, but undoubtedly this would be reported to my employer. I would be dismissed when I had barely had a chance to settle at my new job. Just as in the six months before, I would be hanging around town unemployed. I couldn't go down just like that. How could I avoid them? Nervously, I started playing out different scenarios.

While the elevator was crawling down, I suddenly came up with an excellent plan. I'd knock on any door and ask to use the phone. I'd tell Marina that I might be late. And I'd tell the people at the apartment that I was pursued by strangers and I was afraid to go back inside and ask if I could leave via the window. I was quite happy with my idea and sighed relief.

But the moment I left the elevator cabin, two musclemen materialized from the dark and grabbed me on both sides — this was familiar from the first time in Kharkov — and demanded my passport. I asked for their IDs. They showed something that, even in the torchlight, was illegible. I had bad luck — I didn't have my passport on me. I had left it in my coat at home. Now I had to submit to the demand to follow them to police headquarters.

In the daylight, the two turned out to be the ones on the bench. They passed me along to the third one and returned to their position.

My escort was silent, walking slightly ahead and to the side. He was not afraid I would run away. We followed an odd route — side streets and dead ends — and entered the precinct from the back. I wondered if it wasn't police at all nor the KGB. Perhaps they were common criminals, but what could they want from me?

The sight of a policeman calmed me down.

I was led through lengthy corridors to a small room and handed over to a short, nondescript person. He had a Moscow University graduate pin on the lapel of his gray coat with brownish stripes. He introduced himself as Petr Saràntsev and — proudly, I thought — showed me his KGB ID.

He reprimanded me gently for walking around without a passport. "We could fine you and worse." I read out my personal data. He assured me I would be let go as soon as they were assured that I was indeed who I said I was. And then he started questioning me — whom I was visiting in the building and why.

I told him that my friends were about to leave on vacation. I was about to visit them, but they were not at home. I was still hoping to get away with a slap on the wrist.

"What's your friends' name?"

"I don't know."

"You don't know whom you were visiting?"

"Actually, I'm friends with their daughter. I know her name, I never asked her last name."

Lying has never been my strong suit. Once again, I thought that my job was as good as gone now, with all the effort I put in to get it.

"Really? And what is the name of your friend, if you don't mind? You don't remember that, either?"

"Actually, I do. Lucy." I named the Korenfelds' older daughter, in the faint hope that a common name like this wouldn't mean much.

"I see," Saràntsev said, and added, with deliberate slowness: "You — were — visiting — Lucy."

He invited me to follow him. I stumbled along, realizing I was not doing well at all.

We turned into a half-dark hallway. Stories about the KGB's beatings of Jews flooded my head. The main thing is to cover my head, I thought, so as not to scare Marina. Though there's no getting out of it without blood. And it's almost a new shirt ... I shrank and fell back.

At this moment Saràntsev called me from the back of the hallway, his voice suddenly severe. "Who did you say you were visiting?" He opened a door that was invisible to me, and bright light spread around the hallway.

Barely did I have a chance to get used to it when I heard Lucy's familiar voice with its rolling R's: "Gaaaarik!"

This room was similar to the one we had just come from. A guy sat at the table — like Sarantzev, blond, pockfaced, and about five years younger than me, with the same university pin.

Opposite him on the couch was Lucy — dark hair, bright makeup, and fat knees under the shortest mini imaginable. She was flanked by two of my acquaintances, Leonid Ziskin and Alik Polishchuk.

The trio was delighted to see me. I was not equally delighted. Moreover, I felt scared. The two men were refuseniks, too. They had nothing to lose. As for me, I hadn't even received an Israeli invitation yet. I might never get it — and here I was, getting involved in a story that might very well cost me my job. And there was nothing at home left to sell.

Alik (Arkady) Polishchuk had a terse nickname, The Jew. He was tall, slender, with thick glasses over a predatory nose. Before applying for a visa he was deputy editor of *Asia and Africa* magazine. I had met him once at the Korenfelds.'

Alik would be held in Moscow for another five years. He used the time to attend the trials staged by the KGB for the Jews who tried to leave for Israel. He gathered material for a book. After we left, using a power-of-attorney, he continued to sue my employer for my unlawful dismissal. More than once he was beaten cruelly by the KGB.

In 1980, I found out that he was finally let go. I suddenly saw him on Ted Koppel's *Nightline.* Then he visited Chicago for a few days, and we had a lot of fun reminiscing about that night. Soon after that, he was hired by Radio Free Europe and moved to Munich, and then to Prague.

Leonid Ziskin, forever in love with Lucy, left for Israel, just as the Korenfelds did.

But that night, all this was far in the future.

Saràntsev left, and the KGB man whose name was Boris continued the conversation my entrance had interrupted. "What can I tell you, we really have a heavy workload, especially with your rallies. I haven't had a free moment ever since I got back from Mordovia. I think they'll bring about fifteen people tomorrow." He grinned, pursing his lips.

How does he know the numbers, I wondered. Do they have quotas?

Mordovian camps were famous for their beastly treatment of prisoners. This one couldn't have gone there for nothing. Perhaps to learn more about giving the third degree.

"I have an exam for my master's soon." Boris made a face. "With you guys I don't have any time to study."

What are the exams in? I wondered. How to beat up on Jews and other dissidents? Having recovered from the shock of arrest, I inquired: "For your master's?"

"That's right. I was telling the comrades here. I attend a postgraduate program at night. Writing a dissertation."

"And what's the subject?" asked Alik the Jew, as if reading my thoughts. "How to force the evidence out of a suspect?"

"Not at all," Boris said. "It's about the role of the Party cell in fighting fire hazards."

"What?" I was dying of laughter, momentarily forgetting where I was. "But what does the KGB have to do with it? It's a Party subject."

"Or a fire team's," Alik joked.

"This is soooo intere-sting!" Lucy exclaimed. "Please tell us more."

"So what?" Leonid put in his two cents. He was reeking of liquor. "What does it matter what they write. Who's going to read it? They give out degrees for persecuting Jews and dissidents. Which most of the time is the same thing."

"You're wrong, Ziskin"— Boris made his crooked grin —"our rules are stricter than anyone's. I started working on this when I was still an advisor at the Party Committee. Hence the subject. You really have misguided ideas about the KGB. We have a lot of research facilities, like Army medicine and other stuff—"

"*This is soooo intere-sting!*" Alik imitated Lucy in a reedy voice. "Why don't you research prenatal means of rooting out dissidents? Or scientifically justified torture methods?"

"Your sarcasm is misguided. Stalin's days are long gone. We use force only when necessary."

I wondered what kind of a conversation this was if The Jew was mocking the KGB man so openly.

It had been an hour since I left the streetcar. I became worried. "How long are you going to hold us here?"

"You shouldn't've left your passport at home." Boris was happy to change the subject. "Once your identity is confirmed, we'll let you go."

"With modern techniques, you don't need more than half an hour."

"How do you know?" Boris got wary, eyeing me with somewhat cold eyes.

"So why are you holding me?" Leonid muttered. "I did have a passport."

"So why did you get picked up?" I asked.

"Ask them. I saw those two outside, I went up to the seventh floor and knocked on the door. I had already got in — and then one of these guys put his foot in the door and dragged me out. I showed my passport. Come with us, they say, for 'clearing your identity.' Like parrots, they've just learned one phrase" —

"You shouldn't say that," Boris broke in meanly. "Our guys all have a college education."

"Then they should read the laws." I couldn't hold back, again throwing caution to the winds.

"There's no such thing as ideal legislation," Boris said in an icy voice.

"Who's talking about ideal," Alik said. "We'll settle for what we've got. A friend of mine opened an electrical outlet recently — very carefully, afraid of the current. Bingo, a mike falls out."

Boris was getting more upset. "If we don't break the laws, many people will be able to escape the law." He went on, as if reciting a textbook: "We go outside the law occasionally. We are being charged with using forbidden methods. And what about your Zionists? They don't spare Arabs either. You can't take things out of context."

"Speaking of context," Leonid said. "Garik still has his bottle. Why don't we, er —"

"Excellent idea!" Lucy said.

Boris mechanically opened the drawer to get a glass. Then he remembered and pushed it back. "We can't, citizens. There's an article in the code to that effect. 'Illegal material compensation of an official on duty,'" he recited.

"It says nothing about wasting wine," Leonid said sadly.

We went on trying to talk Boris into it. He even hesitated. But the one who had brought me — Saràntsev — came in.

"People can hear you all over the place. Having fun?"

"Just talking, Comrade Saràntsev," Boris reported, suddenly at attention.

"About sex," Alik said. "What else can we be talking about?"

"I was trying to set them straight, Comrade Saràntsev. I had to explain the role of our Committee to the citizens here. They do not realize that the power of the state lies in strong security agencies."

"You mean there is a difference of opinion on this issue?"

"We thought the power of the state lies in the welfare of its citizens," said Alik.

"Welfare is a relative notion," Saràntsev said, mentor-like. Then, as if climbing the podium, he orated: "Order in the country is an absolute necessity. The Russian people are not ready for democracy. Only fifty years before the revolution they were still living in slavery. They need a strong power, and our Committee is its best support."

The bastard may be right, I thought admiringly. "You are working on a degree, too?"

"I have already got one."

"The subject has to be the protection of personal interests in a democracy," Alik commented.

"What do you mean by 'personal interests?' Don't be a smart ass. Personal interests are subordinate to those of the state."

"I didn't mean anything," Alik retreated. "But you know the people hate your law and your state, too. You've just said that they are suborned by force, as represented by the KGB."

I caught my breath. Talking like this to a KGB man? One phrase like this could easily get you sent to places far away. But perhaps in places like this you can speak your mind. Whatever made me think that?

"Easy, Alik — it's their problem," Leonid said. "Don't get involved. Let them sort it out. We just want to go home to Israel."

"Let me tell you something, Polishchuk." Saràntsev clearly tried to be calm and hold back. "We put forth enormous effort to protect our national interests — including from people like you."

"So why keep us?" Alik pleaded mockingly. "You should let us go."

"Comrade Saràntsev, how do you feel about us opening the bottle?" Leonid persisted.

Saràntsev continued to seethe, ignoring the request. "All right, let's disband the KGB — then what? Chaos and vacuum — don't expect a democracy."

"So what's your ideal — a country of informers?" Alik asked insolently.

"Our agents are respected people and patriots. We don't employ alcoholics, drug addicts, or homosexuals" — Saràntsev paused to catch his breath. "By the way, informing is a built-in part of the Russian character. Maybe you don't know our history. Russia has always lived like this. And the KGB is the main protector of order in the country."

"I do know history," Alik echoed reluctantly. "Every tsar had his own butchers."

Boris, who had been silent, eyed Alik with ill-concealed enmity. He must have taken the last remark personally.

"Would you just stop?" Leonid turned to Alik. "These are their problems. What do we have to do with them?"

"Alik, pleeeez," Lucy chimed in, taking Alik's hand. And then she shot coquettishly: "Comrade Saràntsev, are you married?"

Saràntsev blew up. "You talk too much, Polischuk. No wonder they kicked you out of your magazine. I advise you to behave more soberly."

"Soberly?" Leonid faked concern. "So we'll never get to open the bottle?"

"Enough mockery from you, Ziskin! You already reek like a distillery!"

"Yessir." Leonid tried to salute and collapsed back on the couch.

"As for you, Arkady," Saràntsev continued, "I wish you took stock of your behavior. This could have consequences!"

(It did. A few weeks later, Arkady got a sound beating from these "intellectuals.")

"I'm just sitting here quietly, waiting for my visa," Alik said.

Silence fell. I checked my watch. Marina had to be worried.

"Another point worth noting," Saràntsev said, and recited, as if from a newspaper: "Foreign special services have stepped up their operations, which are becoming more sophisticated, especially in the realm of ideological sabotage. Our Committee — our security organ — protects our country."

"You can't call a good thing an *organ*." Alik went on attacking.

I caught myself thinking that I was envious of refuseniks — of their freedom of speech and behavior, unrestrained by internal censorship.

I didn't know then that Alik was quoting from Solzhenitsyn, who had just been exiled to Germany. Saràntsev the "erudite" must have caught it right away. And, since he probably didn't have a sanction to beat up on Jews that night, he slammed the door and left.

"They'll never let you go like this," Lucy trilled. "Why do you bother debating him? He's just a tiny bolt in the machine. A nothing." Then she caught herself and cast a look at Boris.

Boris had his own thoughts on the subject. "Here you are, complaining about anti–Semitism. Aren't you just making it worse? You organize your rallies and then complain you can't get into college or can't get a job. What is it you don't like here? You're doing all right, all in good jobs. There, it's a foreign country. You'll be nothing but cannon fodder. I went to a briefing. That *Hybrid* language — you can't learn *that*! And I sure wouldn't go to rallies if I was you. That sure plays into our country's enemies' hands."

"Enemies of *your* country," Leonid remarked soberly. "If you let us go to *our* country, we wouldn't have any reason to rally."

I wondered what rally they kept talking about. Perhaps I should listen to the BBC, if the jamming wasn't too bad tonight.

Saràntsev came back. "Let's go, Berkovich. I'll put you on the bus."

"I can make it myself."

"You can't."

It was as if I felt that today was a special day. "How about an apology for holding me this long? It's past midnight! What was my crime?"

The refuseniks stared at me in surprise.

"Go, Garik, before they change their minds," Lucy said. "You're just frazzling Marina's nerves. Remember what happened to my dad when he went to buy milk and Mom and I spent three days calling the morgues looking for him. It's a good thing that Mom saw Alik and me picked up through the window. Don't play with fire, Garik!"

"Listen to Lucy," Saràntsev advised. "The law says we can hold you up to three days."

"I think you owe me an apology." I had no idea why I was so insistent.

"You should go." Alik supported Lucy and added sarcastically: "Our friend here wants to apologize on the way. He's a college graduate, a man of culture...."

"Leave us the bottle." That was Leonid's contribution.

"Before I change my mind," Saràntsev said menacingly. "If you promise to go directly home."

Once again, we made our way to the bus stop in silence through unknown, dark side streets. Suddenly, Saràntsev said in an abrupt metallic voice: "We have a deal, right? You are going straight home — no other place." Then he added in a softer tone, "You shouldn't be messing with these rallies."

"I don't know what you are talking about."

"Come on, come on — the one tomorrow outside the American Embassy. Kissinger's coming! You shouldn't go. Maybe this way you'll leave sooner rather than later."

"Where?"

"You shouldn't play games with me. We know where — Isra-*el*." For some reason, Saràntsev stressed the second syllable. "People sit quiet, people don't stick their necks out — people get visas. That's the tactic you should adopt, too."

For sure he would call my employer. And I hadn't been there a month yet! I was as good as gone. No, wait! He doesn't seem to know I haven't even applied for a visa yet? So they don't know everything, after all. And in the confusion they might even forget to contact my employer.

After midnight, buses did not run often.

Saràntsev still could not settle down. "You and your friends do not realize a simple thing. Our Party and state are a mechanism of compensating for the slips of the Communist theory!"

Wow! He actually attacked the great infallible religion! Could he be a hidden dissident himself? Oh sure. But how could he deem this important to me, who was about to leave? In that case, whom was he talking to — himself?

"You keep talking about totalitarianism. But once you pull it out, this country will fall apart — uncontrollably. Do you understand?"

Oh boy. Something really bugged him about that conversation. It looked like they debated this a lot behind closed doors. They must be worried about the survival of their system!

I was terrified. Graduates of Moscow University, postgraduates, our future leaders.... They were nothing like the major in Kiev and certainly not like the lieutenant in Kharkov. I hoped I'd leave before they took over.

Mika

One night in the fall of 1974 a man knocked on the door of our Moscow apartment. He was about forty, unshaven, and wore clothes that were crumpled and unseasonably light. Off the bat he declared that his name was Mika, that he was the son-in-law of our Aunt Liza in Odessa, and he was about to spend the night with us on his way home. We knew that this relative existed — my wife's cousin's husband — but we had never met him before.

In Odessa he worked as a contractor. The only resemblance between a Soviet contractor and an American one is that both deal with construction. But a Soviet contractor's main skill was knowing how to steal payroll money and construction materials. There were good and bad contractors. Good ones never got caught.

Mika's story was a gem.

One morning, a month previously, he stopped by his construction site, a nine-floor residential tower made of reinforced concrete panels that was almost finished. He made sure that the painters showed up and went to a matinee movie show. He came back at lunchtime. There was no tower. He made out a heap of bent panels in a cloud of dust.

Amazingly, Mika did not panic. Luckily, he got paid the day before. He grabbed a cab to the train station and bought a ticket to Vladivostok on the Pacific Ocean. You could not get any farther away than that.

After a month, the money ran out and he called home. On hearing his voice, his family realized he was alive and well. They were both happy and enraged, too, having spent a whole month looking for his body in the ruins. The main thing they told him was that he was not to blame. It was the geologists' fault. They got paid for the soil borings report, but instead of doing the job, they sent in a copy of the study done for another lot. They just changed the address.

Thank God that no one died, the family told him. The building collapsed right after the paint crew left for the liquor store, which did not open before eleven.

Tomsk

In the summer of 1975, my studio head Konstantinov asked me to his office. He took his time getting to the point — "I know you've been moonlighting quite a bit" — but soon cut to the chase. "A place called GìproRech-Tràns" (GRT) — River Transportation Designs — "asked me to design a river terminal for them in Tomsk, Siberia. I don't have time for it — and it's somewhat below my rank, too. I gave them your name. They wanted me still —

mostly to hide behind my Lenin Award, I guess — but it's an urgent project, so they are stuck with you. I used to work with those guys. They are not bad — they won't welsh.

"So what if you never designed a river terminal? Big deal! You need money? You can charge them all you want — they are up the creek without a paddle."

The next day, which was Thursday, I visited the GRT place and got all the information for the design, including geological studies. I promised I would go over it through the weekend and would start sketching next week.

They called me back Friday morning: they needed sketches by Monday.

My wife Marina and I had planned to go visit our daughter at summer camp on Saturday. On Sunday I had promised to take our son to the zoo. Yet the voice of the man from GRT suggested that something dramatic had happened. Well, I reasoned — so much the better. I'll get it done sooner. My wife was aghast, but she could do little but to go on to the camp without me.

Back home in the evening, she was stunned to see the sketch almost ready. In the morning I had nothing.

After I went over the requirements and the site description, I realized that the structure had to stretch along the bank, with as many promenades as possible. I followed the precepts of my once-idol, architect Ginzburg. I diagrammed passenger traffic, keeping local and long-distance separate as they went through the ticketing area. In the center I placed a two-story-high waiting room and a restaurant with a huge Soviet-style kitchen. The second floor would be taken by a few hotel rooms. In order to keep the scale, I drew huge circle windows, so the whole thing looked like a beached cruise ship.

Marina was not fond of my design, and wondered if the sketch of a terminal as a ship would be perceived as mockery. I assured her (and myself) that this was merely the first idea. While they considered it, I would create something more serious and substantial. I had no intention of lowering my standards just because the job was "on the side."

Monday morning, as agreed, I showed up at GRT with the sketches. No one paid them any attention. I was told that tomorrow we were flying to Tomsk to show the design to the client. The tickets had already been purchased, and Konstantinov had been told I would be absent from my job.

Aboard the plane I sat next to GRT's director Schevelev. Gradually, I pieced together the sources of this farce. GiproRechTràns had been busy designing the terminal for years, and all the money had long been spent. The client — Tomsk River Authority — had rejected all the previous designs for a simple reason: they could not get green-lighted by the local architecture board.

Tomsk was a booming area of oil and gas production. The oilfields could be reached either by air (helicopters) or by water (in winter, on ice). "Under these conditions, a modern river terminal is no luxury, but a necessity," Schevelev recited.

He also told me that local Party Secretary Yegor Ligachev — the czar of the region — was an up-and-coming Brezhnev favorite who wrote his boss a letter of complaint against GRT and was expected to follow it up with a tête-à-tête with his boss on his upcoming trip to Moscow.

Brezhnev's advisor on water transportation held up the complaint and alerted his own pal, the river transportation minister. The latter called the department head and the latter called Schevelev. All of them ran the risk of Party reprimands, if not their very jobs.

Schevelev called my boss Konstantinov for help. He figured that if "local architects" turned down a design by a Lenin Award winner, it would absolve GRT of any blame.

Schevelev didn't care that the actual design was mine, rather than Konstantinov's — it was assumed that Konstantinov had supervised the project. I learned that Konstantinov had told Schevelev over the phone that he liked my design, neglecting to mention he had never seen it.

The situation was more farcical than Schevelev realized. An invitation from Israel was in my pocket, and we were about to file for exit visas any day. And here I was, designing a highly prestigious project "on a site," and at my boss's request, too. Truly, the Soviet Union was a Wonderland.

The river people in Tomsk set up the discussion of the project in such a way as to get around the local architects, starting right off with the Party Committee. If the design failed, they also risked Party reprimands.

The next morning the council convened. Altogether there were sixteen people: the regional council chairman, city party secretary and his two advisers, two regional Party committee functionaries, the chief city architect and his assistant, the local Architects' Union secretary, the director and chief architect of the Tomsk Civil Engineering Board and the Moscow guests, the GRT director, chief engineer, section chief and me.

Ligachev entered the room and slowly walked past the lined-up participants like a general receiving a parade, shaking their hands. As he approached me, he paused. "Who is this new character?"

I deemed his tone offensive. "I'm not a character. I am an architect who designed this project."

The room became very, very quiet. Schevelev was on the verge of fainting.

"You've got a big fucking mouth, architect. What are you showing off for?" He offered me his hand. "Ligachev, Yegor."

I shook his hand. "Berkovich, Gary."

"Big mouth you got, Gary," he repeated. "Let's see if your stuff here is as big." He stepped up to the stand with my sketches.

The local architects who had used the delay to cut my design to shreds were now rubbing their hands, expecting a debacle. The pale Schevelev was

The River Transportation Terminal for the city of Tomsk, Siberia, as seen from the river. Rivers in Siberia are a major form of transportation all year around. In the winter, frozen rivers are transformed into convenient roads for trucks and cars. The terminal in Tomsk is located in the downtown area on the right bank of the river Tom'. The complex includes waiting rooms, a restaurant, and a group of resting rooms for crews (there were no night trips) and a high-rise hotel. All places in the terminal are designed as multipurpose rooms (exhibitions, meetings, lecture halls, etc.) for use during winter when passenger flow is lower. Moscow, 1976.

held by his chief engineer and department head. In contrast with them, what did I have to lose? My career was in the West! And yet even I caught the bug of the nervousness that pervaded the room.

Ligachev turned abruptly. "Comrades!" He spoke loudly, as if addressing a Party rally. "What does all of this mean, Comrades? It means that once I put some fucking pressure on you, you can do a fucking good job, after all! Why did you waste all this time and keep bringing us all that shit! I should have your Party cards on the table and your balls in the wringer! Why couldn't you have Comrade Berkovich design it in the first place? Is it because we here in Siberia are not good enough for you Moscow farts?"

He turned to the city architect. "What do you say, architect?"

Never had any of my projects been showered with praise so unanimous. The same ones who would not give me the time of day minutes earlier were now fighting for the privilege of pointing out the perfection of the planning and the beauty of the facades.

Moved, Schevelev shook my hand heartily.

I was in a panic. If this moron adored my sketch, then Marina was right —

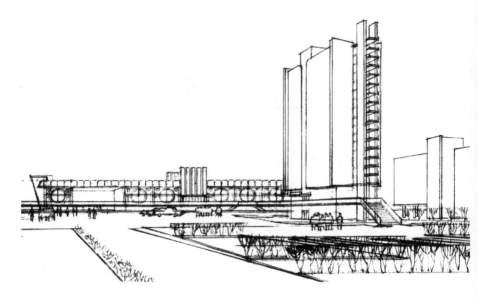

The project for the River Transportation Terminal for the city of Tomsk, Siberia, as seen from the city. Moscow, 1976.

this was not my best effort. But once the design was confirmed, there was no going back on it. As if to make things worse, a short elderly man named Dreysin, the local architecture preservation official, approached me and quietly poured oil on the fire: "What are you trying to do — raze our only stone structure from the eighteenth century?" The ruins of the merchant warehouses got in the way of building a plaza in front of the terminal.

When the debate died out, Ligachev said to me: "You listen here, if these assholes keep fucking with you, you call me right up. I'm gonna fry their shitty little asses."

I used this moment to mention that out of ignorance I had planned to raze some historically important structures. I was thinking of an alternate solution.

"Don't you fucking welsh on me! *Historically important* my ass! Anything those capitalists built, the Party can build thousand times better! Am I right, comrades?"

The man was a natural. Wherever he was, he was on the podium.

Afterwards Ligachev invited everybody for dinner at a suburban restaurant. En route we were joined by a local author named Georgy Markov, a Socialist-Realist mastodon whose opuses had won every Lenin Award there was and were absolutely unreadable.

Ligachev introduced me. "Berkovich — a fucking architect from Moscow. What's your first name, I forgot?"

I reminded him.

Markov looked as if he had eaten a lemon at having to shake hands with a Berkovich, but Party loyalties and thoughts of more money and cars and trips abroad overrode his natural dislikes. I was not enthusiastic to extend my hand to this anti–Semite, either. Yet we shook hands.

Berkovich Ph.D.

In February 1973 I finally defended my Ph.D. thesis. The defense went well, with a bit of praise and a bit of criticism. The secret vote couldn't have gone better, with 16 ayes and 2 nays. With a vote like this, a thesis is rubber-stamped by the High Accreditation Commission (HAC).

Yet my dissertation was sent for an additional review to the so-called "black" — or secret — reviewer. A "black" reviewer name always remains a secret, which means he can criticize without concern for his career. More-over, the harsher the criticism, the more work he will get.

HAC's own rules allowed for five months' consideration. In my case I waited for nineteen months before I got an answer with an invitation to HAC's Expert Council.

Through the grapevine I learned that the review had been authored by a Platònov, a doctor of architecture from Leningrad. I had to bring a written rebuttal to his critique to the council. Actually, the meeting went well. There was nothing to rebut: Platònov's review was positive, with little criticism of substance. The council members praised the thesis. Then my wife Marina and I were asked to step outside.

In the late evening, the hallway of the Higher Education Ministry, where the meeting took place, was abandoned. With every sound resonating through the "closed doors," we could follow the discussion without extra effort.

At first they were quiet. Perhaps they were waiting for someone to jump in first.

Finally, someone said, "What shall we do, Comrades? We can't confirm it, right?"

"Platònov really screwed it up," someone else chimed in. "No one warned him?"

"He should have known."

"Someone should talk to him. Who needs this holier-than-thou attitude?"

Suddenly, someone said something unexpected. "Comrades, I went over the thesis before this meeting. It should be confirmed and published. No need to dump on Platònov. He acted in good faith. We should be thinking about something else. It is no problem to table this for a couple of years. But what if this Berkovich starts pushing for his rights and someone upstairs will look at us dragging our feet and conclude we are putting obstacles in the path of an important economic project? I don't think we'll be praised for it."

After a long silence (or a subdued conversation) someone exclaimed: "That's what we'll do then. An excellent solution. Ask Berkovich to come back." And I was told I would have an answer in writing.

Six months later I got a letter that my thesis was being directed to yet another "black" reviewer.

By then the whole Ph.D. business no longer seemed relevant. Back in the spring of '74, after six months of unemployment due to the suspicion that I was about to emigrate I realized that emigration was inevitable. Yet I kept pushing, out of sheer curiosity and stubbornness.

The second review in the fall of '75 — a record thirty-two months after the defense — was an exact copy of the first one. The difference was that I was simply told that my work was "in the process of being reviewed."

Three months later, I wrote to the HAC, asking for an explanation. Almost three years had passed, two "black" reviewers had sent in positive reviews, and the discussions at the Experts' Council were devoid of even the vaguest questions. Why was it not confirmed? Were they waiting for me to file a lawsuit?

Finally, in March 1976 — over three years after the defense — I was informed that the Experts' Council had ruled in my favor. Yet the celebration was premature. Two months later I learned that, since my thesis was sent now to the highest level, the term allowed by the HAC for its confirmation was unlimited.

By then I knew that the original delay in my case was exacerbated by a curious political sideline. As it turned out, in December 1973 the HAC received a letter stating that I was about to emigrate to Israel — by Soviet rules, a mortal sin.

Yet they had plenty of time to approve my thesis before they got that slander letter. The favorable Platònov's review of my work came in July of '73. Well, now it was history.

I learned that the thesis was with "black" reviewer number three, named Zmèul. He was chairman of the State Construction Committee (SCC) and at the same time chairman of the HAC's architecture section. Using him for review was a brilliant coup for the buck-passing council members. If I left the country with a Ph.D. in my pocket, it would not be their fault.

I wrote Zmèul a complaint: a work crucially needed in the national economy had been delayed for three years. Unexpectedly, he asked me in for a talk.

Zmèul received me quite good-naturedly, which was rather atypical for a boss of his rank.

"Please take a seat, Comrade Berkovich. I have been meaning to talk to you for some time, ever since I read your thesis. I just couldn't find you. At the office where you had been working, they said they didn't know how to find you. You had a fight with them, didn't you?

"This is a very good project you did. A timely one. We need to publish it by all means. We are considering a number of measures in automating the design. We don't want to lag behind the West. Over there, they have been at it for some time. So we do need to promote research like yours. It's a shame it has been sitting at HAC for three years. It's unforgivable.

"What happened at your former office? They wrote a letter to HAC that you were planning to emigrate to Israel. This is absurd. Clearly, you could never implement research like this over there. It's not the same scale. And why would you be waiting all this time for your thesis to be confirmed? Tell me straight: Are you planning to leave for Israel?"

Ah, Comrade Zmèul. I wished you had posed me this question two years earlier in the spring of 1974 when I indeed had no intention of going anywhere. I ran from one design office to another looking for a job. And at each stop I heard that they already had "too many Jews."

Or how about even earlier, right after my thesis defense in February '73, before my work — without the slightest pretext — was sent to a "black" reviewer.

How come I was not asked this question when the reviewer sent in a positive review and yet my Ph.D. was not confirmed? Or when this happened again?

You could have asked the question another three years earlier when all the Jews from my office had been crossed off the list of applicants to travel abroad.

Better yet, you should have asked me in August 1968, before the Soviet Union occupied Czechoslovakia, and I, along with many others, lost all faith in the regime. Never mind that that was not directly related to anti–Semitism.

The question would not have been out of place in 1964 when I was barred from continuing the project — one you praised so much — and sent to Siberia to work in the land utilization business.

Actually, you could have asked the question eleven years before that, in 1953, when — illegally — I was not included in the group of the top five percent of the trade school's A-students who could go on to college, omitting the obligatory three years' work, and without the entry exams.

Alas, Comrade Zmèul's question was a quarter century too late. But more importantly, this quarter of a century had made me a different person. One who now could look Zmèul straight in the eye and say without blinking, "No, I am not planning to go to Israel."

Which, technically speaking, was true. We were planning to go to the United States. But I am not sure I would have been so "inventive" twenty-five years earlier. Comrade Zmèul's ilk had made me what I now was. So they were not in a position to complain about "Jewish tricks and deceptions." Didn't the authorities know that our invitations were from fictitious relatives to begin with? These are the rules they had made, so how could they complain?

"That's fine. In a few days I'll submit your papers for confirmation. Then I have to go on a business trip abroad. But I'll be back in a month and then you should come by — we'll discuss the publication of your project and your future work in the same direction. We'll include it in the plan of the R&D Residential Design Institute. Let's get going on this — we have lost enough time as it is."

And he called the secretary to schedule our next meeting.

Departure

I have always believed that I knew well the state where I was born and lived. I read a lot about the USSR and I knew people from all social strata, from workers and scientists to the military and intellectuals. I knew the ropes of the system and how to pull them. I went through the Navy, trade school, and college. I traveled through Siberia, the Far North, Central Asia, the Caucasus, Russia, Ukraine, and the Baltics. And yet I had to admit that my knowledge of the country was superficial.

Once, in a heated dormitory discussion, my friend Dmitry Radygin gave a very precise definition: "Individuals can be good or bad, but the mob is always shit." Soviet Communism was built on manipulating the crowd and succeeded by creating a new type of people who were primarily the part of the whole, rather than individuals. This is why its leaders — people brought up on its philosophy, who represented and used the power — have always been hopeless mediocrities. It is no accident that sticking out in the crowd was the deadliest sin of Soviet times.

The atrocities of the Gulag days are explained by Stalinist repressions. When we were leaving the Soviet Union in the late 1970s, those were long forgotten. But the people — the mob — were still there. Once we declared our intention to emigrate, we stuck our heads out. Now we saw the other side of the people. Former colleagues would not even "breathe the same air" with us.

The Jewish emigration from the USSR was limited by various Draconian laws.

In theory the émigrés were traveling to Israel to join their close relatives.

The purpose was to limit the numbers of those leaving. The authorities did not mind that the invitations were fictitious (what's another lie in Russia? You live with lies, and you leave with a lie, too). That opened the door to corruption: people were ready to pay any money to buy their Jewishness, from arranged marriages to forged papers.

Émigrés were not allowed to bring valuables — gold and silver jewelry, silverware, and gems. Everything that had been earned by years of back-breaking work or kept as a family memory had to be sold, and the proceeds had to be used for absurd fees, like one for "rejecting Soviet citizenship," which was imposed on émigrés. The cash left after this state-sponsored robbery could not be taken out of the country and had to be hastily spent on items of putative resale value that — since no one knew anything about life abroad — often turned out to have no value at all.

We were also forbidden to bring out anything that would prove our professional status abroad. In our case that meant not only education diplomas, but also photos of projects and buildings, our own etchings and paintings — even my six-year-old son's drawings.

The only exception was made for books, if they were published after 1948.

All these limitations bred massive corruption among the officials with any smidgen of power, from common customs officers to transportation workers. All of them knew: the Jews were afraid that their visas would be cancelled without any explanation at any time. Hence the customs became the seat of robbery and humiliation.

Only a few exit points were designated for leaving the country. The best known ones were the Sheremètyevo Airport in Moscow, for those who took the plane, and Brest terminal in Belorussia, for those who took the train.

We took the plane. Our family of four had few personal belongings: just a few suitcases with personal effects and a bundle of bed linen. We were lucky with the customs. They found little of value in our belongings and therefore didn't take much. Perhaps in frustration, they scattered everything and did not give us a chance to pack it back nicely. I had packed our collection of family slides along with two 8-mm reels of popular cartoons. They were taken away for over an hour. When the customs officers came back, they told us with great relish that the entire shift had had a lot of fun watching the cartoon. Apparently the slides were left alone. I wished I had put in the slides of my projects, too.

I shipped our library separately. I neatly packed it into a large wooden box, in accordance with the rules, and brought it to the freight customs a week prior to the departure. The customs officers scattered the contents on a large desk and went through all the pages, then dropped the books into the box every which way. They took whatever they liked, and I dared not say a

The author's daughter Lana and son Slava on the eve of departure. Moscow, 1976.

word. I knew from the experience of others before me that an attempt to get justice could lead to the disappearance of the whole library.

The address label on the box read, *New York, Berkovich.* Our official destination was Israel. The official said indifferently, "Aren't you going to Israel?" I said I thought New York was in Israel.

This was part of the Soviet game. The customs were instructed to ignore the New York address. A reliable rumor circulated that American Jews bought us out from the Soviet government. Figures ranged from two to ten thousand dollars a head.

My kid brother Gena and his family traveled by train and were leaving through Brest.

Gena was not a dissident. He was not leaving because he could not get along with the Soviet state for political reasons. In fact, he got along with it fine. He was a businessman. His underground business did very well, but it could not go on forever. The semi-legalized racket on the part of officials was getting worse and worse. He decided to leave for a place where he could make an honest living, where business was a legal and even an honorable occupation.

Gena had never had idealistic notions about our country. It so happened he had spent his adult life dealing with thieves and cardsharks and other antisocial elements. Human meanness could not impress him. Yet in the process of his departure even he was stunned by how much robbery and humiliation had become the norm under the Soviet authority. He often told me that this experience opened his eyes to the essence of Soviet power.

Of course the departure of Jews from Russia was unlikely to be more dramatic than escapes from Cuba or North Korea. Jews who left Egypt or Iraq or Yemen in the 1940s didn't have an easy time either. Yet we were taught (Russians are still being taught) that we lived in a civilized country. Scales started falling off our eyes from the moment we applied for exit visas, but we saw our country's real animal scowl only when we were crossing the border. We shuddered with horror when we saw that the emperor was naked. We had lived in a third- or perhaps even fourth-world country, we realized.

Gena recalled that their train arrived in Brest about five in the morning. It was still dark. In the window he saw a porter who was haggling with a local woman over her two suitcases. The moment the porter learned that Gena had more luggage, he kicked the poor woman's suitcases off his cart and called a couple of his pals, who did the same to their passengers and rushed off to load up Gena's luggage. Porters loved émigrés who had a lot of luggage and paid well. The Jews knew well that haggling with (to say nothing of fighting) porters could end badly at the customs. The porters were known to share their earnings with customs officers.

Upon checking the luggage in, Gena paid the porters 100 rubles (in those days a schoolteacher's monthly salary) and settled in the waiting room with his family — his wife Marina; Igor, 14; and Masha, 7. Suspicious-looking men in plainclothes milled about and even sat next to them. One felt surrounded by "eyes" and "ears." This meant that only very general things could be said.

At 1 P.M. the doors opened, and the porters rolled in their luggage. Gena and his family rushed behind them.

Customs was a huge room with a large, iron-plated, ring-shaped table in the middle, which consisted of two halves. Within it was a smaller table, also iron-plated, with customs agents working around it. The second floor had a gallery along the perimeter, where other agents observed what was going on downstairs.

Gena's luggage took up half the oval table. At first they were told to show the jewelry entered in the declaration: wedding rings and earrings. "That's it?" asked the young agent. "We'll see." He called a female agent, who took Marina and Masha away.

Then he took Gena and Igor to a special room. He removed Igor's overcoat, coat, pants, shirt, and shoes. He inspected these things thoroughly, though for some reason missed the twenty rubles Igor's grandfather had stuck in his pocket when saying goodbye.

Then it was Gena's turn. He was undressed and his clothes were examined, with a passion. Wherever the agent was in doubt, he simply tore up the cloth. They found a silver-plated cigarette case, which they took away, while breaking the cigarettes in half. Then the agent took out a pocket knife to force off the insoles. All this time he peered at Gena, muttering, "If we find gold or diamonds, you'll be traveling in the opposite direction."

"Whatever you find, you get half," Gena said.

The agent did not say anything, but seemed to relent. At the end he didn't find anything, and, clearly irritated, yelled at Gena to dress faster.

His wife Marina and seven-year old daughter Masha went through the same examination — plus a gynecological one.

Now the crew of seven or eight agents started working on the luggage.

First was the box with toys. Its contents were dumped on the table and got the full treatment. Every toy was dismembered; every doll's head was screwed off. Everything was torn up and destroyed. Having found nothing, the agents went on to tear up cardboard containers, kicking up their bottoms and forcing off suitcase handles. The contents were thrown every which way, and it was impossible to put them back in any semblance of order. Some things were taken away, and not everything came back. The agents were clearly getting a kick out of acting with impunity.

The train departure was close now, and only half the items had been cleared. The inspection speeded up. Now items were simply dumped in a pile; if something fell on the floor close to Gena, he could still pick it up and put back in the suitcase; but if it fell on the agent's half of the table, chances were it was gone. At a certain point Gena grabbed a porter who was putting his watch in his pocket.

Gena was still trying to pack the cleared items as the porters started to carry the rest aboard.

Part of the belongings was already on the platform. The border guard paid no attention and pushed Gena aboard the train.

The train came into motion. The porters fought to the exit over the suitcases that took up the corridor and jumped off as the train gathered speed.

The train approached the border river of Bug. The border guards who stood on the steps jumped off. The train went over the bridge slowly. The Berkoviches were out of the country — just a regular Soviet Jewish family, one of hundreds of thousands that went through Brest.

Index

Milton Keynes UK
Ingram Content Group UK Ltd.
UKHW032234020824
446485UK00014B/141

9 780786 441396